HOW TO **paint**
fast, loose & bold

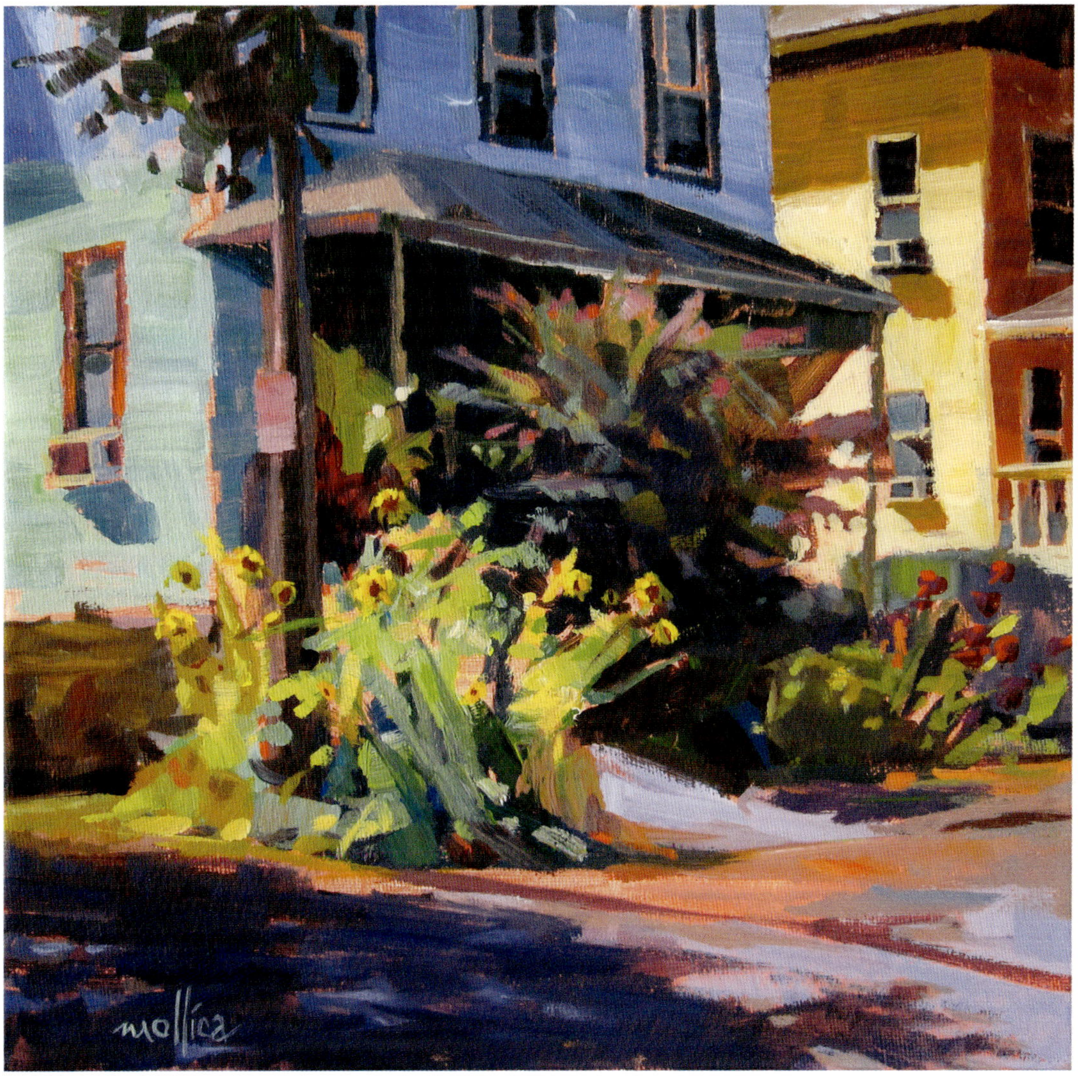

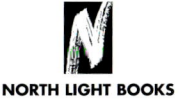

Simple Techniques for Expressive Painting

Patti Mollica

NORTH LIGHT BOOKS

Contents

WHAT YOU NEED

Surfaces
Hardboard panel or canvas board, white mat board

Pigments
Alizarin Crimson, Burnt Sienna, Burnt Umber, Cadmium Lemon Yellow, Cadmium Orange, Cadmium Red Light, Cadmium Yellow Light, Cadmium Yellow Medium, Carbon Black, Cerulean Blue, Diarylide Yellow, Green Gold, Manganese Blue, Neutral Gray N6, Payne's Gray, Permanent Violet Dark, Phthalo Blue (Green Shade), Phthalo Green, Quinacridone Magenta, Raw Umber, Sap Green, Teal, Titanium White, Ultramarine Blue, Yellow Ochre

Brushes
¼"–2" (6mm-51mm) flats or filberts, 1/16" (2mm) script brush

Other
black and white vine charcoal, color wheel, eraser, value scale

RED UMBRELLA | 8" × 10" (20cm × 25cm) | Acrylic on canvas | Private collection

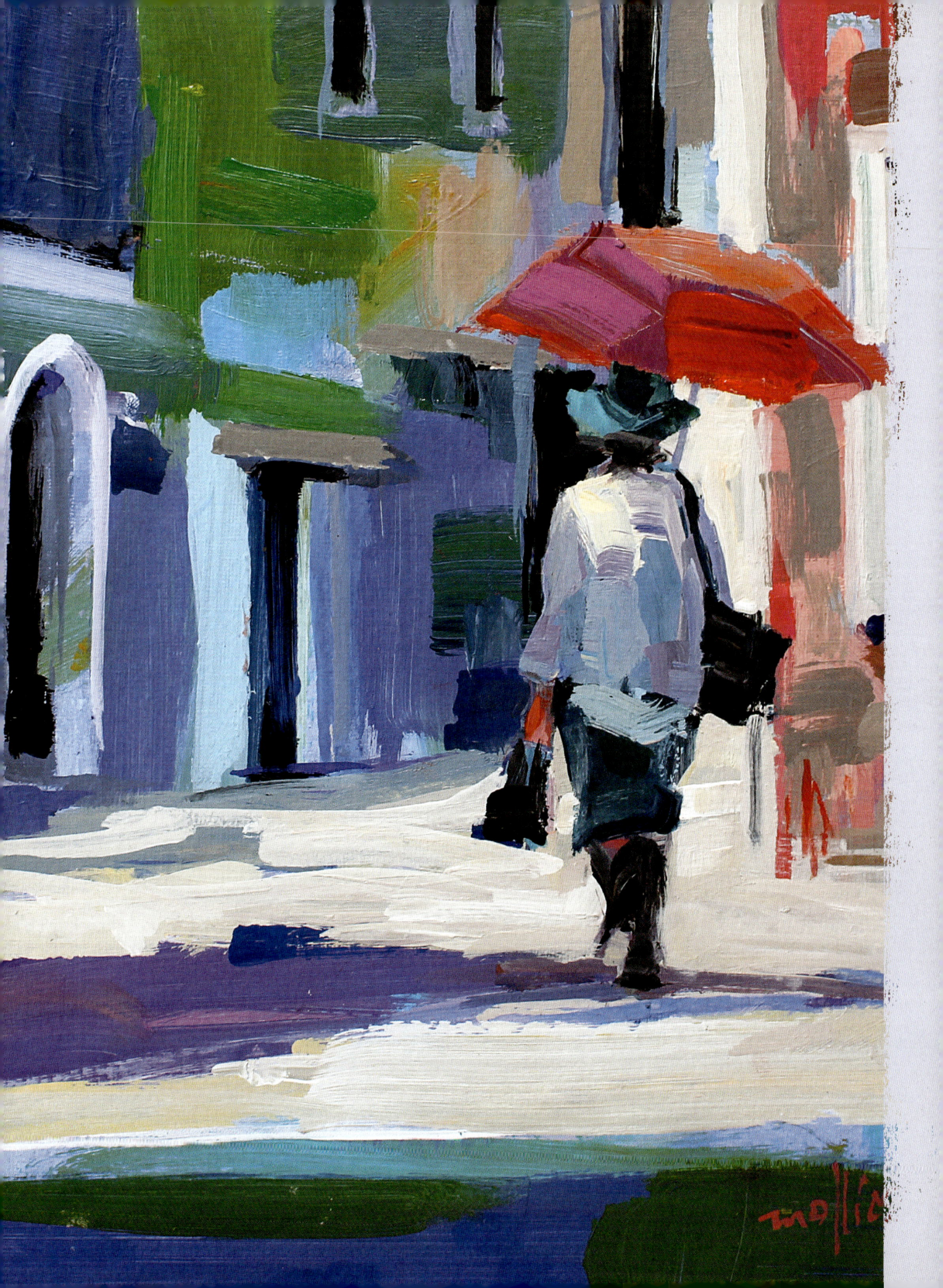

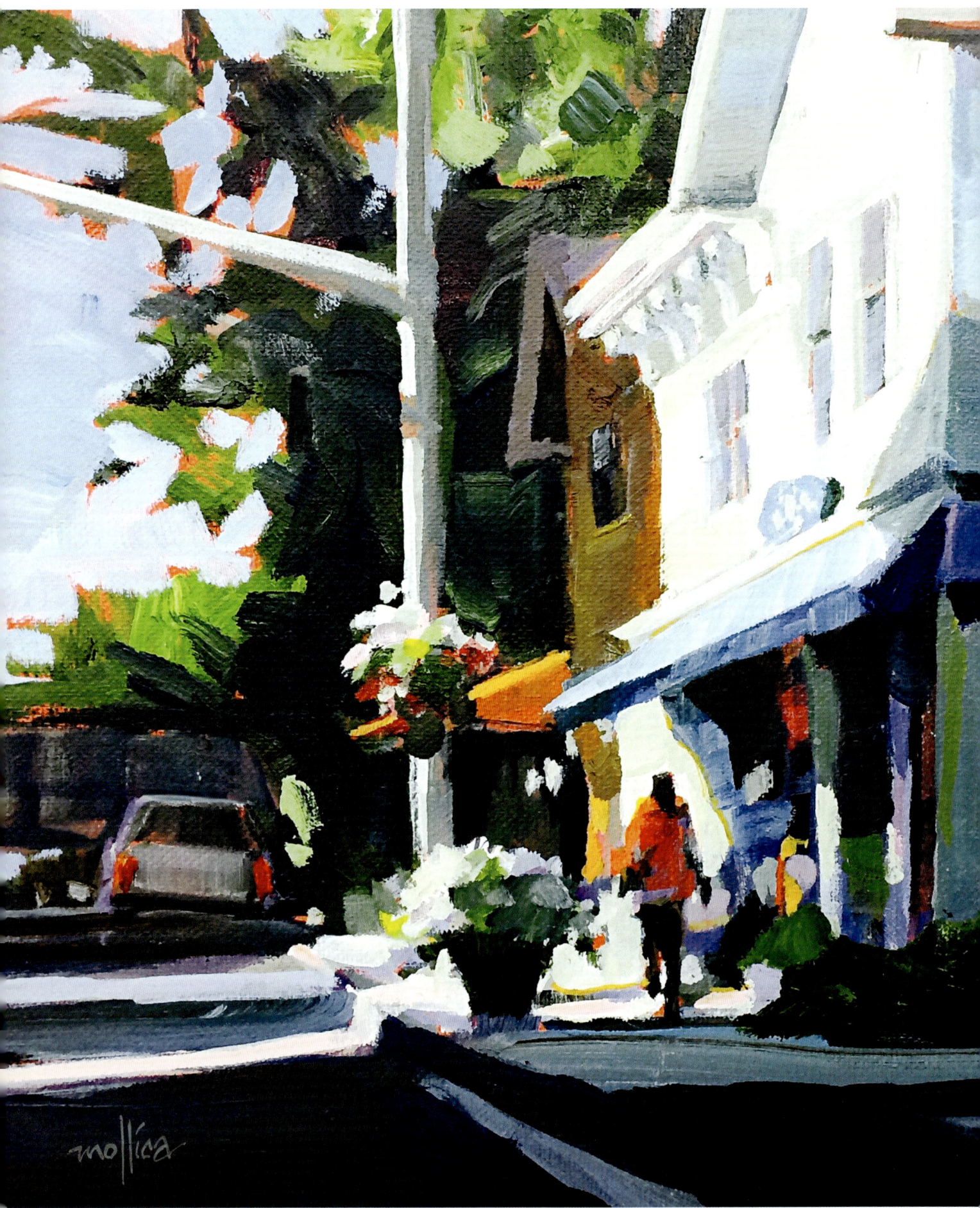

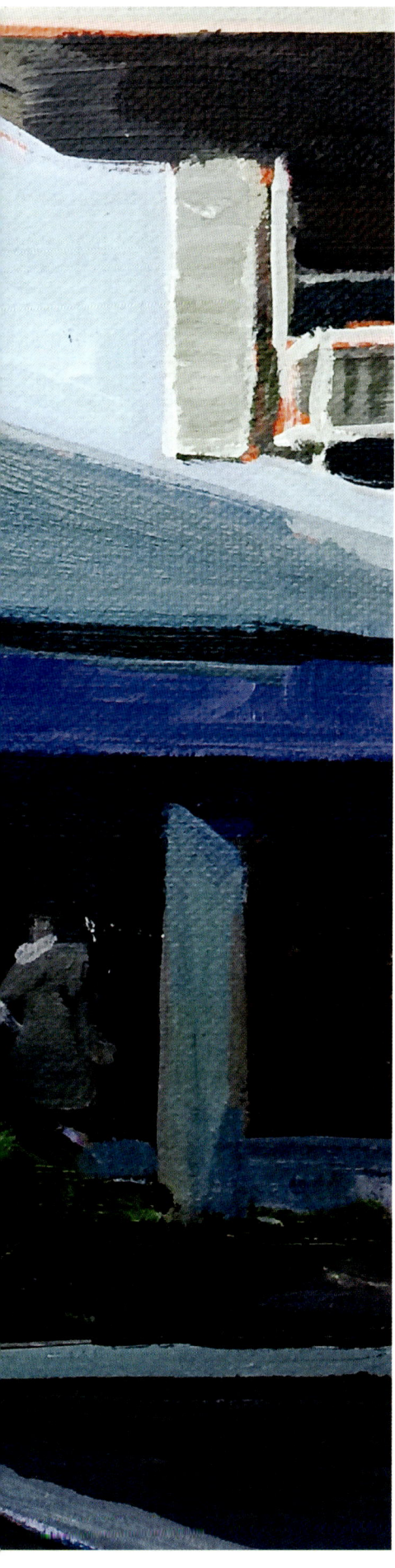

Introduction

PAINTING FAST, LOOSE AND BOLD is what happens when you approach a painting with confidence. When you feel confident in your method and process, it shows in the finished painting. Fast: If you work with a value plan, a painting can be executed relatively quickly. Loose: If your color values are matched correctly, you can lay down definitive brushstrokes that have an overall looseness, without over-working. Bold: If you use fresh, unexpected colors that are matched to a strong well-composed design, your painting will read well from a distance and exude boldness.

Many people show up to my workshops with the impression that they will be learning to paint fast and furious. Yet, my approach would be better described as mindful. After all, anyone can paint fast and furious—just give some paint to a two year old and watch the speed and energy that ensue. My method, however, is mainly geared toward representational painters who want to let go of all those little details that hold them back from being more expressive.

The question then becomes, how do you gain the artistic confidence that is required to produce paintings that look fast, loose and bold? It took me many years to hone the essential skills that helped me become a consistently better painter. *Consistent* is the key word here. You want your paintings to succeed on a *consistent* basis. For that to happen, you have to lay the necessary foundation on which to build strong, successful paintings.

My painting method is based on several building blocks that offer a solid foundation for painting with confidence—values, color and brushwork. Once you are able to understand, practice and implement these basics, the door will open wide to a much freer painting experience. In this book, I will guide you through these fundamentals so that you, too, will be able to approach your paintings with confidence and enthusiasm.

RYE CORNER
Acrylic on panel
12" × 12" (30cm × 30cm)
Collection of Colleen Ulrich

Choosing Supplies

Here is an overview of the materials you'll need to get started. These suggestions are based on my own experience and preferences, but feel free to experiment with various tools and supplies to find what works best for you.

Paints

Use a lot of paint! Many students want juicy, luscious paintings, yet put out only dime-sized dollops of paint on their palettes. If you want your paintings to look painterly, you need to use lots of paint!

For acrylic painting, I prefer to use Golden Heavy Body Acrylic paints, which are excellent quality and professional-grade. If you're on a budget, you can buy student-grade paints. Just keep in mind that they will dry more dull and transparent because they contain less pigment. If you are a beginning painter, student-grade paints might be more conducive for experimenting without worrying about your budget.

I always have the following pigments on my palette when I paint. All these pigments are also included in the materials lists for the painting demonstrations in this book, even if they are not all used in the paintings.

- Burnt Umber
- Cadmium Red Light
- Cadmium Yellow Light
- Cerulean Blue or Phthalo Blue (Green Shade)
- Quinacridone Magenta
- Titanium White
- Ultramarine Blue
- Yellow Ochre

Optional colors I often use, depending on the subject matter, are:

- Alizarin Crimson
- Cadmium Orange
- Cadmium Red Medium
- Cadmium Yellow Medium
- Carbon Black
- Dioxazine Purple
- Green Gold
- Medium Gray
- Sap Green

If you are put off by the fast dry time of acrylics, there are several brands that allow a slower dry time. I have only experimented with Golden OPEN products, which have a dry time up to seven times slower than their Heavy Body counterpart. These paints have a slightly more fluid viscosity, so experiment to see if that feels right for you.

However, my preference is the (fast drying) Heavy Body paints. They are creamy and retain the brushstrokes when dry, so the ridges of the bristles are visible. I used Heavy Body paints in all the acrylic examples shown in this book. Other manufacturers in addition to Golden offer slow-drying acrylic options. Do a little research to see what suits your preferences and budget.

For oils, my favorite professional-grade paint is Williamsburg. I use colors that are the equivalent of

PAINTS
The paints in my container pictured here are: Phthalo Blue (Green Shade), Ultramarine Blue, Manganese Blue Hue, Teal, Green Gold, Neutral Gray N6, Cadmium Yellow Primrose, Cadmium Yellow Medium, Yellow Ochre, Burnt Sienna, Sap Green, Cadmium Orange, Cadmium Red Light, Quinacridone Magenta, Alizarin Crimson, Carbon Black and Titanium White.

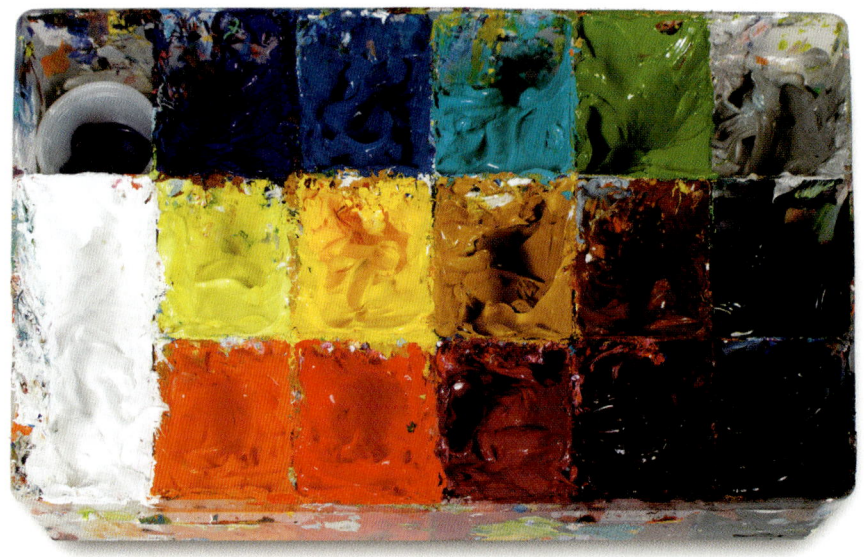

the names mentioned for acrylics. Galkyd Lite is my medium of choice because it improves the flow of my mixtures and facilitates a faster dry time.

Supports

I like to paint on a variety of surfaces. Stretched canvases, canvas boards, gessoed Ampersand panels and Strathmore Mixed-Media Board (with two coats of gesso) are all good supports for painting. For quick paintings and demonstrations, I've found it's best to work with small sizes like 8" × 10" (20cm × 25cm), 9" × 12" (23cm × 30cm) or 12" × 12" (30cm × 30cm).

If you are strictly experimenting, I recommend using a 12" × 12" (30cm × 30cm) Strathmore Acrylic Pad.

Brushes

I use flats in various sizes. My favorite brushes are Catalyst Polytip brushes made by Princeton. Not only are they suitable for both acrylics and oils, they have a wonderful spring and retain their shape after repeated use. The bristles are similar to hog's hair in that the ends of each have small split ends for the purpose of holding more paint.

Palette

I recommend using disposable palette paper such as Grey Matters by Jack Richeson. Mixing your colors on the middle-gray toned paper will help you to judge the values more accurately. If you work on a white palette, the light- and middle-value mixtures may appear dark, which might cause you to paint in values that are too light.

Paint Containers

You can use something as simple as a plastic bead box from a craft store to hold your paints. Fill up each compartment with an entire 2 ounce tube of paint. If you only put small dabs of paint in the compartments, you can be sure they will dry out quickly. It also helps to spritz with water during painting sessions.

The container is not airtight, so after you finish a painting session, close the lid and place the entire container in a 2 gallon resealable plastic bag. Include a wet paper towel placed on top of the container to keep the atmosphere within the bag moist. Your paints will

stay buttery for a long time. (Though, they will lose some moisture eventually.) It's also a nice way to make sure your paints will be ready to go when you are. It's not a perfect system, especially if you are a stickler about keeping your colors perfectly clean—but it can result in some happy accidents!

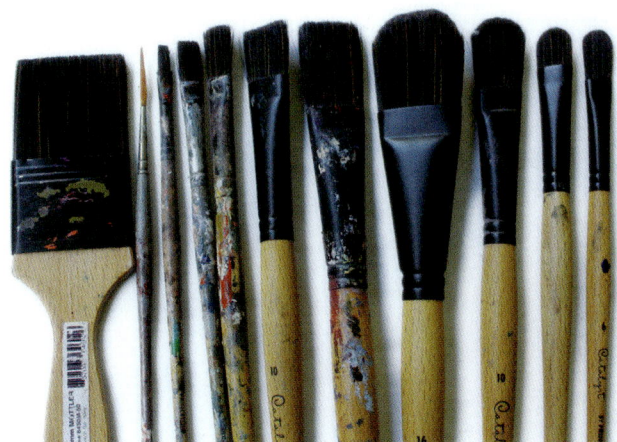

BRUSHES

The most important quality to look for in a brush is that it springs back to its original shape when wet. Also, the ends should be tapered so you can get fine lines, even on a wide brush. If your bristles splay outwards from the center, you will have a difficult time controlling where your brush makes contact with your painting.

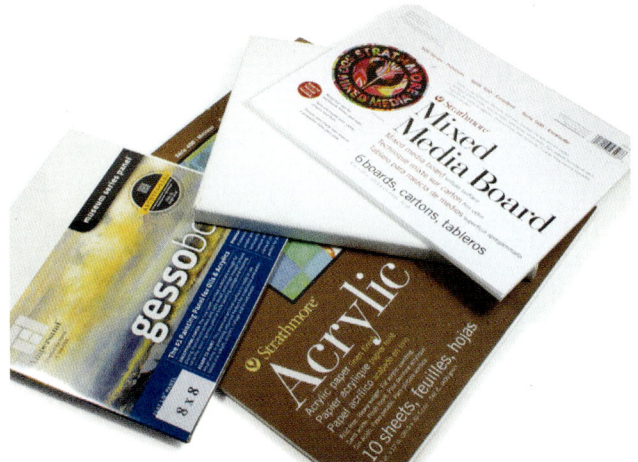

SUPPORTS

There are several painting surface options available including canvas, panels and mixed-media papers and boards.

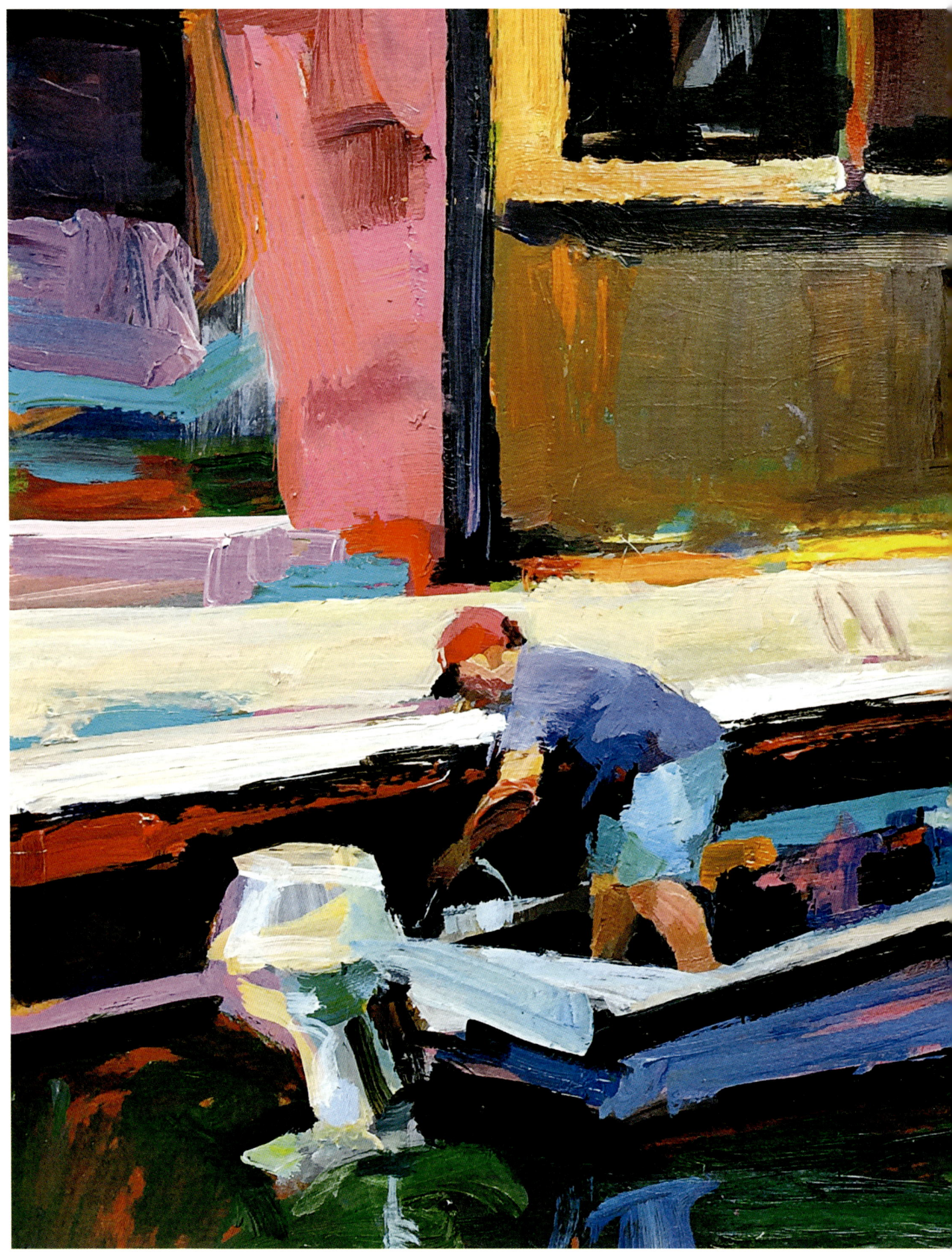

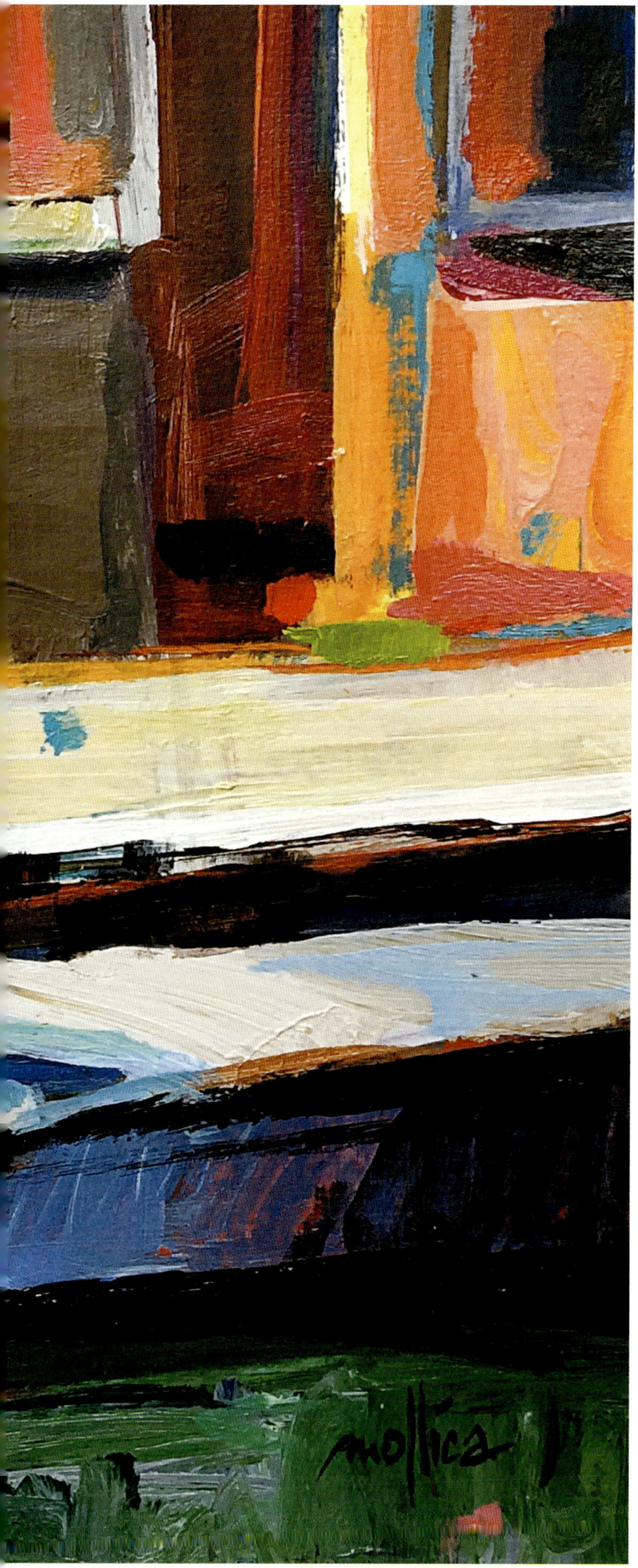

Creating a Strong Foundation

A strong composition is the foundation of a successful painting. And learning to identify, simplify and compose the values in your paintings as the basis for strong compositions. No matter how well you can draw or paint, without knowing how to design your compositions, your paintings will lack drama. In my opinion, the key to creating bold paintings is to start simply with a strong value plan as the foundation for your overall composition.

BURANO FISHERMAN
Acrylic on panel
12" × 12" (30cm × 30cm)
Private collection

Understanding Value

For many years I heard the word "value" tossed around, and was told how important it was to see and identify correctly. Value, by definition, means the relative lightness or darkness of a color. I understood that it was important to be able to identify approximately where a color's value fell on a scale of 1 to 10, but didn't understand how this would make my paintings any better. Understanding how to identify a color's lightness or darkness is a good start, but the ability to simplify values and organize them into well-designed patterns and shapes, which for the basis for a strong composition, is much more important. The ability to take what you see, modify the values as necessary to create a stronger, more readable image is key.

Seeing With Your Artist's Eye

This principle is important to an artist because rather than simply record what is seen, you learn to become a designer. An artist can take advantage of artistic license to design the composition rather than simply transcribe what is actually there. Often the subject is not placed or lit perfectly. There may be no drama, objects might blend together, everything could be too light or too dark, etc. As artists, we have to give ourselves permission to move mountains and change values in order to make our paintings read well. We have the artistic license to do so, and we need to use it.

My Ah-Ha Moment

One day after laboring over a large painting for weeks, I realized it simply didn't work. It was a painting of an intersection in Times Square featuring crowds of people, cars, buildings, signage, lights and billboards. The proportions were correct. The perspective was accurate. The colors were crisp and vibrant. The brushwork was lively and gestural. The subject matter was appealing. It had movement and felt energetic. There was plenty of interesting detail. How could it not work? The more I studied the painting, the more perplexed I became.

A few days later I decided to take another look. From across the room, seeing it fresh, I realized I was looking at a hodgepodge of colors and shapes, but they did not hold my attention. In fact, I did not know where to look, or what exactly I was looking at. There was no center of interest, no sense of distance, no cohesion or continuity, and no real composition. All I saw was a collection of brightly colored shapes and marks scattered around the canvas that didn't seem to create an actual setting.

I had painted a profusion of surface details, but no major shapes or patterns that might give the piece a foundation to hold it all together. It was all icing and no cake! I had copied what I saw in the photo, but I had not created a work of art.

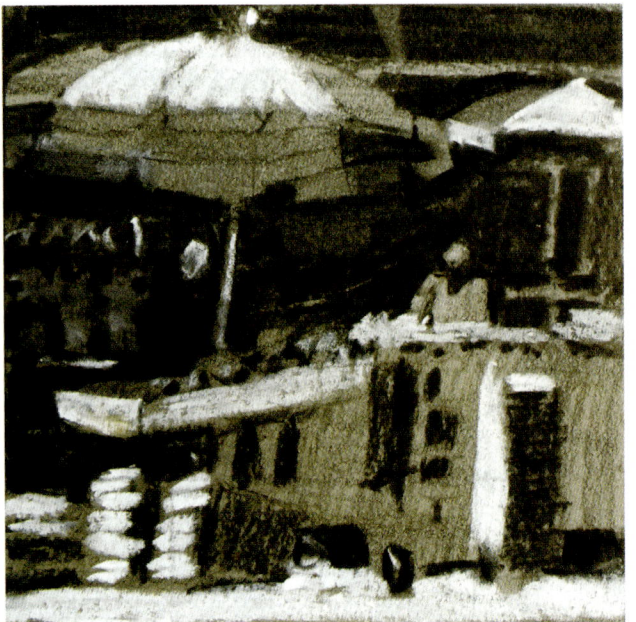

START WITH A VALUE SKETCH

This value sketch was created using only three values: light, medium and dark. If you can learn to compose small studies and simplify the range of values, you will be on the road to consistency. Notice that this value sketch has no intricate detail, only simplified basic shapes that depict the light-dark pattern.

I create these small sketches in charcoal so I can easily change my mind by erasing or smudging. With one swipe of my finger, I can turn a dark passage into a medium passage and judge whether I like it better or not. If I create a sketch that reads well, especially in a small thumbnail size, I can proceed to painting with confidence!

That was my ah-ha moment. I realized that successful paintings are based on an ability to simplify the subject down to its essentials rather than paint it in great detail. Design and composition are the solid foundation that a painting must rest on. Values must be simplified. Colors, shapes and patterns must be organized and arranged harmoniously to support the focal point and lead the eye to it. Visual order must be brought to the scene, by massing and simplification.

When I delved further into this realization and compared my good and mediocre paintings side by side, it became clear that the successful pieces had an underlying simplicity to the values and shapes. Now, I understood the value of values loud and clear.

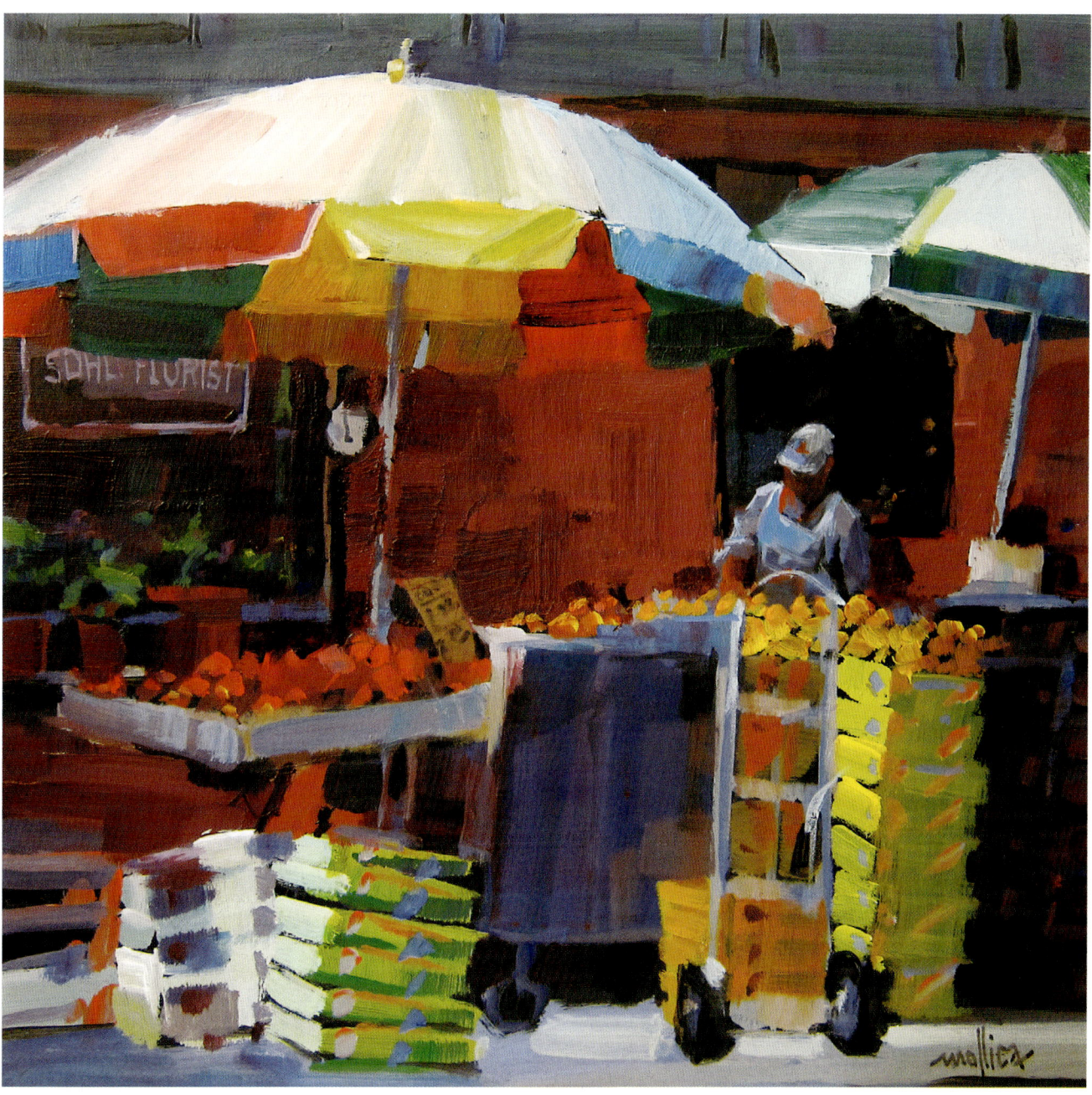

SOHO FLORIST
Acrylic on panel
12" × 12" (30cm × 30cm)
Collection of Elizabeth Garribaldi

Defining Value

Value is defined as a color's relative lightness or darkness. When we look out at the world—or look at nature, an urban scene or a bowl of fruit—we see an infinite number of objects each with varying degrees of lightness or darkness. For instance, a garlic clove is considered a light value, an orange a middle value and a pepper a dark value.

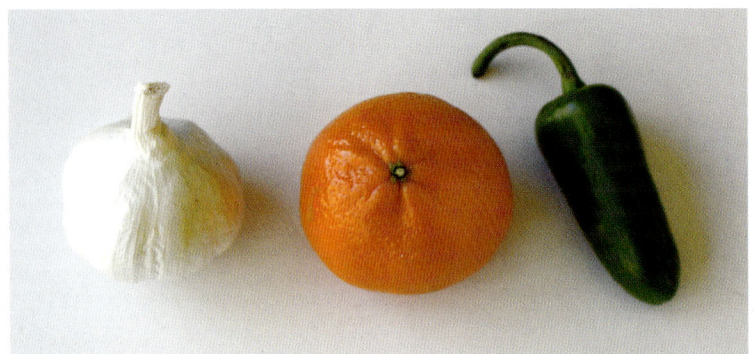

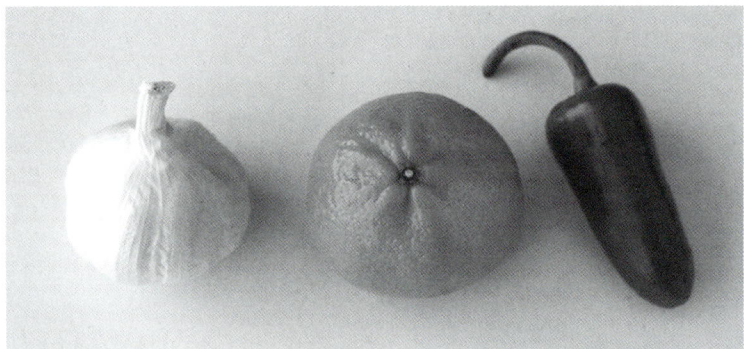

USING TEN VALUES

The eye can perceive millions of subtle gradations from light to dark. As an artist, it is imperative to be able to translate complex visual information made up of thousands of value variations into understandable shapes and patterns using a limited number of values. Many accomplished artists reduce this infinite amount of information down to a scale of nine or ten shades, ranging from white to black. This helps simplify the process because the range of values that can be perceived by the eye is far greater than what we can actually produce with the pigments in our paint palettes.

Using ten values will give you a realistic representation of the subjects in your painting. For a bolder, more dramatic composition, reduce the value simplification to three: light (white), middle (gray) and dark (black). When painting a natural landscape, allow yourself four values: white, light gray, dark gray and black.

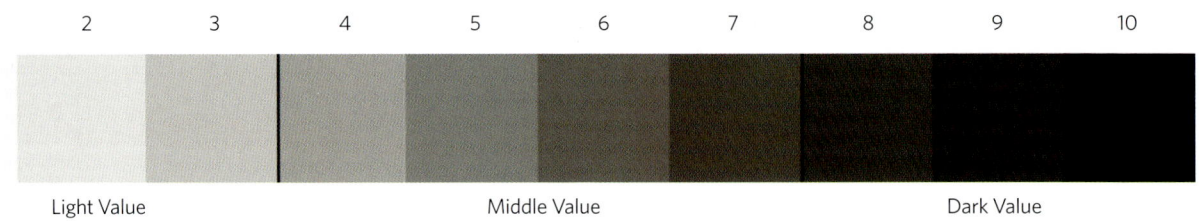

| 1 | 2 | 3 | 4 | 5 | 6 | 7 | 8 | 9 | 10 |

Light Value   Middle Value   Dark Value

TEN-VALUE SCALE
Here is a ten-value value scale showing incremental graduations from light to dark.

Simplifying Values

The concept of simplifying values might sound like it should be easy, but it takes patience and the ability to stop and really think about your light, middle and dark shapes before you jump into color. When your painting is based on a value sketch that has been organized, simplified and worked out, it rests on a strong foundation that shows in the end result.

It's understandable if you to want to jump in with color right away. Who doesn't? However, painting without thinking about values and composition is like jumping into a car to drive cross-country without a road map, and hoping you'll reach your destination.

Squint

The best way to see value relationships more clearly is to squint. The image in front of you will automatically appear more simplified because there is less light being perceived, which makes the large shapes appear to mass together. This will help you see and identify the overall pattern—minus the small details.

Remember, small details can hinder rather than help the overall strength of the painting. They should be considered finishing touches rather than structural, weight-bearing beams. When you see the big shapes that make up your subject, you can start to block them in and make decisions about how to simplify what you see. Squinting also de-emphasizes color. The lack of light cuts out color so you mostly see fuzzy black and gray shapes.

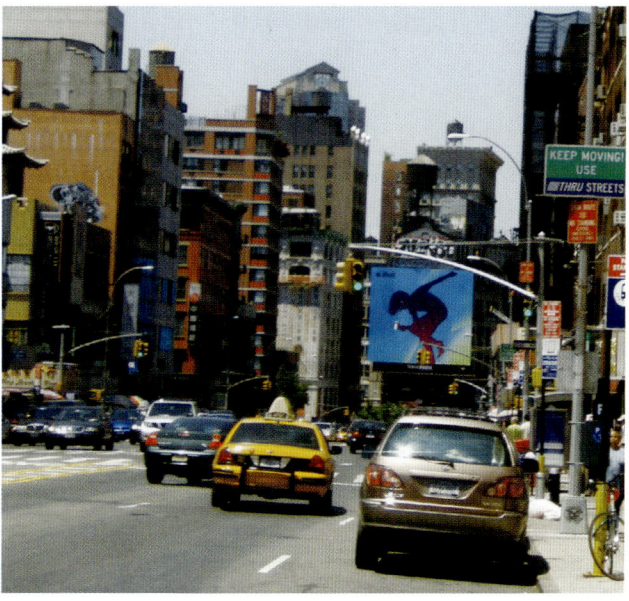

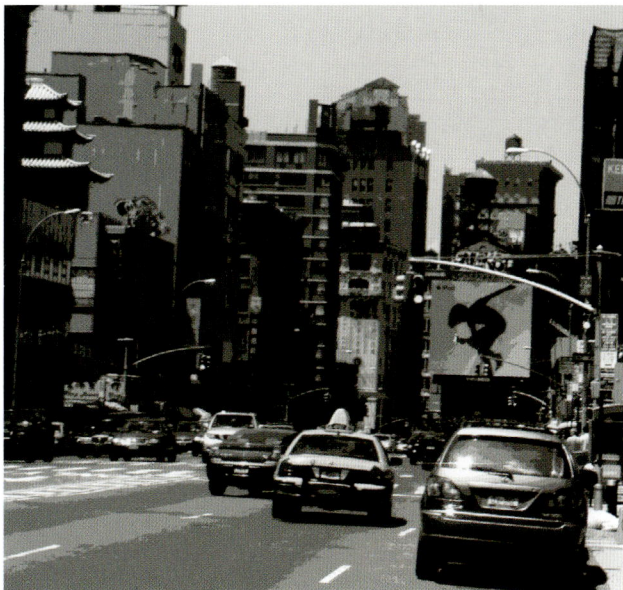

SIMPLIFIED TO TEN VALUES
Compare the color photo to the grayscale photo. The number of values on the grayscale photo has been reduced to ten, which helps to simplify the chaotic scene by massing together similar values.

Get Some Distance

When you go to an art museum, do you only view the paintings from a foot or two away, or do you look at them from more of a distance? A painting should look cohesive and readable from across a room. Many artists, especially beginners, tend to work very close to their paintings. This leads to focusing more on tiny details than on the general relationships between big shapes.

When creating a preliminary value sketch, it is important to consider how the final painting will read from a distance. Walking away from your work and viewing it from 10 feet away will help you to decide whether it reads well. Squinting does the same thing, as well as looking at a very small thumbnail image on your computer screen.

If you are having problems with a value sketch and can't judge whether the subject is reading clearly or not, try stepping back several feet and squinting. If you can't tell what the sketch is depicting, or if too many similar values are merging together causing the subject to get lost, continue working with the shapes and values until it reads more definitively.

It's not a simple process, but it's necessary to work out this foundational stage to your satisfaction before moving on to color.

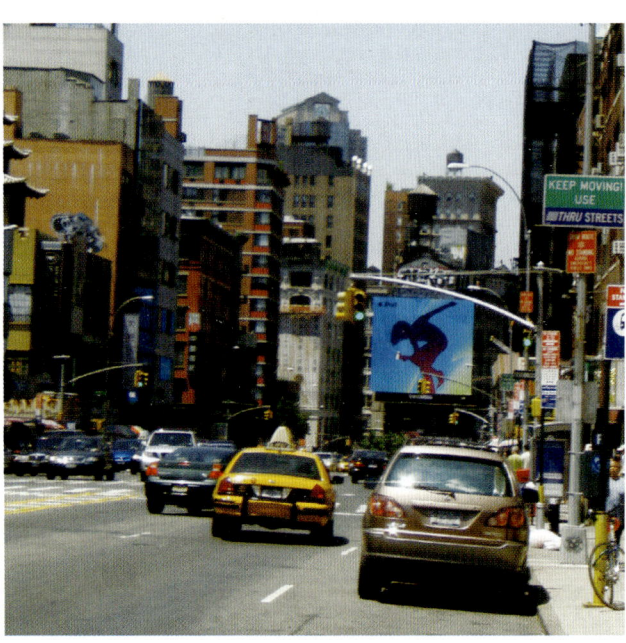

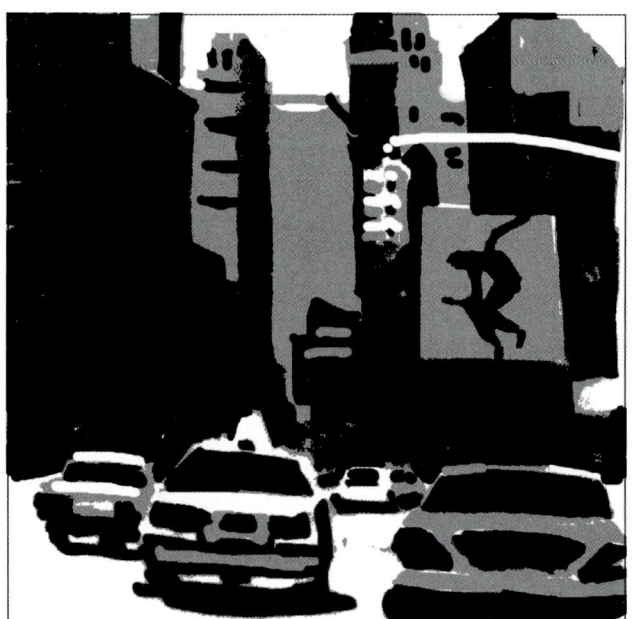

SIMPLIFIED TO THREE VALUES
Now the complex urban scene has been translated to just three values to create a simple and strong composition. You can and should use your artistic license where necessary to clean up chaos. Detail can be added later during the painting stage.

Creating a Value Sketch

Creating a preliminary three-value sketch before you start painting will help you see the overall light, middle and dark patterns so you can make decisions about design and composition—the foundation of any painting. It only makes sense to plan ahead before you spend hours, days, weeks or even months working on a painting.

Mass Shapes

Create one or even several value sketches of your subject matter and try to simplify your composition into a few recognizable shapes and values. Be willing to veer away from what you actually see and change shapes, modify values and anything else you deem necessary in the interest of creating order and organization out of visual chaos.

Use Artistic License

Keep your eraser handy because you will try out ideas and change your mind often. This is part of the design process. Remember, you are not working with numbers; you are working with visual information that is being filtered through your personal sense of aesthetics. What do you think looks good? Does it convey your subject clearly? Will it be readable from a distance when you squint at it? These are all questions you will need to ask yourself.

Color Won't Save You

Many artists do not plan ahead and just start painting what they see in the hopes that color will save the day. I do not recommend this. In fact, there is a popular saying, "Color gets all the credit, but value does all the work."

If you work out your composition as you paint, making changes and revisions with hues, values, shapes and placement, your colors will become overworked and muddy. Muddy colors are the result of changing your mind so many times that the colors all start to blend into gray-brown. Having a game plan for value organization is not only the key to strong compositions, it's also one of the keys to cleaner colors.

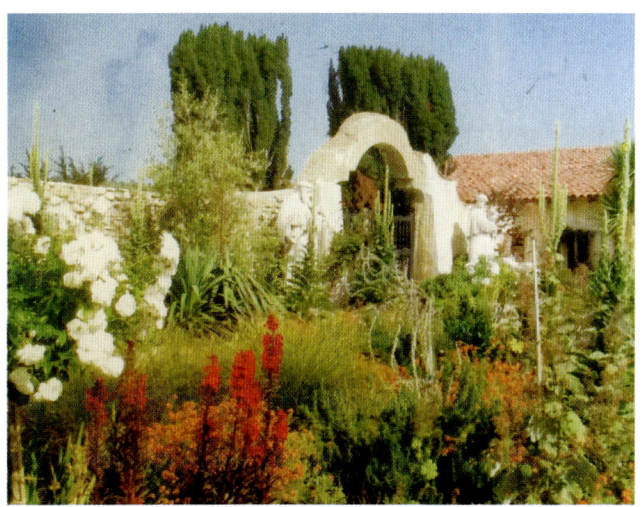

ORGANIZE AND SIMPLIFY
There is a fair amount of complexity in the scene, but a quick value sketch shows you everything you need to organize and simplify.

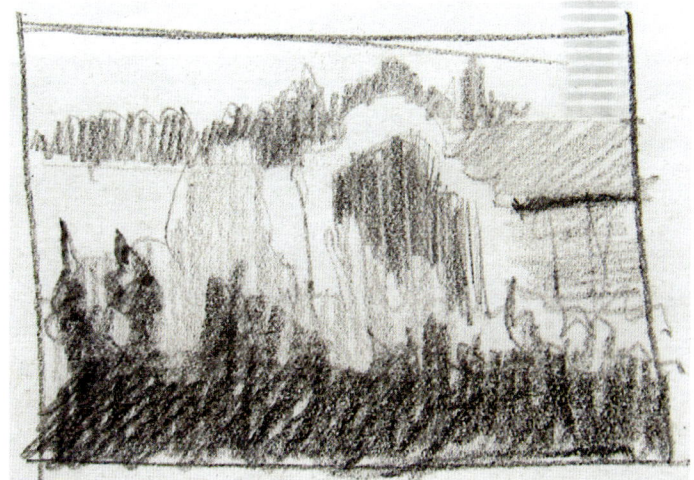

Follow Your Plan

When you have completed one or more sketches, decide which composition you like best and move forward with the painting. Keep your value sketch in plain view while painting so you can refer to it and ensure you are following your plan and sticking with the decisions you made earlier. When mixing your colors, make certain they correspond to your value plan. (See Chapter 2 for more information on this.) Having a value "map" in front of you will allow you to loosen up and paint with more confidence because you will have laid the groundwork for a strong foundation upon which the painting will rest.

It does take some time and effort to compose these value sketches, depending on how complex your scene is, but if you can't simplify the composition in black and white, it will be far more difficult to do it in color.

A value sketch should not be large or overly time consuming. Fifteen minutes for a 4" × 5" (10cm × 13cm) sketch is all you need. Don't make the mistake of doing a large, elaborate rendering. That defeats the point of learning to simplify. A quick visual guideline is all that is necessary to keep you on track. Keep it simple!

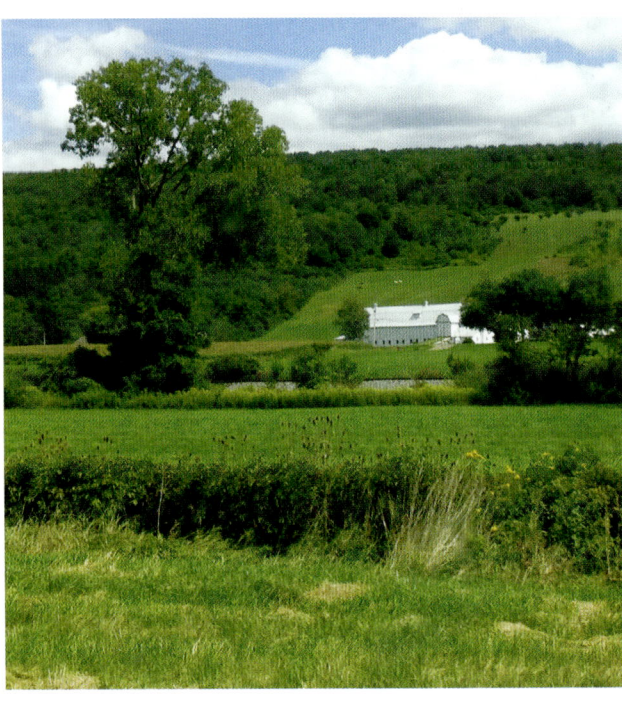 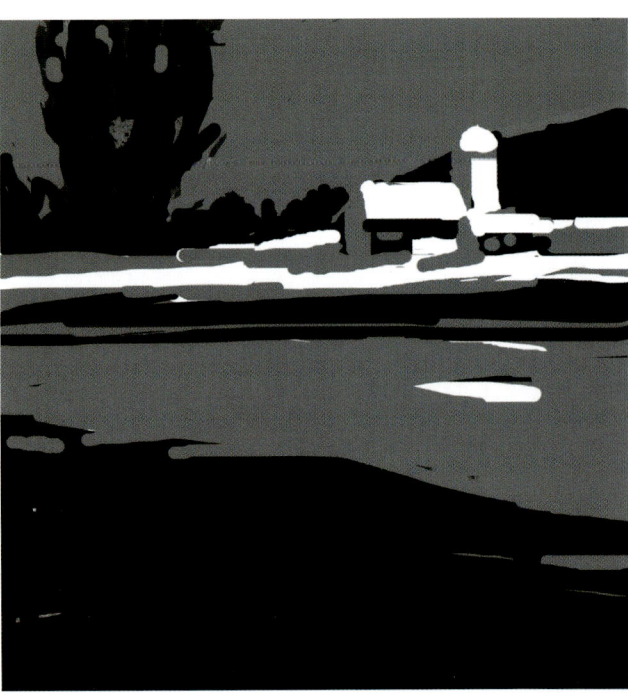

SOME SCENES MAY REQUIRE SIGNIFICANT CHANGES
This landscape has been translated and simplified down to a handful of values. In the value sketch you can see that significant changes were made to the overall composition and its elements. These decisions were made according to my artistic license; what I thought the painting needed.

Each artist has to decide for themselves what, if anything, should be done to strengthen their composition. You may like this scene exactly the way it is. Personally, I felt that the background hills merged with the large tree, so I changed the angle of the hills to a diagonal and lowered it altogether to emphasize and separate the tree. I thought the ravine in the foreground looked like a stripe and broke up the composition too much, so I unified the whole lower area into one shape and value.

Your decisions may differ completely. There is no absolute right or wrong—it depends on your artistic preferences.

Value Sketch vs. a Sketch

Let's explore the differences between a value sketch and a typical sketch.

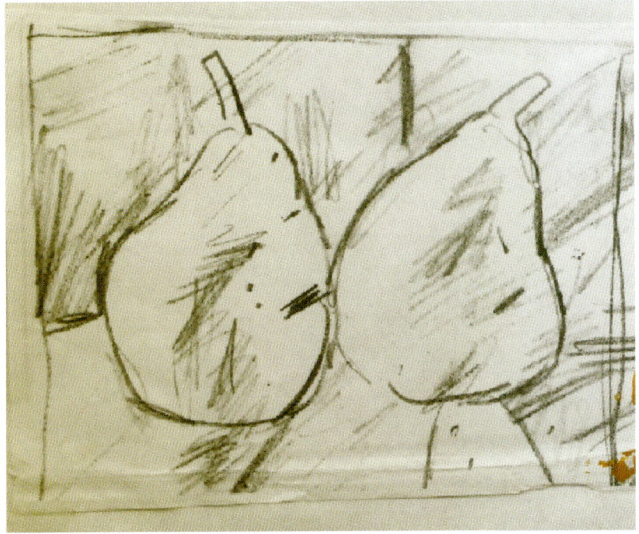 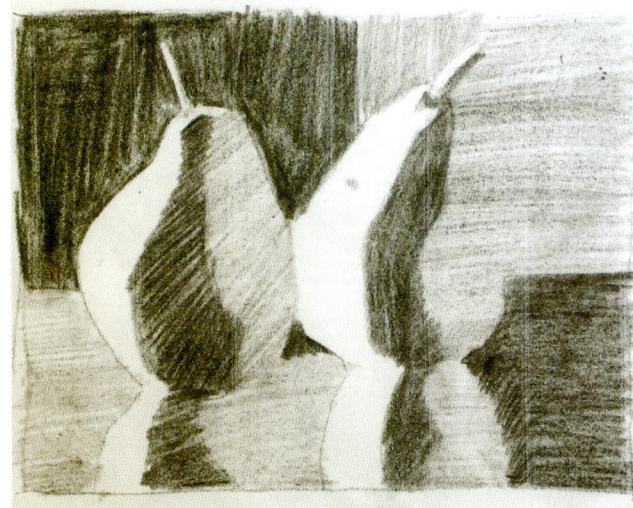

SIDE BY SIDE COMPARISON

The pears displayed on the left are considered a typical sketch. The basic shape and delineation of the foreground and background are indicated by lines. The shapes are not filled in with solid gray or black. There is no indication of the dark-light pattern.

The image on the right is considered a value sketch. There is a clear, readable dark-light pattern. Each area of the picture has a value attached to it, like puzzle pieces that all fit together. No area has been left undecided.

Just Do It!

It is important to emphasize that the point of the value sketch is in "the doing." As artists we make decisions visually, not theoretically. Many students want to skip this process and simply mentally theorize on what they plan to do in their value sketch. Unless you have spent years working out artistic compositions with limited values, such as in the capacity of a graphic designer or a printer, this approach will work against you.

As visual composers, we must make our decisions and judgments by seeing, reacting and revising. It is a visual process. We need to *see* how the shapes and values work together, or not. This is not something that can be done by theorizing. As the motto goes, *Just Do It!* Talking about what you are going to do without actually doing it defeats the entire point. The time you save by skipping the value sketch now will be added tenfold when you are struggling with a weak, unresolved painting later.

If you are new to this process, be patient with yourself! Learning to simplify values is not easy, nor is it easy to teach. Because of this, many teachers limit their critiques to pointing out drawing inaccuracies. But no matter how accomplished your drawing skills, if your values are weak or disorganized, you will not end up with strong, dramatic paintings. As much as possible, practice reducing your values down to three or four.

Interpreting a Subject Into a Value Sketch

Squint at the pear photo below and notice how the light background in the upper left corner is almost the same value as the yellow light-struck part of the pear. This needs to be worked out in the value sketch. Should they be kept the same value or should a darker value be assigned to the background? At what point should the light value of the background turn into a middle value? Where should the line of demarcation go between light and middle? Do they change along a vertical or diagonal axis? What about the spots? If made dark, will they contribute to or detract from the pear shape? These are the sorts of questions you should ask as you design your composition. Try to work out these issues in a value sketch rather than in your head.

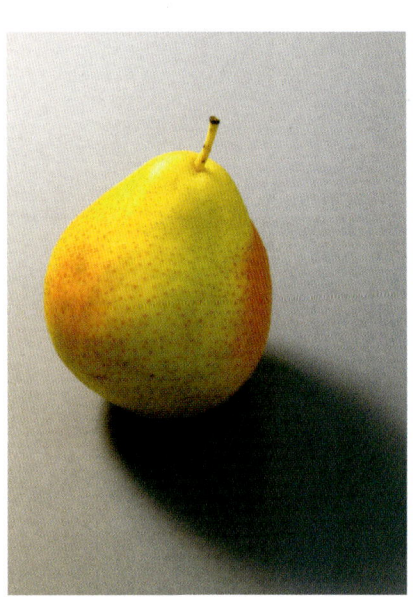

THE TRICK PEAR
I call this photo "The Trick Pear" because my students often get hung up on the color spots in their attempts to simplify. Some of them have even told me that it is impossible to break this down into three values.

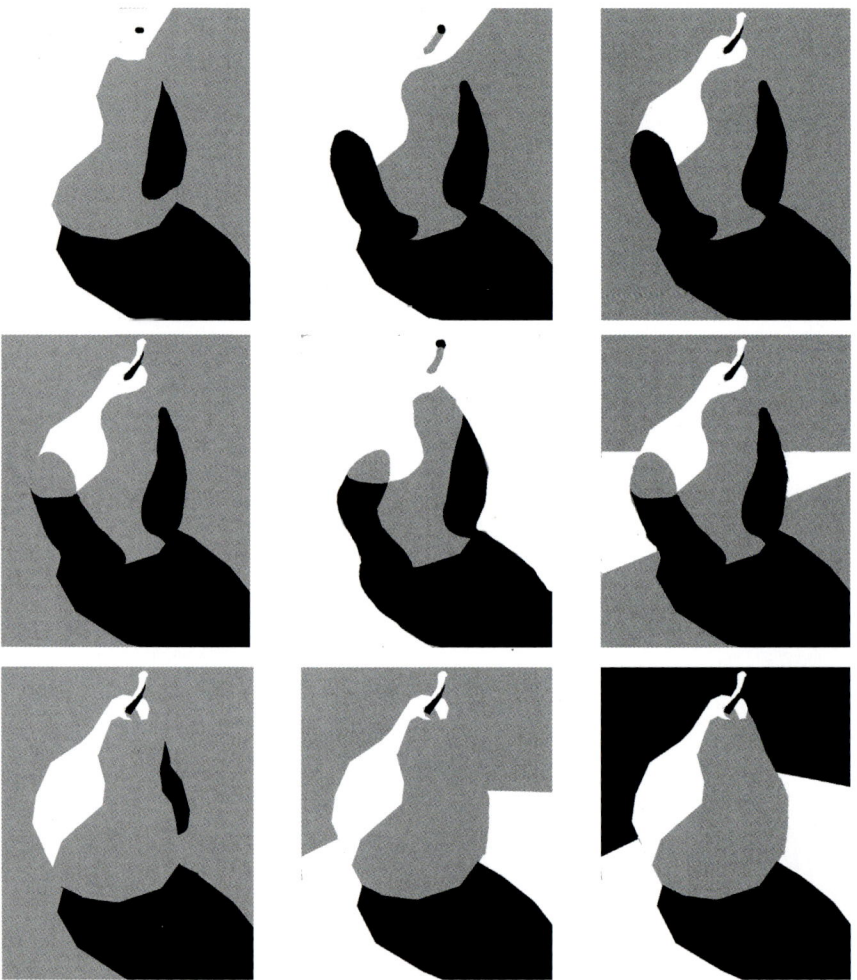

VARIATIONS OF THE TRICK PEAR IN THREE VALUES
Impossible? Not at all! Here are a few variations on translating the photo into three values. The first pear is what you might create if you were basing the value sketch on what you actually see. If you look at it from a distance, however, it may not read as a pear at all. Remember—it's about creating an image that works—not replicating what's actually there. Squint at each one, or view them from a distance, or both. Which one reads most easily as a pear? There is no absolute answer, only opinions. Try different variations to determine your preference for how to best simplify.

If you decide to remove the spots in your value sketch, it does not mean that they need to be absent from the final painting. It simply means that the color of the spots will be consistent with the value you have assigned that area in your sketch. (We will discuss this further in the next chapter.)

Avoiding Pitfalls

Let's take a look at a more complex subject: flowers in a vase. In the example below you can see that there are many shades of tonal values. How would you translate this subject into just three values? As I mentioned earlier, the best way is to pull out your sketchbook, start chipping away at it, and explore some variations to see what looks best.

The biggest mistake students make when learning to compare values is hyper-focusing on the subject rather than squinting at it. They then proceed to break each small area up into light, middle *and* dark values by comparing every value with whichever value is directly next to it. This will result in a value pattern that is disorganized and very busy with lots of tiny shapes. Your goal is to simplify—not to make things more complex.

Squint and look at the larger general areas of light and dark. Compare values all over the painting. Ignore the tiny details by squinting them out of sight. If you hone in on every little value and compare it only to the value directly next to it, you will soon find yourself in a maze of confusion and frustration. The resulting image will be more decorative and chaotic than structural. Squint and generalize. Compare the big shapes, not the tiny fluctuations. I can't stress this enough.

It is also important to take visual cues from the light-struck planes of your subject and compare with the areas in shadow. Assign a different value to each. That will give you a more structural, dimensional depiction. Any part of your subject that is in light cannot be the same value as the portion in shadow.

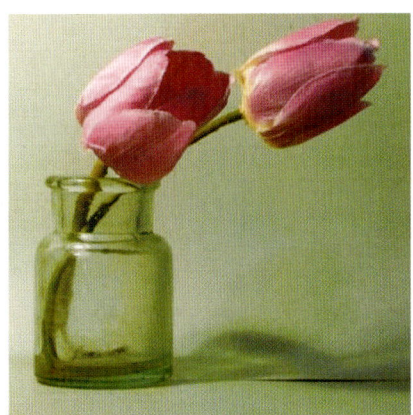

IDENTIFY PROBLEM AREAS
From a value standpoint, this photo of tulips has the same problem as the pear photo. The upper left background is the same value as the light pink on the left tulip. You can see that the tulip separates from the background only due to the difference in their colors. But since you can't use color in the value sketch, you will have to create a composition that works without relying on color.

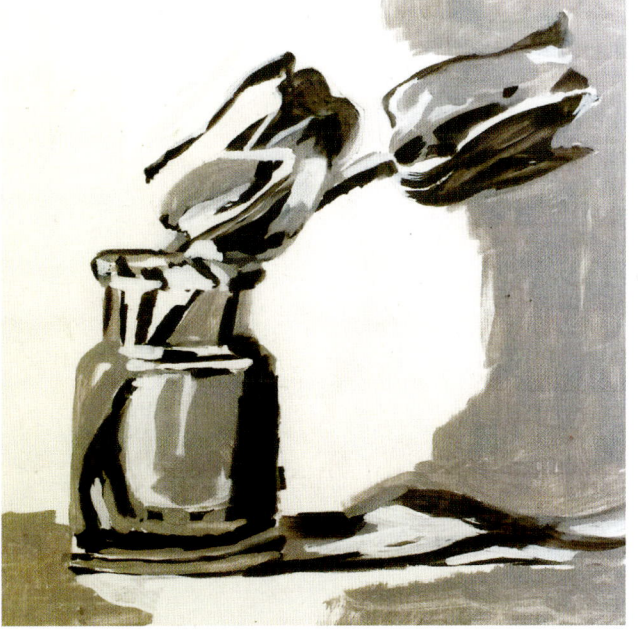

WHAT NOT TO DO
Here is an example of an unsuccessful value sketch. The drawing is fine, and the three values separate clearly from each other. However, the form has been broken up into too many detailed pieces. It is visually quite busy, and there are spots of the three values scattered around every part of the image. Although the background in the photo on the previous page seems to get darker on the right side, translating that shift into a middle value gives the composition an awkward and off-balance feeling. Remember—it's your job to design how the scene as it *should be,* not copy it as is.

SIMPLIFY AND MERGE VALUES

Your goal is to simplify and merge values together that are close in both proximity and value. These examples are more effective at communicating the form and structure of the tulips—with less tiny shapes and more simplicity.

Be aware of plane changes and how to use values to imply three dimensions. Wherever there is a plane change from light to shadow, there is also a value change. The tulip flower has a cylindrical form. When being illuminated by one light source, the plane struck directly by light must be a different value than where the plane has turned away from the light and is in shadow.

This is what you want to communicate as simply as possible in your value sketch. Try to avoid rendering every superficial nook and cranny. Only render the details that you consider to be essential to your painting.

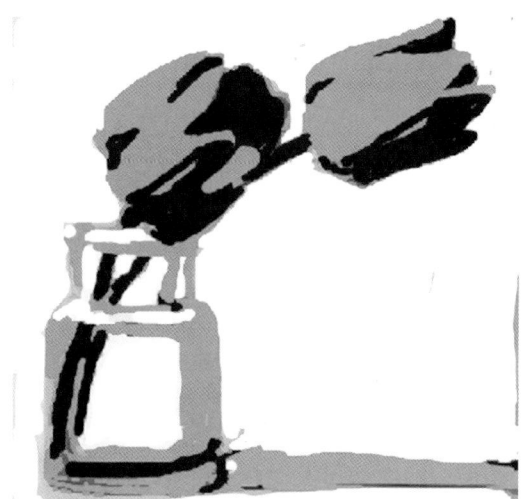

Light Background; Middle and Dark Flowers

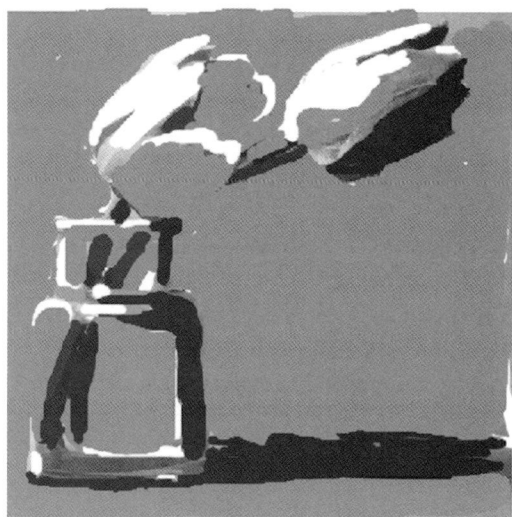

Middle Background; Light and Middle Flowers

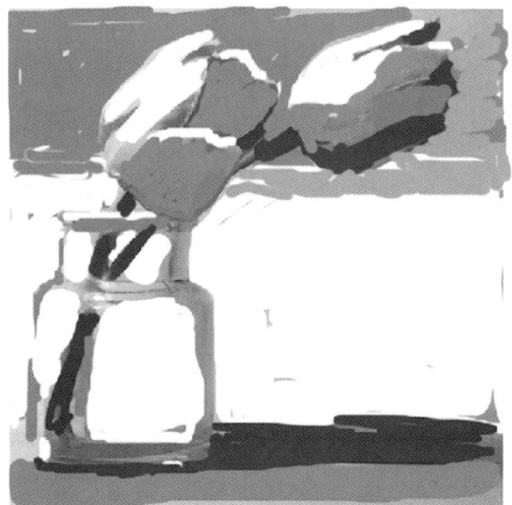

Light and Middle Background; Light and Middle Flowers

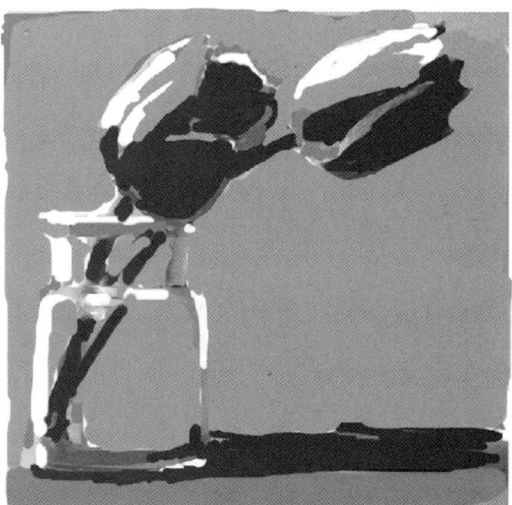

Middle Background; Light, Middle and Dark Flowers

Composition

When composing your value sketch, consider the following basic guidelines to strengthen your design and overall composition.

Dominant Values

Make an effort to design your sketch so that one of your values will take up most of the picture area. The boldest compositions have a dominant value. Try to avoid having equal amounts of each value in your composition.

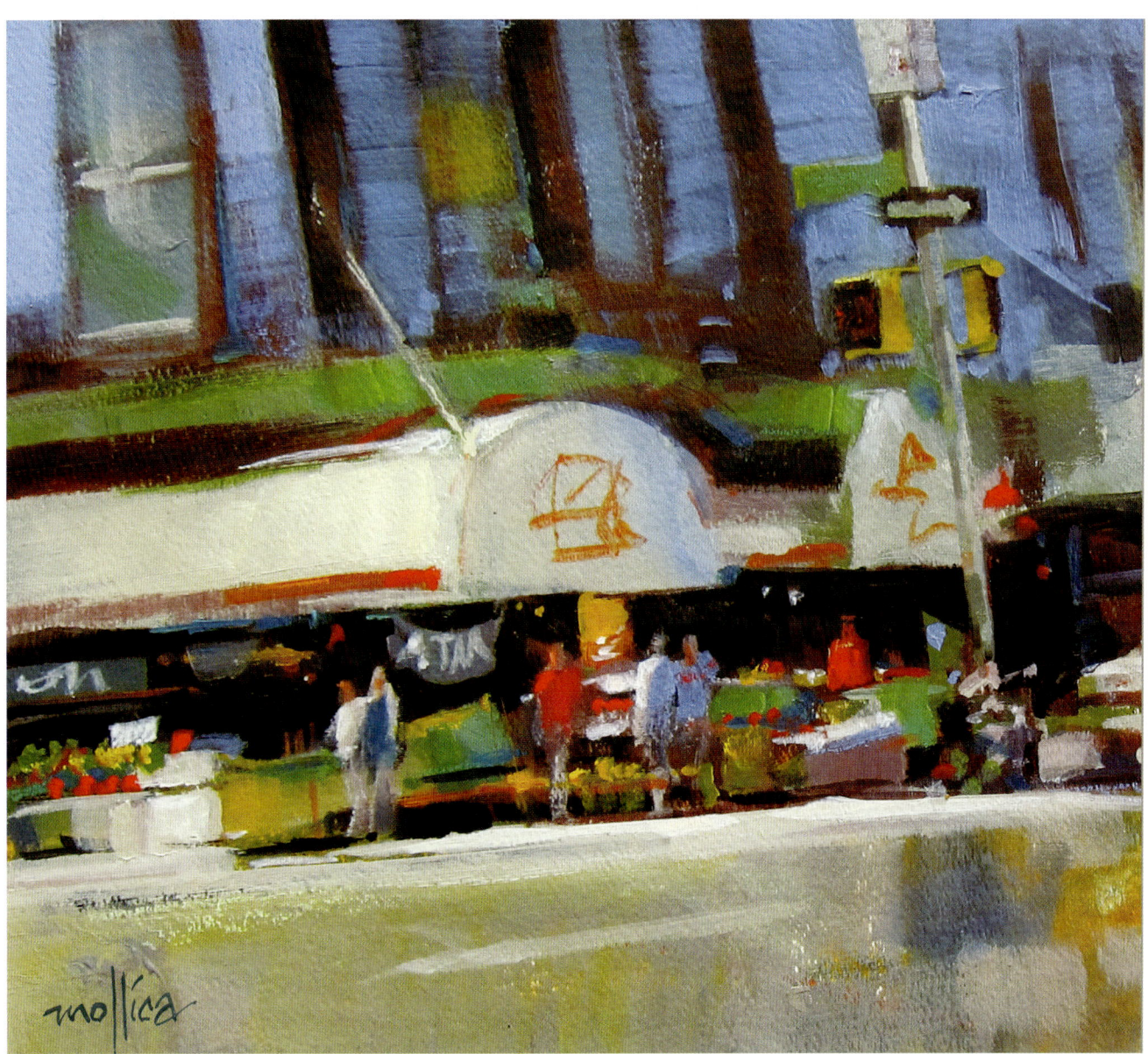

DECIDE ON A DOMINANT VALUE

There is a dominance of middle value and dark value, with very little light value. The large light shape of the awning hemmed in by dark shapes above and below leads the eye to the figures. The strong directional lines of the windows also lead the eye downward. The large middle value shape of the road frames in and provides a contrast for the light-value streak of sidewalk, again bringing the eye to the figures.

BLUE BUILDING ON TENTH AVE.
Acrylic on panel
16" × 16" (41cm × 41cm)
Private collection

Focal Point

Decide where you want the viewer's eye to land—that will be the primary area of interest in the painting known as the focal point. A properly designed composition will lead the viewer's eye right to it. Although this is more relevant in landscapes than still life paintings, your focal point should be supported by your design and the value patterns that lead up to it. Elements of color, value and directional shapes should be employed and emphasized so that there is a pathway leading around your painting to the focal point.

The eye will automatically be attracted to the area of the painting where the lightest and darkest values are in closest proximity to each other. If the values are scattered and don't offer any type of path toward the focal point, the viewer won't know where to engage with the painting.

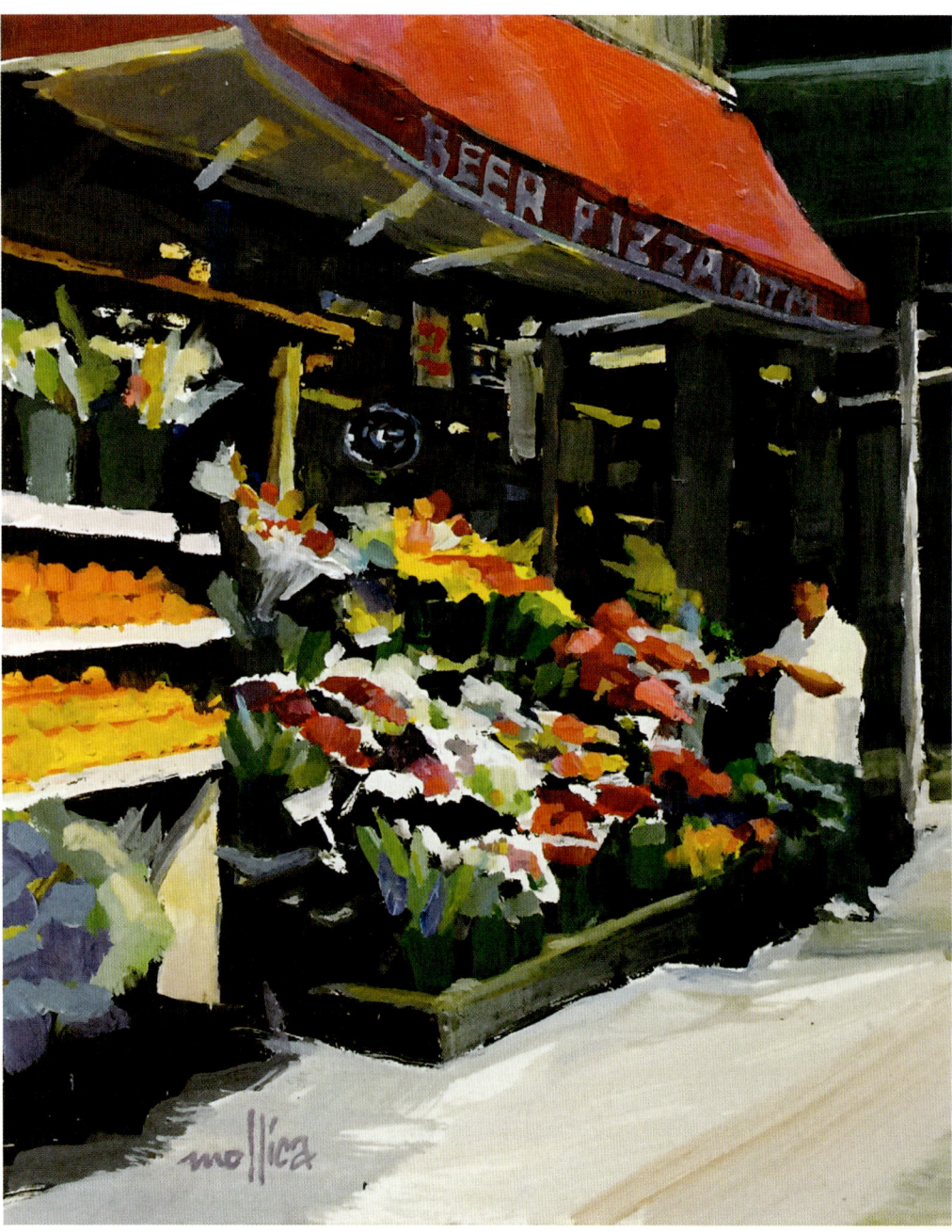

LEAD THE VIEWER'S EYE
Notice how the perspective lines of the fruit, flowers and sidewalk lead the eye directly to the figure, which is the lightest value surrounded by the darkest value. The viewer's eye is immediately drawn to the strongest areas of contrast in the painting. Use this strategy when establishing your focal point.

FLOWER DUDE
Acrylic on panel
16" × 12" (41cm × 30cm)
Private collection

Cropping

Many beginner painters make the common mistake of positioning the entire subject smack in the middle of the canvas, floating in space. Cropping some elements slightly off the picture area is much more interesting and creates more variety in the negative space.

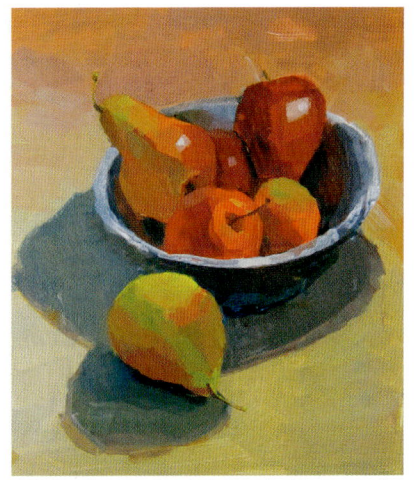

POOR CROPPING

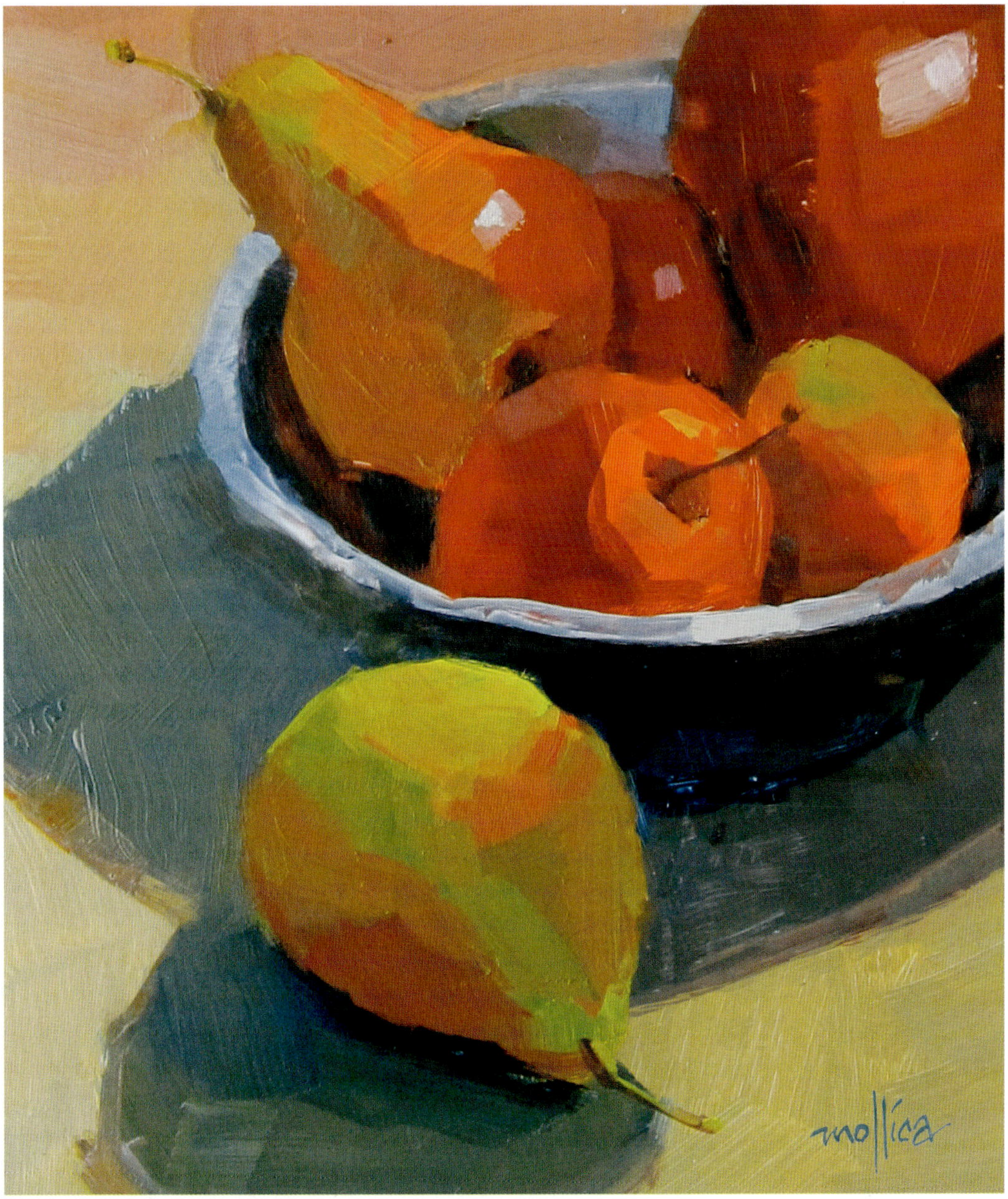

CROP WISELY TO KEEP THINGS INTERESTING
Cropping the painting with the fruit positioned exactly in the middle have created awkward tension in the composition.

FRUITFUL
Acrylic on canvas
10" × 8" (25cm × 20cm)
Collection of Laura Thompson

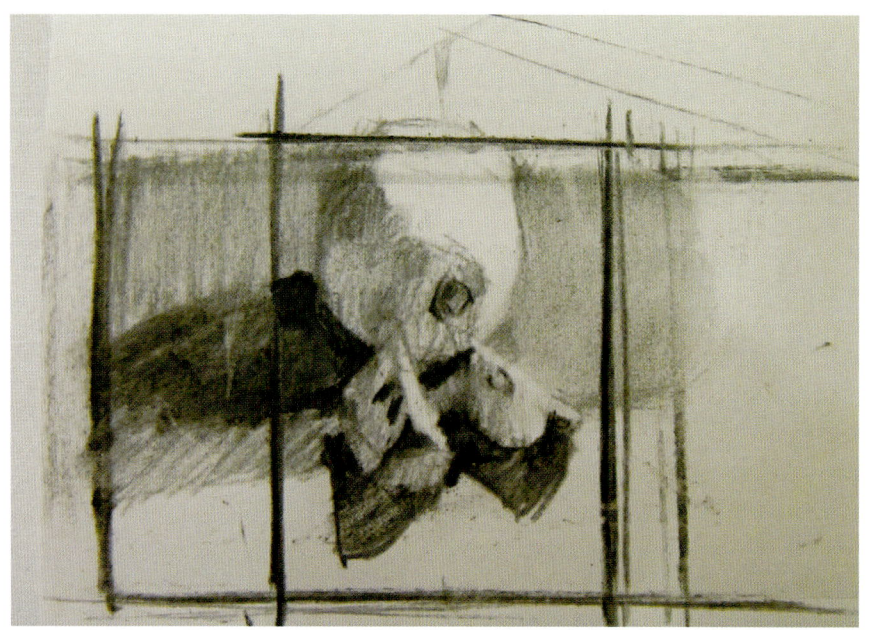

TRY VARIATIONS

Note how the top of the orange and the cast shadow get cropped off the picture area. This is more compelling than having every element centered within the picture boundary.

Try cropping your sketch so that the space around your subject (i.e. negative space) has interesting and unequal-sized shapes. Decide in your sketch how to crop your subject to see where it should be positioned on the canvas.

My initial idea was to position the orange and slices on a horizontal format. But after looking at my sketch, I decided it might be more interesting in a vertical format. Try different variations; change your mind. Just be sure you do it all before you start painting!

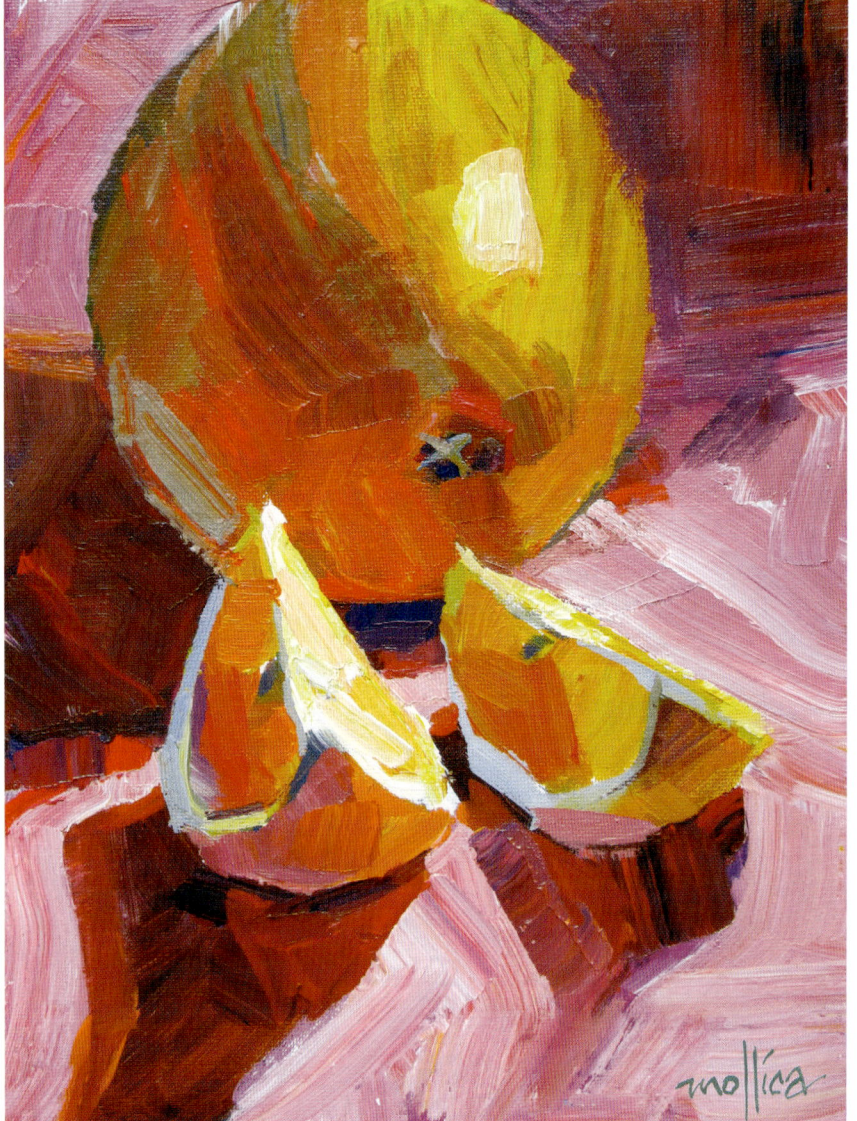

PINK ON ORANGE
Acrylic on canvas
12" × 9" (30cm × 23cm)
Collection of Mark Hagan

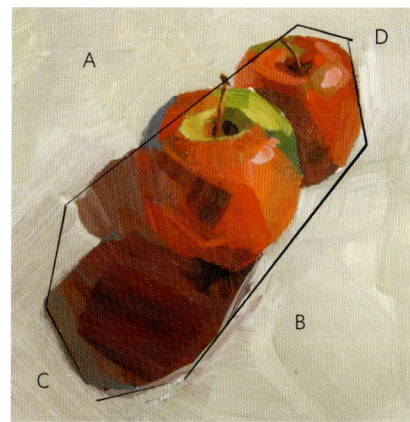

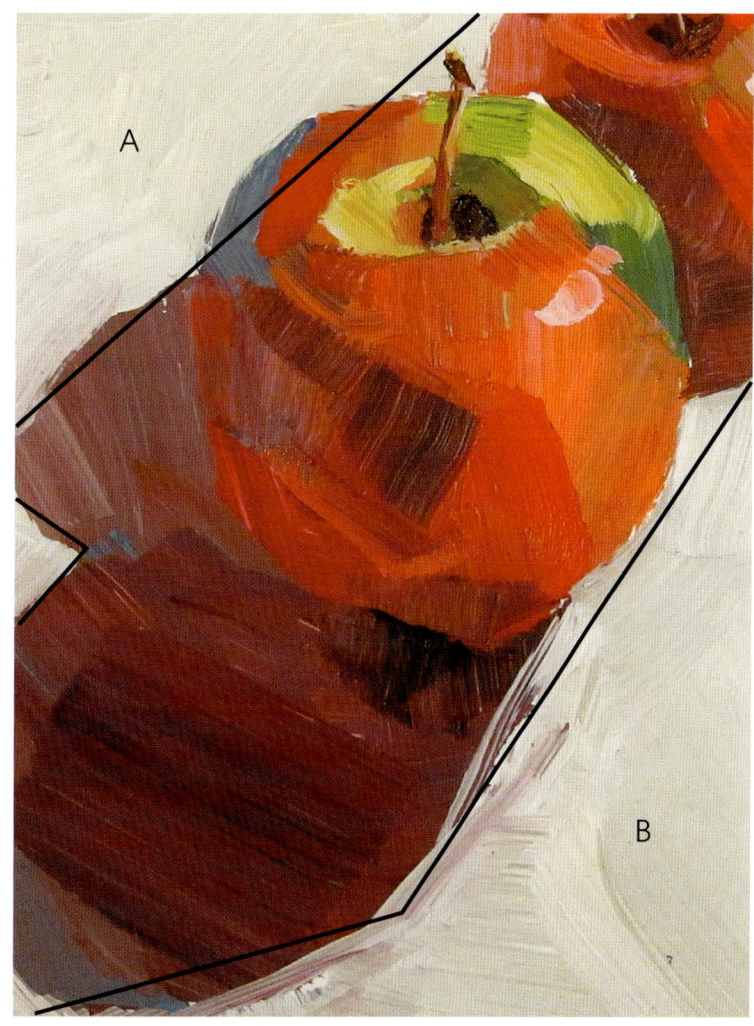

GOOD CROP VS. BAD CROP

With a square formatting (above) the space around the apples is equal. A = B and C = D. In the example to the right, the shapes are unequal and therefore more interesting. Also notice that although the apple sits in the exact middle of the canvas, the cast shadow and the background apple are cropped so that they go beyond the borders. This diagonal movement offsets the static quality of an object placed in the middle of the canvas.

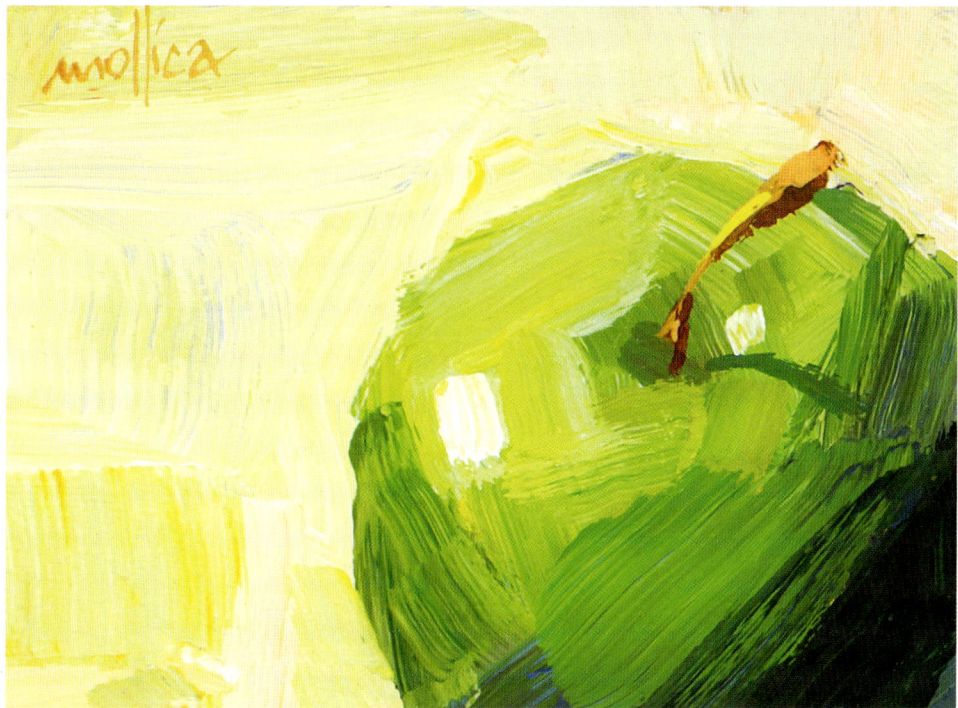

GRANNY SMITH
Acrylic on board
6" × 8" (15cm × 20cm)

Here is another example of interesting cropping and placement of a subject.

Rule of Thirds

The Rule of Thirds states than an image is most pleasing when the subject or focal point is placed along an intersection of imaginary lines that divide the image into thirds—both vertically and horizontally.

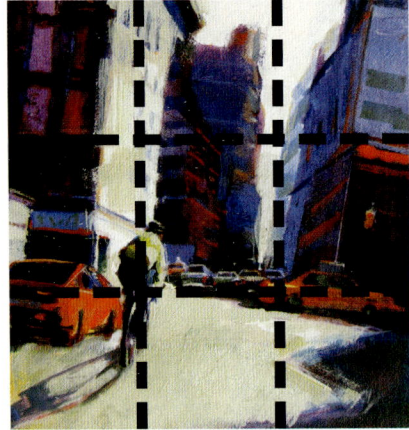

THE IMAGE IN THIRDS

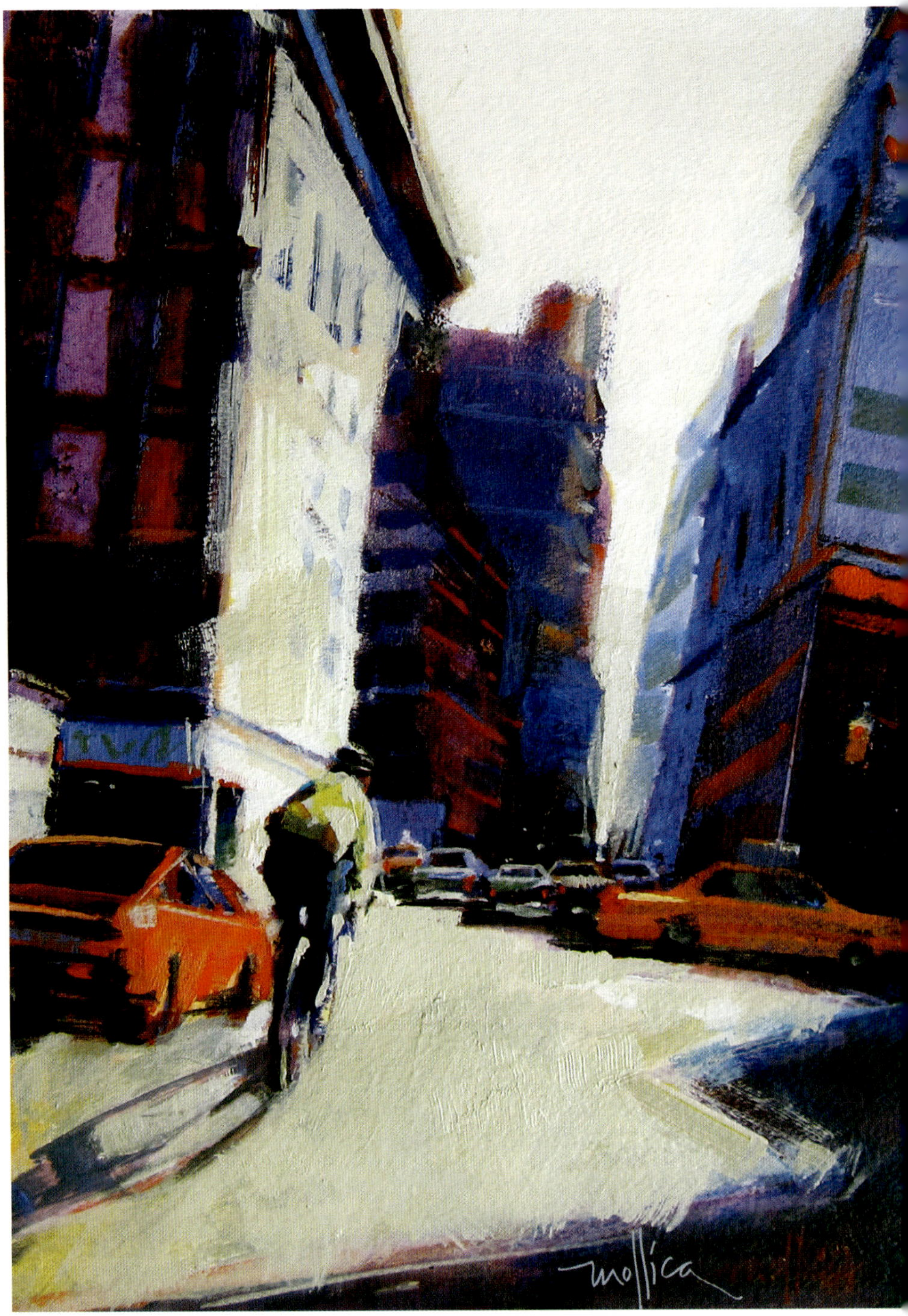

HORIZON AND FOCAL POINT PLACEMENT IS KEY

Try to avoid splitting the composition of your painting in half, vertically or horizontally. It is more interesting to place your horizon line either high or low on the canvas. Your focal point is best positioned anywhere but directly in the middle of the canvas.

ZIG ZAG THROUGH MIDTOWN
Acrylic on canvas
24" × 18" (61cm × 46cm)
Private collection

Overlapping Objects

When composing your setup, try overlapping some elements to create a more dynamic sense of space and better relationships between the elements. When objects are placed evenly apart with no overlapping, the resulting composition can be boring and flat.

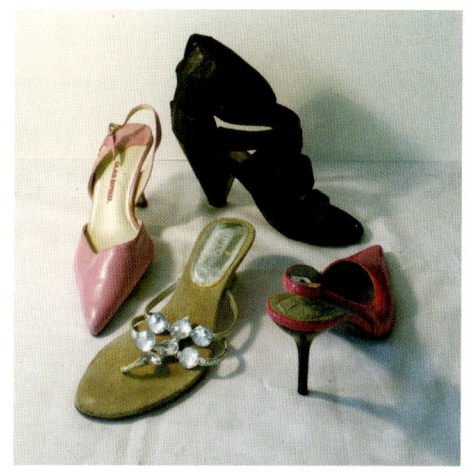

POOR COMPOSITION

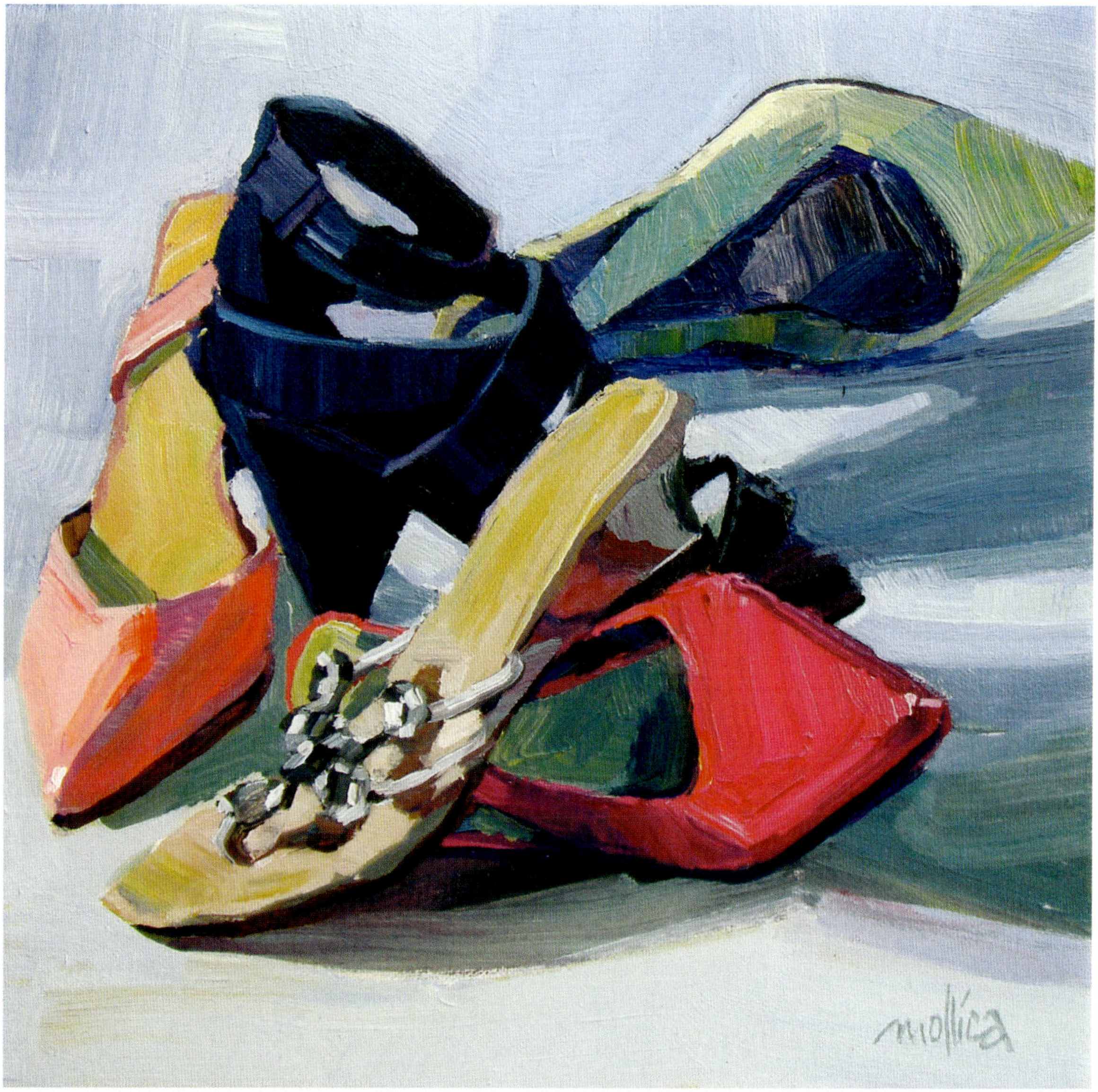

GOOD COMPOSITION

A sense of space and distance is created when objects in a composition overlap. If the objects sit alone, the composition feels flat with no sense of dimension.

STRAP HAPPY
Acrylic on canvas
12" × 12" (30cm × 30cm)
Collection of Ute Spatz

Variety

The eye loves variety. It is intrigued by unequal divisions of space and alignment, and differences in shapes, edges, textures, directional lines and size. Try to create compositions that are dynamic by the conscious inclusion and arrangement of pictorial elements that play off each other. Here are a few suggestions:

- Make the divisions of space around and between objects unequal and uneven.
- Avoid aligning objects on a horizontal or vertical axis.
- Include a variety of shapes, sizes and proportions in your painting. If the composition feels overly geometric, consider adding or emphasizing an organic shape for visual contrast. Alternate your brushwork edges. Contrast hard, sharp edges near the focal point with soft, feathery edges in the subordinate areas.
- Enhance smooth or solid color passages with busy, tactile areas.
- Contrast a dominant horizontal composition such as a flat landscape with strong vertical or diagonal elements like a telephone pole or tree.

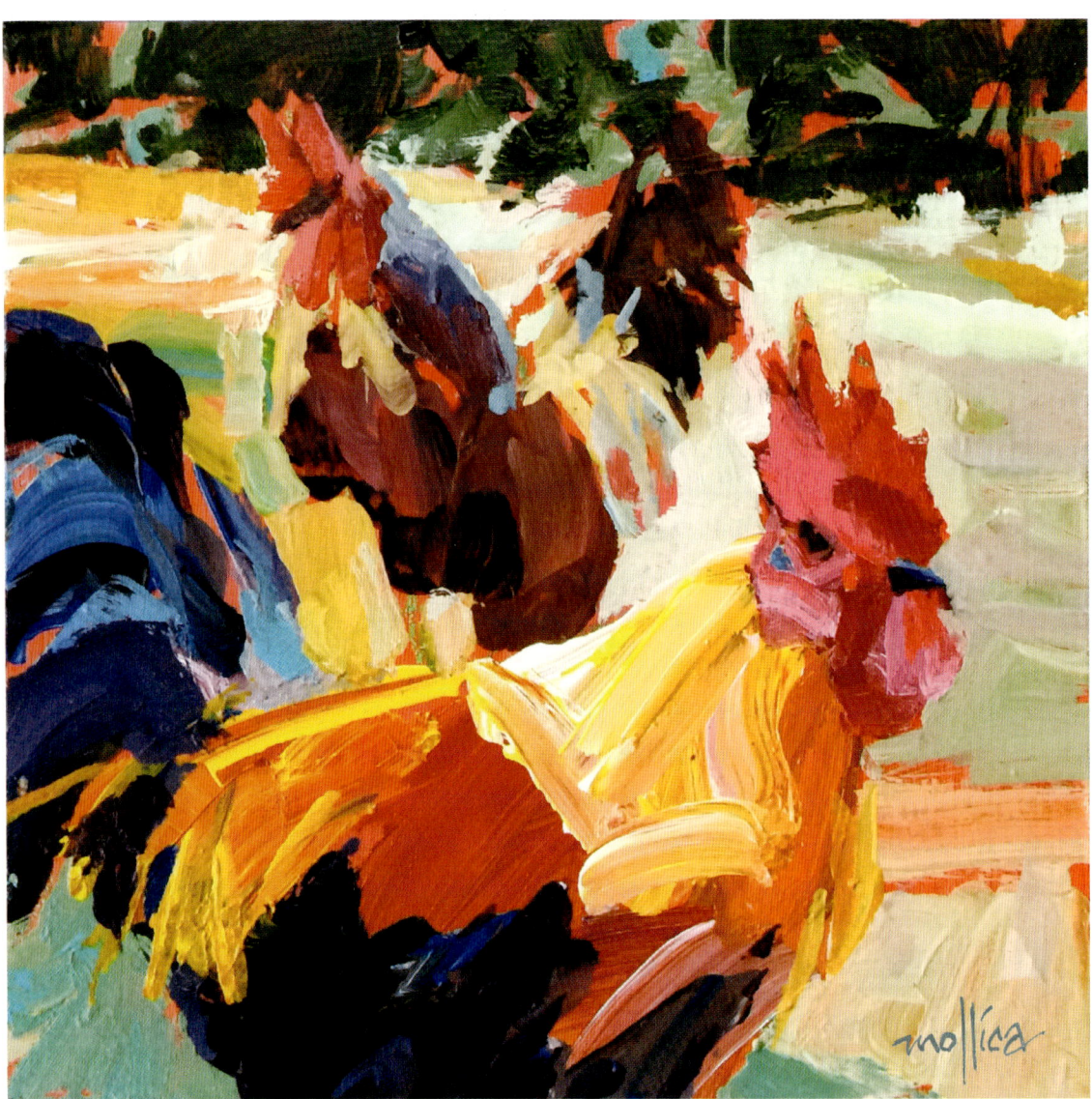

CREATE VISUAL CONTRAST
Notice the variety in linework, angles, shapes, textures and unusual cropping.

CHICKADEAUX
Acrylic on panel
8" × 8" (20cm × 20cm)
Collection of Susan Martin

Materials for Creating Value Sketches

Each artist has their own preferences for how they execute their value plans. There is no best way; it is a matter of what you find most comfortable and effective. Here are some options.

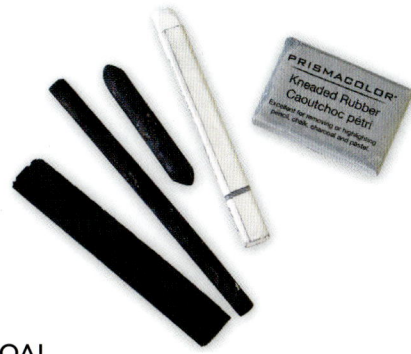

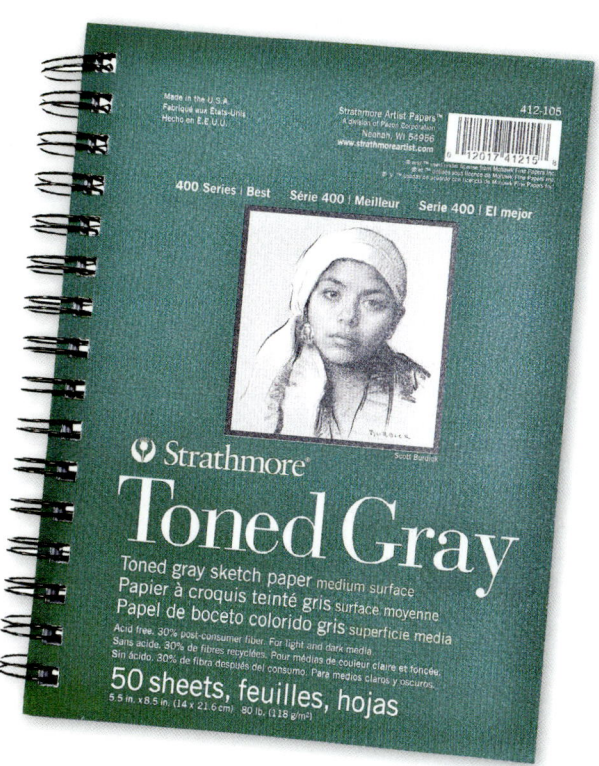

SOFT VINE CHARCOAL AND GRAY TONED PAPER

I use soft vine charcoal and white pastel on gray toned paper to create my value sketches. The gray paper serves as the middle tone. When pressed down, the vine charcoal creates dark black tones. The white pastel indicates the lightest tones.

For many years I worked on a white sketchpad, simply using the white of the paper as the light value. This is a good method because the vine charcoal is so easy to erase—you can change your mind and revise quickly and easily.

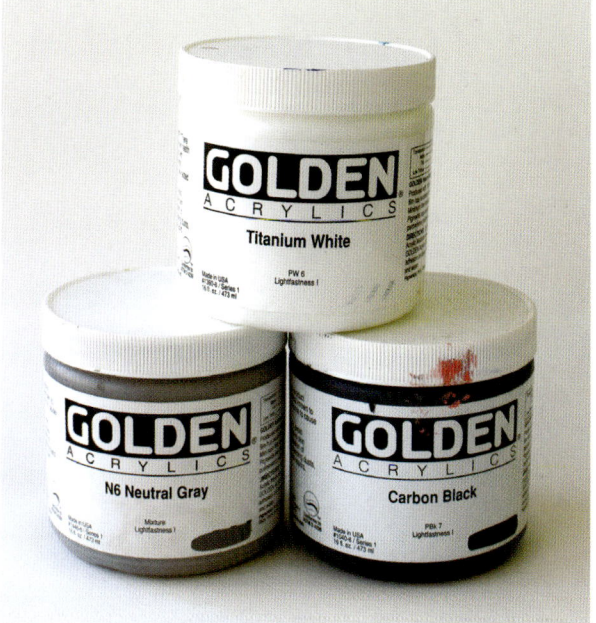

PAINTS

Some artists prefer to create their value sketches in paint, using black, white and middle gray paint on inexpensive canvas boards or gessoed paper. This is a perfectly valid approach, although things can get a bit messier when you change your mind. Often students who use this approach start creating more than three values, so just be careful that your three values don't gradually turn into ten.

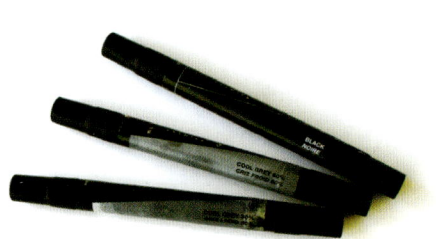

GRAY MARKER AND WHITE PAPER

Some prefer a black and gray marker on white paper, with the paper serving as the light tone. If you want to try other designs you will have to start again from scratch, since the marker does not erase. So be prepared to do several variations.

You could also work on a vellum paper that is slightly transparent. You can use your initial sketch as a template so you don't have to re-create each time.

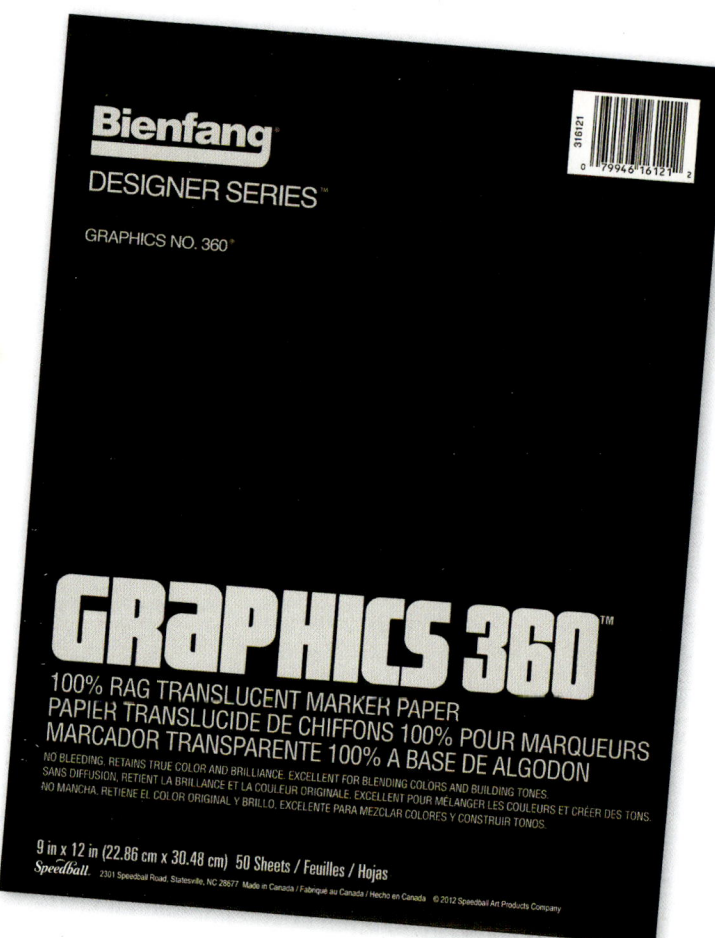

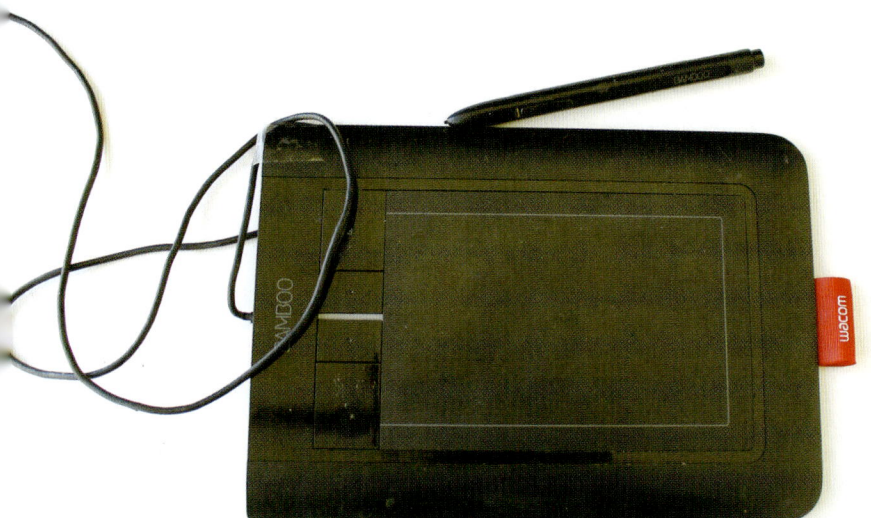

DIGITAL

If you are comfortable with digital technology, there are many digital painting and sketching programs such as Procreate®, ArtRage®, Photoshop® and others. It is fast and easy to create a sketch using a digital brush or a pressure-sensitive stylus to "paint" in your black and middle gray tones. The benefit is that your values will be clear and definite—no mixing or smudging occurs. It also allows you to explore many versions easily and quickly.

Tools for Seeing in Limited Values

If you are having trouble breaking down a scene into simple shapes and limited values, there are tools that can help. Some filter color and turn it into various shades of gray. Others limit the number of values to whatever number you choose. Here are a few of the most popular tools and methods to experiment with.

- **Viewfinders.** Often a scene is so complex it can feel overwhelming, especially in a plein air setting. Looking through a "window" automatically simplifies the amount of visual information by isolating or cropping a scene within a rectangular area.
- **Red gel filters.** Some artists use a red gel or red-tinted acetate to see values better. When you view a subject through the gel, it filters out the color so that the values are more clearly perceptible. There are also products that offer red gel in addition to some other helpful compositional tools for easy reference, such as a value scale.
- **Values finder app.** There is a mobile device app called ValueViewer that can be purchased and downloaded off the Internet. This software will allow you to upload any photo from your mobile device, or take a new one, and then run it through a filter designed to break the image into the number of values you choose.
- **Photoshop.** If you are familiar with how to use Photoshop or any other digital editing software, you can apply various filters to your images that will interpret values.

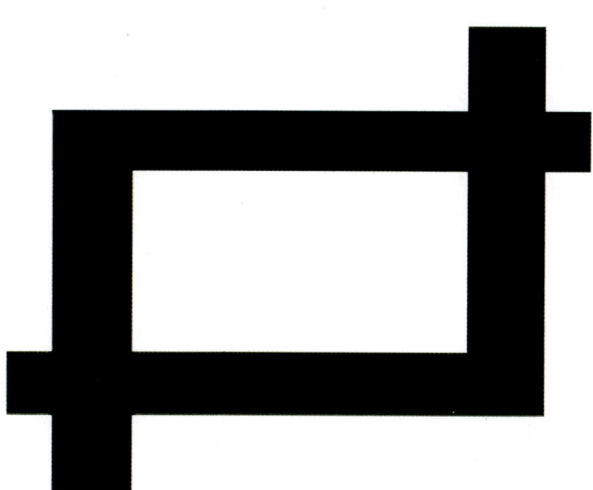

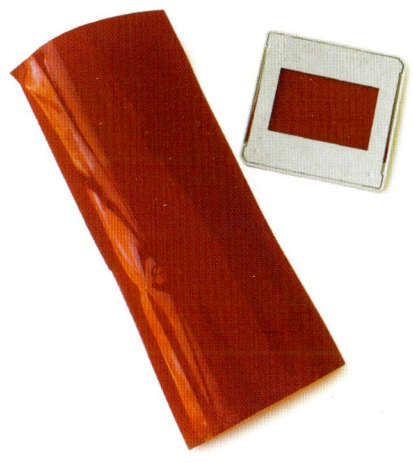

VIEWFINDERS

Look at the scene in front of you while squinting through a viewfinder. You can find an interesting arrangement of shapes simply by moving the viewfinder around in any direction, as well as moving it closer to or further from your face as you would if you were looking through a camera with a zoom lens.

You can purchase a viewfinder or make your own out of two pieces of mat board, adjustable to any size or format. Your viewfinder window should be adjustable to accommodate different size ratios to correspond to the canvas proportions you are using. For example, if you are working on a 9" × 12" (23cm × 30cm) canvas you would adjust the viewfinder window to a 3" × 4" (8cm × 10cm) format.

RED GEL FILTERS

Red gel filters tend to work best in landscape settings that are mostly green, because the red acts as a neutralizer.

Become a Designer

I hope this chapter has shown you the importance of learning how to design your compositions using only a few values. Although some artists find digital tools helpful, it is important to remember that technology does not have an artistic eye. These devices and their software make calculations based on mathematical formulas. As artists, our job is to interpret what we see and filter it through our sense of design and our own aesthetic goals. This comes from within. No app can do it for you.

It is reasonable to use digital tools in an effort to teach yourself how to see values more clearly, but these aids are no substitute for developing your own ability to identify and simplify values. In my opinion, it is better to just put in the time and learn through practice. That way you will own your abilities, and your work will truly be all yours. The examples below will illustrate why it is best to rely on your own artistic eye, rather than digital tools.

As with most things, the best way to learn is to practice. Make a point to do several value sketches every day, and you will develop the ability to create rather than simply copy. It's a big leap, but you will start to see a striking difference in your paintings.

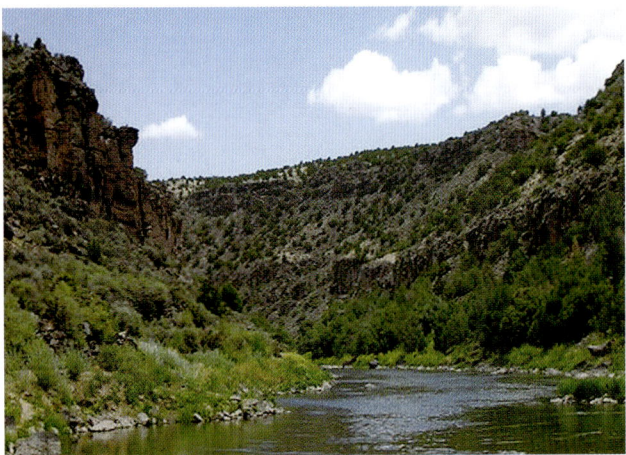

REFERENCE PHOTO
This midday landscape has even, flat lighting coming from directly above. This lighting does not show much depth or aerial perspective. There are no interesting structural shadows to play with.

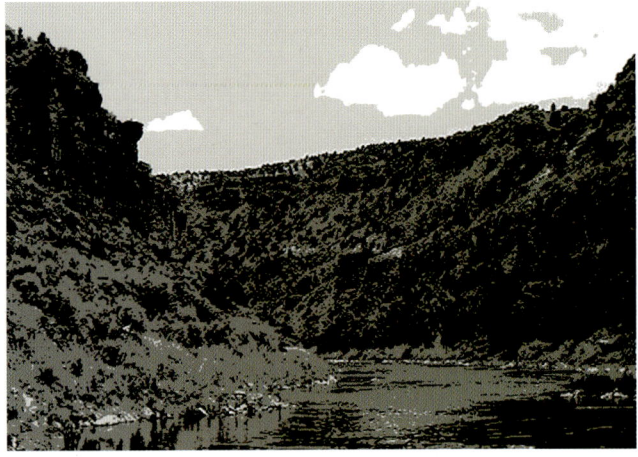

VALUE SKETCH FROM DIGITAL TOOLS
Do you think a digital app will save the day? Take a look at the result when the photo is translated into four values using a values finder app.

ARTIST'S VALUE SKETCH
No digital tool can create a pattern of light and dark shapes that will be anywhere near as interesting and cohesive as what you can achieve by applying your own artistic license. In many cases, nature will not provide you with a perfect and well-defined subject to paint. The design needs to be coaxed out, and it is your job as the artist to do it. It is far better and more empowering to hone your abilities rather than rely on tools that merely interpret, but can't compose. There are no shortcuts.

Learn the fundamentals and own them!

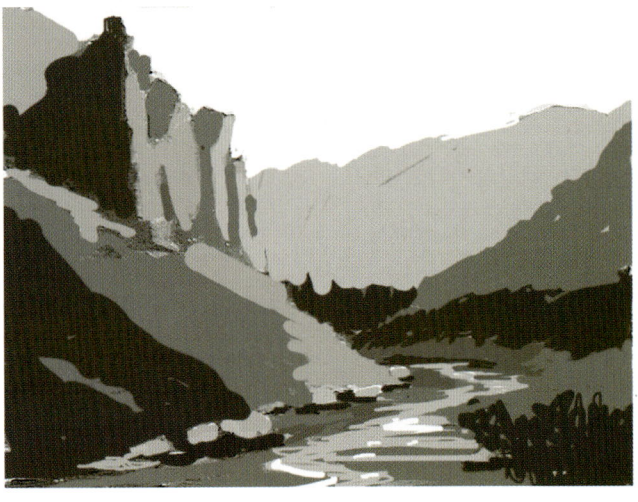

Experiment!

Feel free to play with color and experiment with your own color schemes. Just make sure to get your values right!

In the next chapter we will explore methods for translating value into color, how to work with traditional harmonic color schemes and much more.

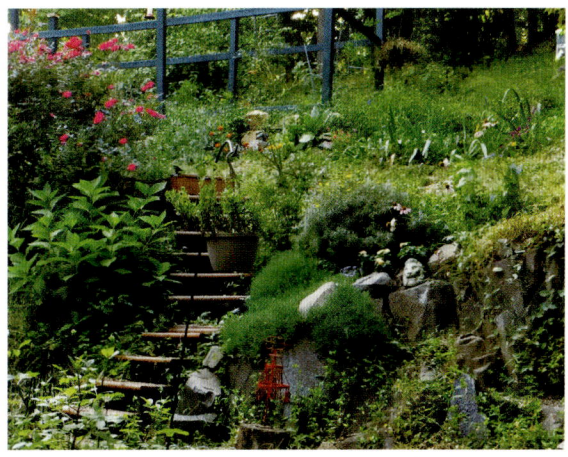

REFERENCE PHOTO

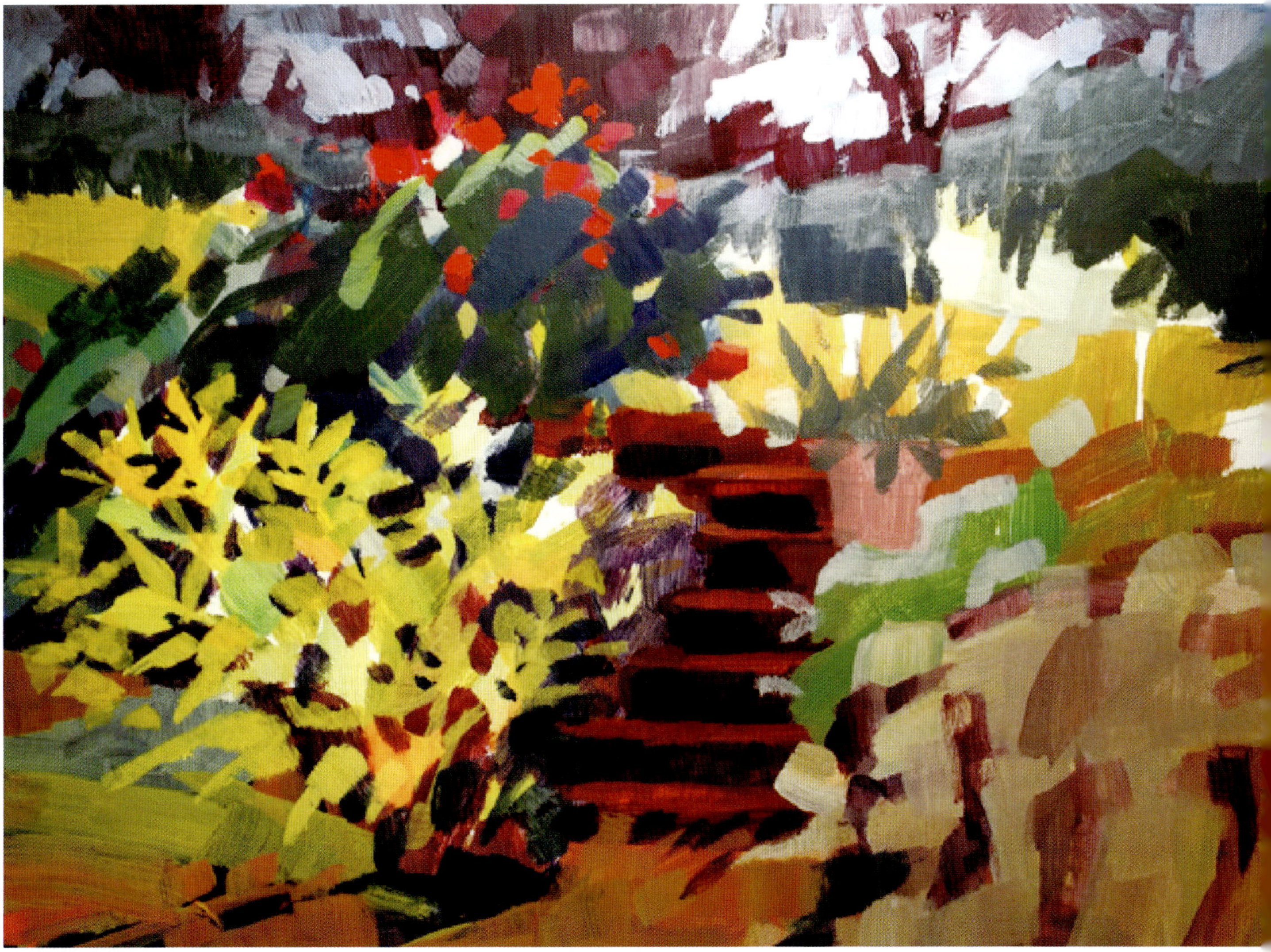

OUR BACKYARD
Acrylic on canvas
9" × 12" (23cm × 30cm)

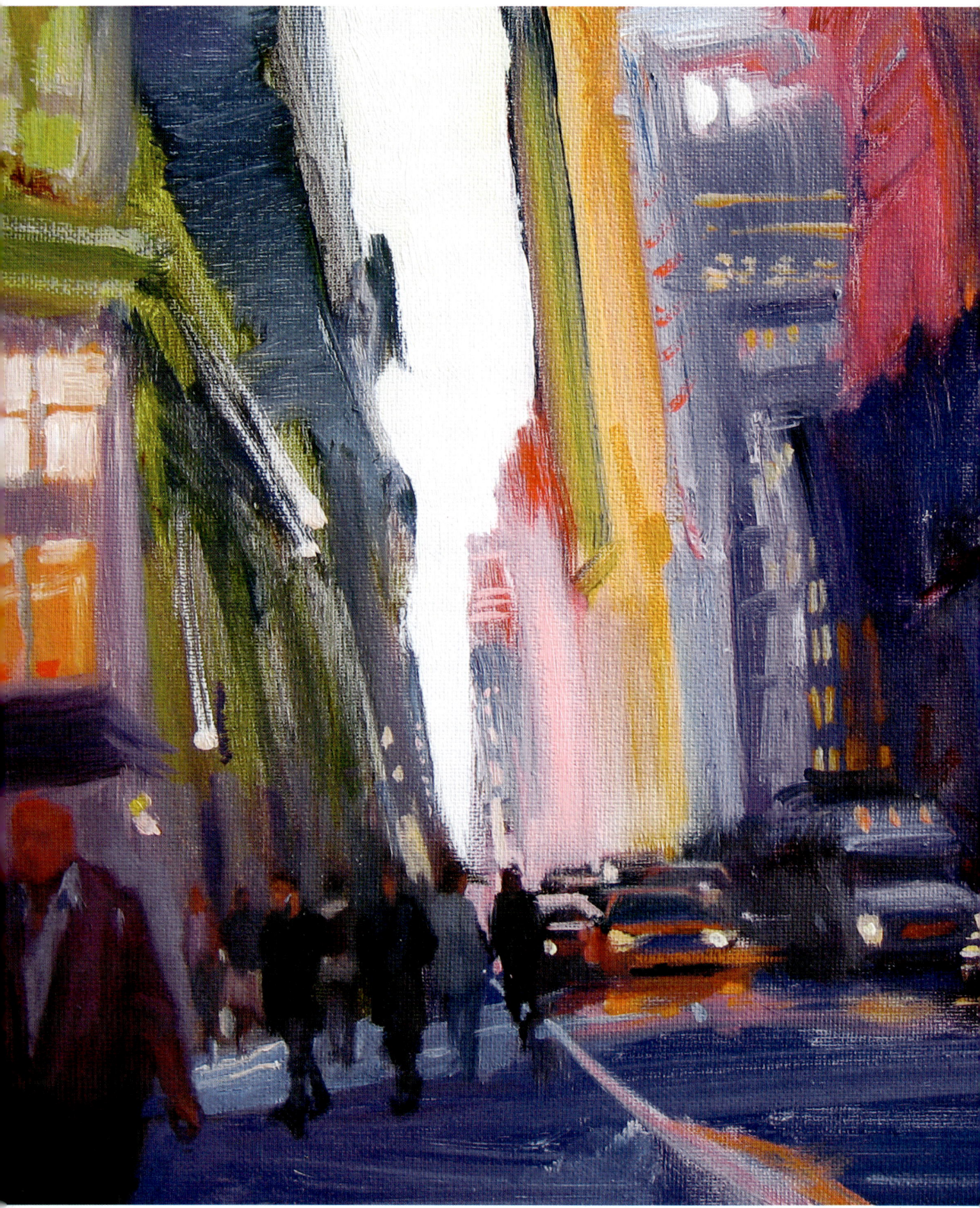

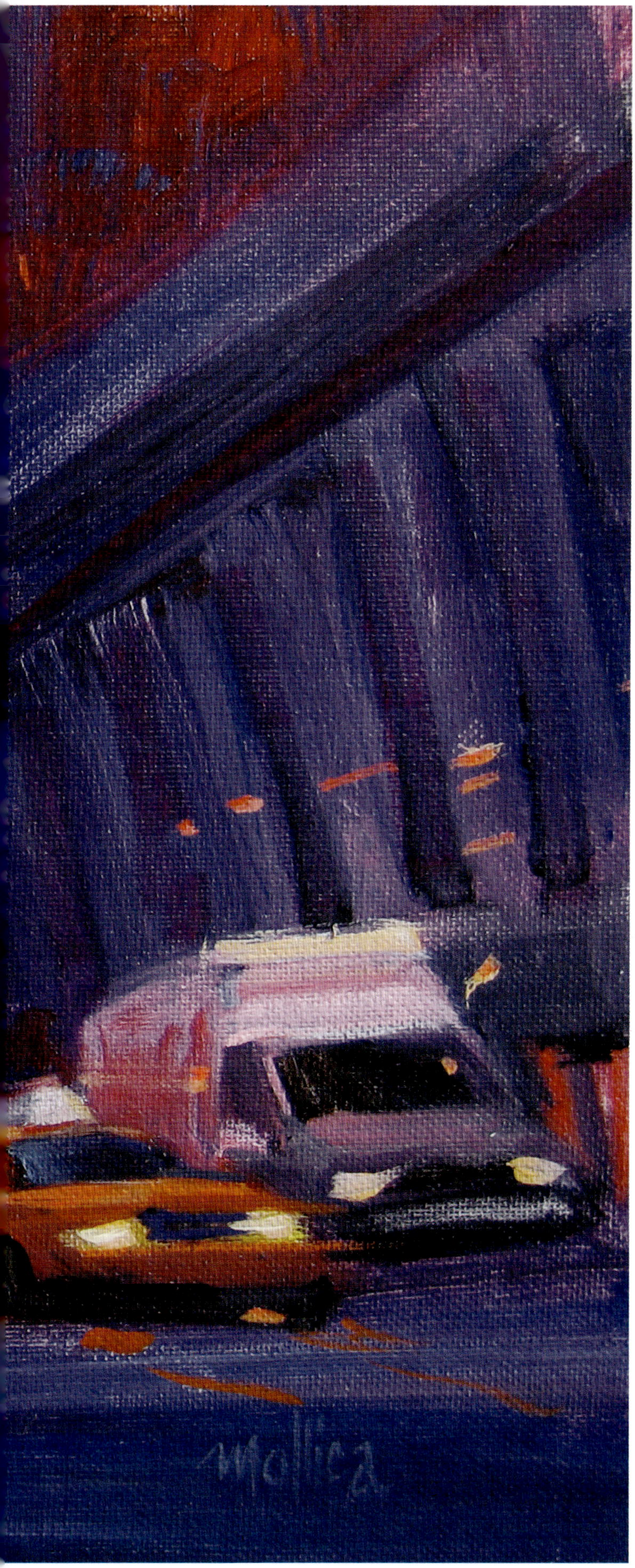

From Value to Color

In the last chapter, we discussed the importance of having a value plan worked out before you jump headfirst into your colors. If you delve into color without having a value plan to refer to, you will find yourself modifying colors to adjust their values throughout the painting process. This constant modification can result in an overworked, somewhat dull painting. It will also take twice as long to finish due to all the revising and indecision. What I have found to work best is: value first, color second.

It may be tempting to skip this important step, but it is in your own best interest to do some planning up front, take the time to consider the important decisions that will affect the overall result, and allow your inspiration to be unleashed after you have laid down a tonal foundation. As I tell my students: If you can't create in black and white (and gray), don't expect color to save the day.

57TH STREET AT DUSK
Oil on canvas
10" × 12" (25cm × 30cm)
Private Collection

Making & Using a Value Checker Tool

MATERIALS

Surface
white mat board

Pigments
Cadmium Red Light, Carbon Black,
Titanium White

Other
flat brush, value scale

Once you are clear on your value plan, you'll need to be sure that the colors you're mixing fall into the correct values. My students often have a difficult time with this, so I devised a simple value-checker card to aid in this task. Follow the steps to make your own.

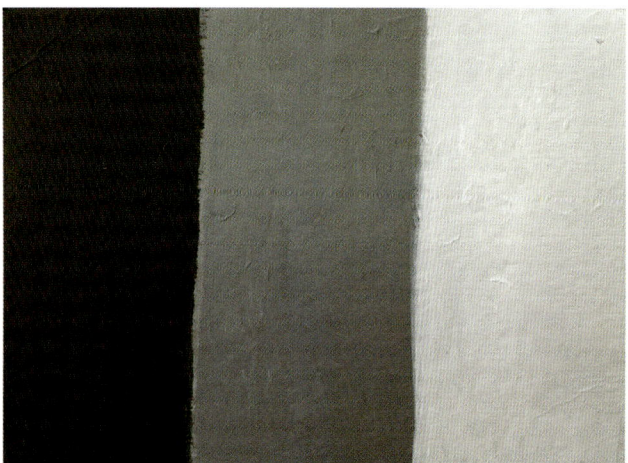

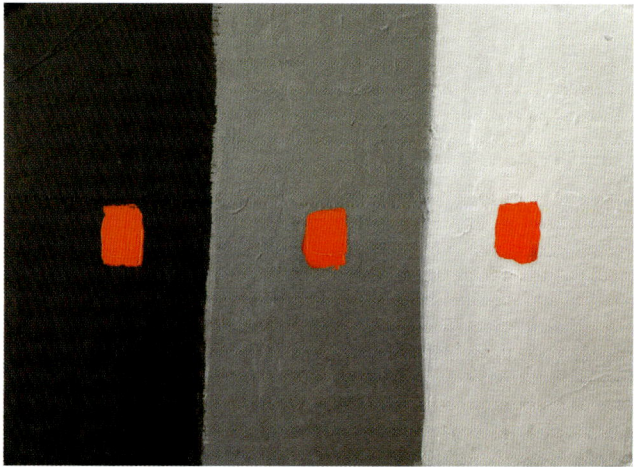

1 PAINT THE VALUE STRIPS
On a piece of mat or canvas board, paint strips of three values—very light gray (approximate value #2), middle gray (approximate value #6) and dark gray (approximate value #9). Be sure to make the strips solid, not streaky. All three values can be mixed from Titanium White and Carbon Black paints.

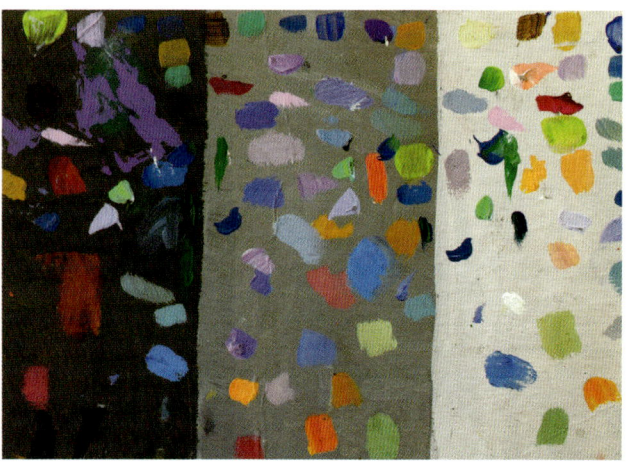

2 MATCH COLOR TO VALUE
Mix any color you want to use. To identify its value, paint a dab of the color on the strip that you think is the correct value for that color. If you are not sure, place a dab on all three strips. The correct value is the strip that the color blends into when you squint. If the color "jumps out" visually on any of the strips, the color is *not* that value.

Keep in mind that the most vivid, saturated colors (such as the Cadmium Red Light shown above) will always pop out of any gray background, even when they are perfectly matched with the value they are on. You will not always get a perfect match. Sometimes your color will be a value that is in between the strips. In that case, you can adjust your color to go a bit lighter or darker so that it blends into the lighter or darker value.

3 REPEAT AS NEEDED
When your card gets full of with color dabs, you can paint over it with the three gray values for a clean area to dab on. Make your dabs of color a reasonable size. If they're so tiny you can barely see them, it will be difficult to judge their value.

Using Realistic Colors

The beauty of still life scenes is that you have full control over the subject matter, colors, lighting and composition. So there is no real reason to change the colors in your painting, since you have the ability to orchestrate the scene according to what you want. In cases like this, I generally recommend sticking with the actual colors and values that you see.

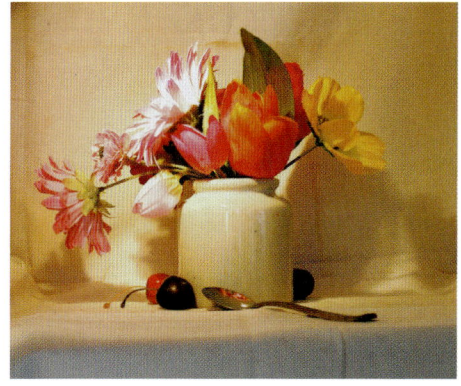

REFERENCE PHOTO

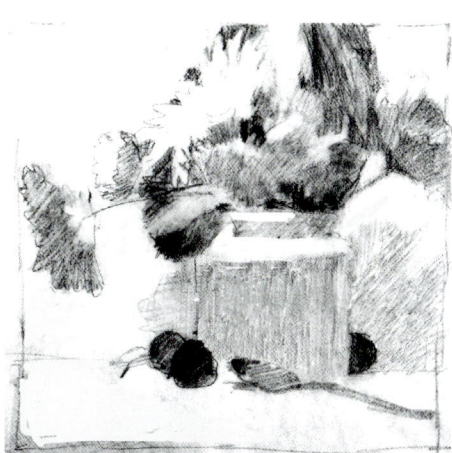

VALUE SKETCH

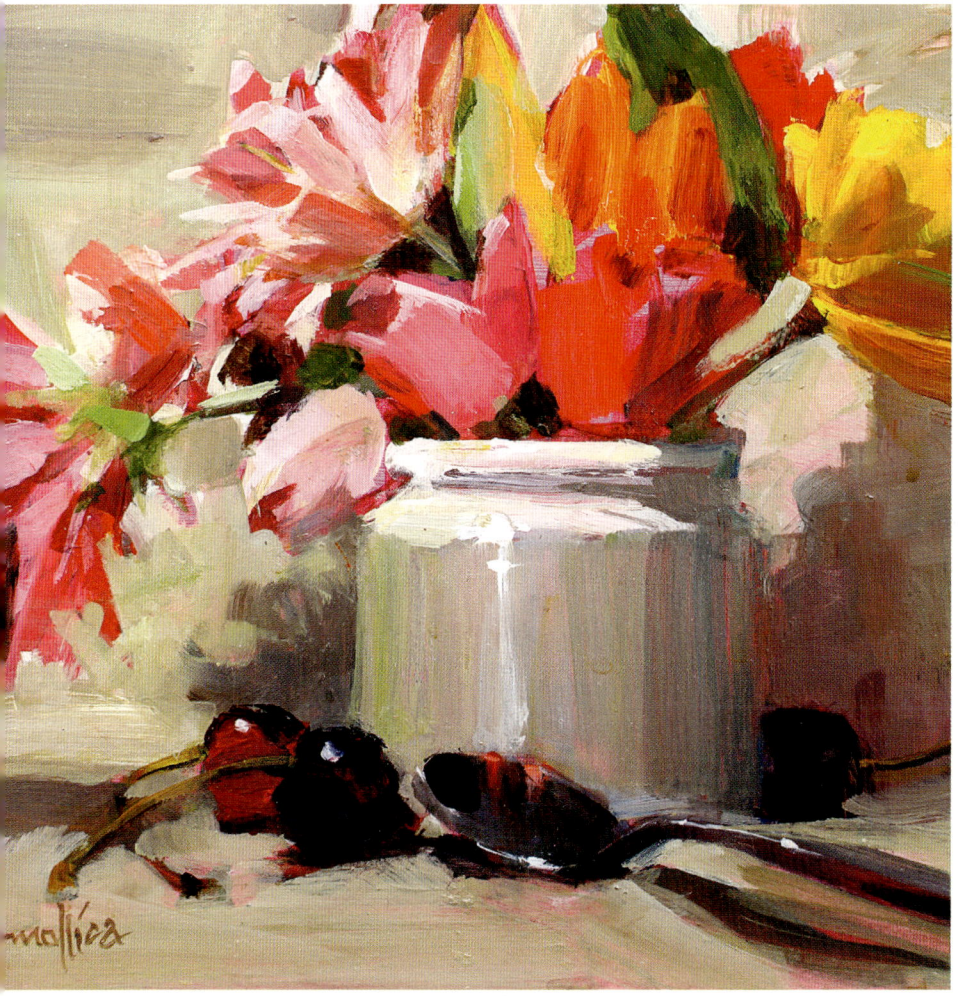

PINK SPOTS II
Acrylic on panel
8" × 10" (20cm × 25cm)
Collection of Denise Antil

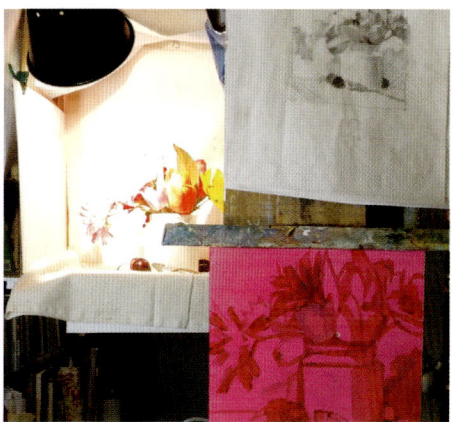

SETUP

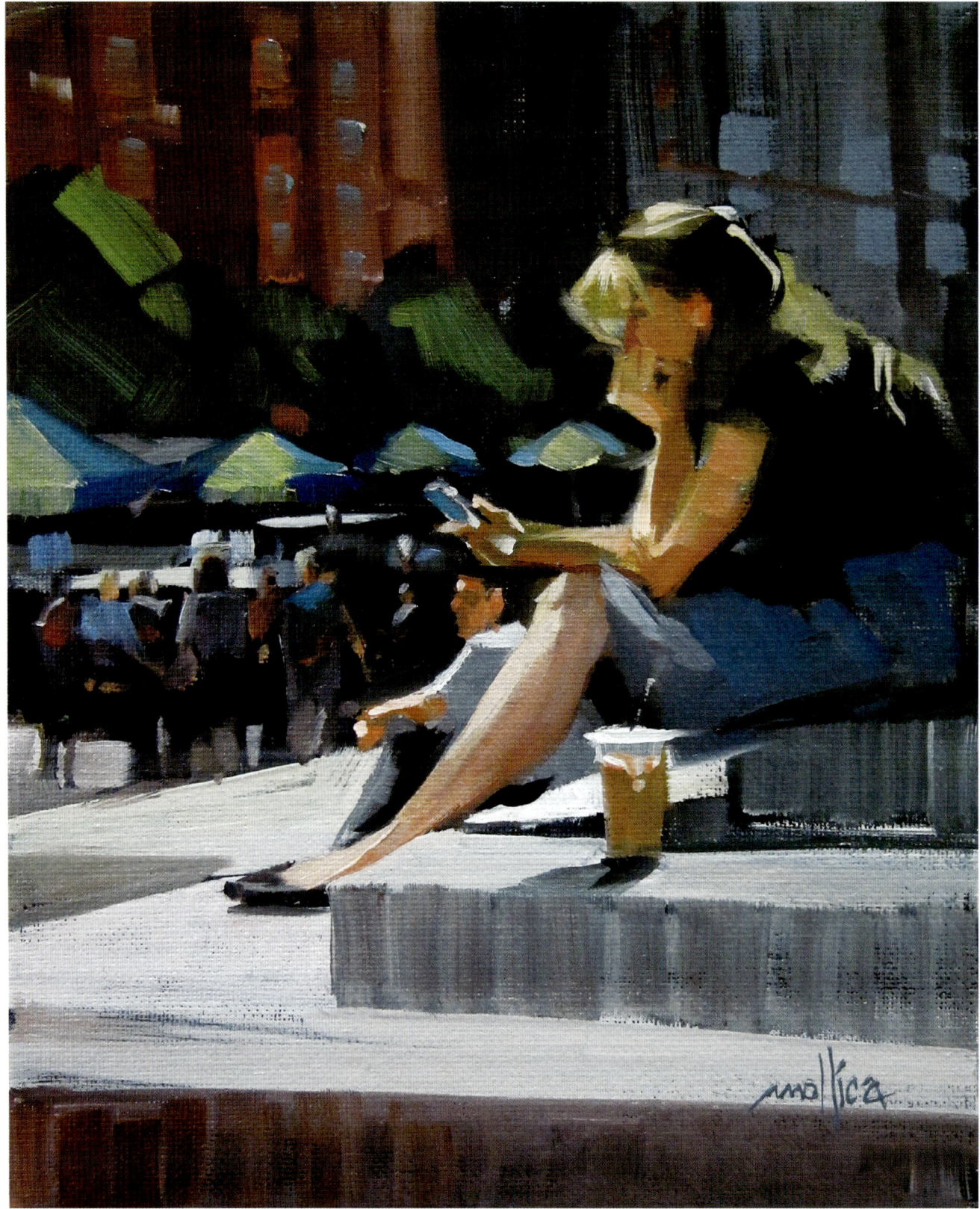

REALISTIC COLOR PALETTE WITH MINOR ADJUSTMENTS

Here is an example of a painting completed with a realistic color palette, with a few composition and color modifications. In the scene above, I basically worked with the colors I saw with just a few minor changes to the buildings.

LATTE BREAK AT THE MET
Oil on canvas
10" × 8" (25cm × 20cm)
Collection of Ann Self

Modifying Colors

When it comes to translating value into color, there will be times when the actual colors of the subject or scene won't convey the mood or feeling that you want to communicate. In those cases, you might choose other colors to suit your own preferences. In the case of landscapes, figure painting or working from reference photos that have poor colors or composition, take advantage of artistic license by adding, deleting or changing colors altogether to strengthen the painting and give it more drama.

The key to switching from a realistic color palette to the colors of your choice is making sure that you have analyzed the main values and then matched your colors to the same values that you see. This allows you to experiment freely with color. There is only one rule: Keep the values correct!

In the example of the cathedral below, a value sketch was created to decide the dark, middle and light values before experimenting with several random color palettes. Making the value decisions up front, before moving into color, is the best way to guarantee a strong design regardless of which colors you choose.

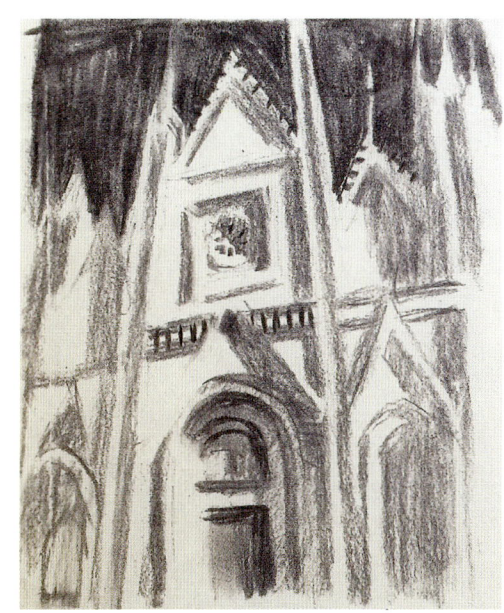

VALUE SKETCH

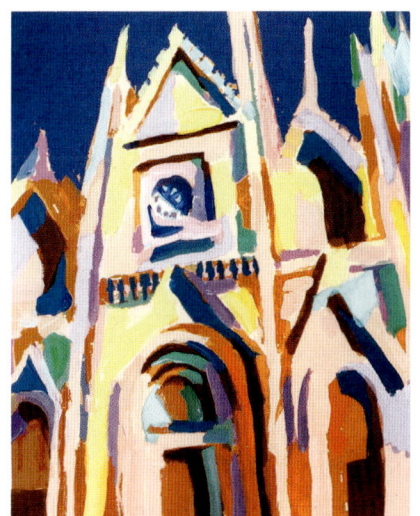 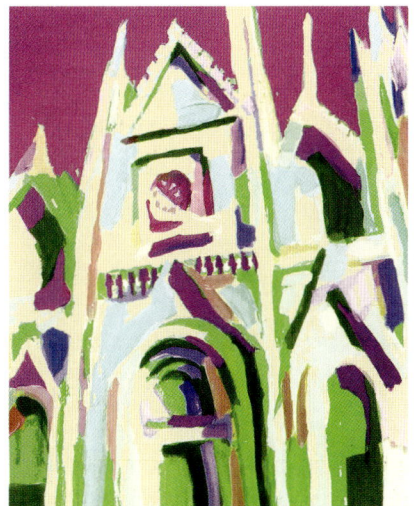 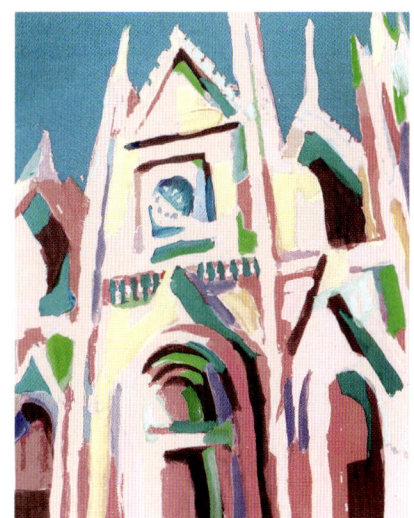

EXPERIMENT WITH VARIOUS COLOR PALETTES

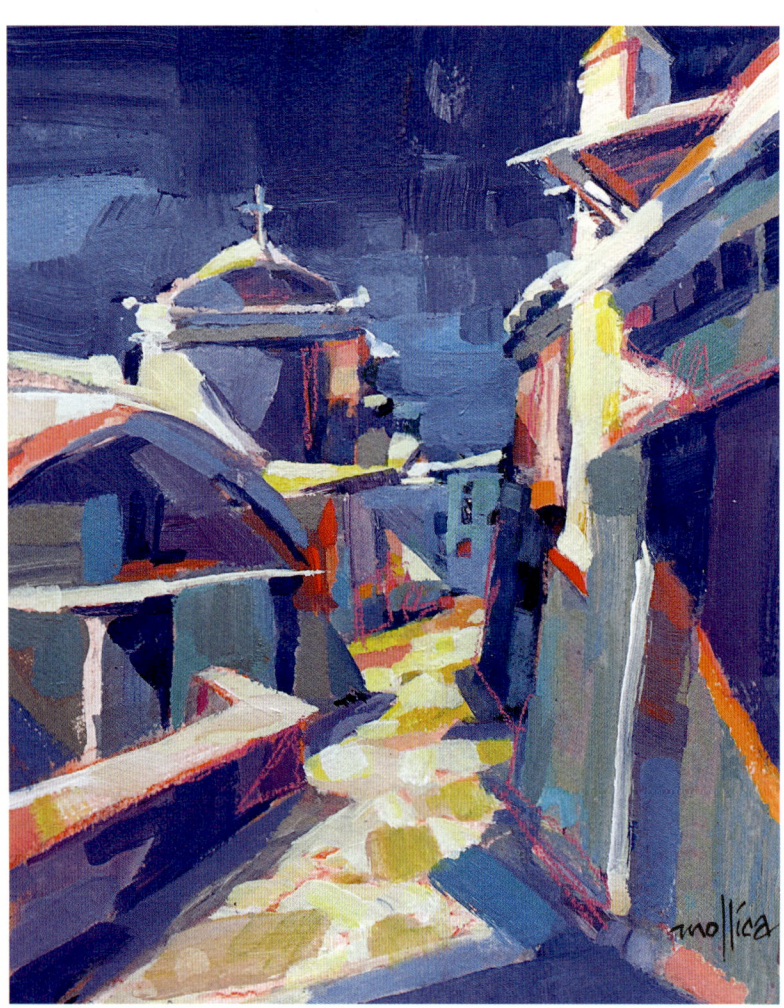

APPLY ARTISTIC LICENSE

In the reference photo for this piece, a warm golden color dominated the setting. However in this interpretation, the cool blues dominate and the warmer hues play a subordinate role.

To achieve my artistic vision I ended up diverting completely from the actual values of the reference photo because I wanted the path to be the focal point.

GREECE HILLTOP
Acrylic on panel
12" × 10" (30cm × 25cm)
Private collection

RANDOM COLORS

The colors in this painting of a pug are very random. They were not organized in a methodical fashion and were chosen according to their inherent value. Working this way leads to fresh and unpredictable color choices, based on your preference and mood.

PERSONABLE PUG
Acrylic on panel
8" × 10" (22cm × 25cm)
Collection of Alisa Dale

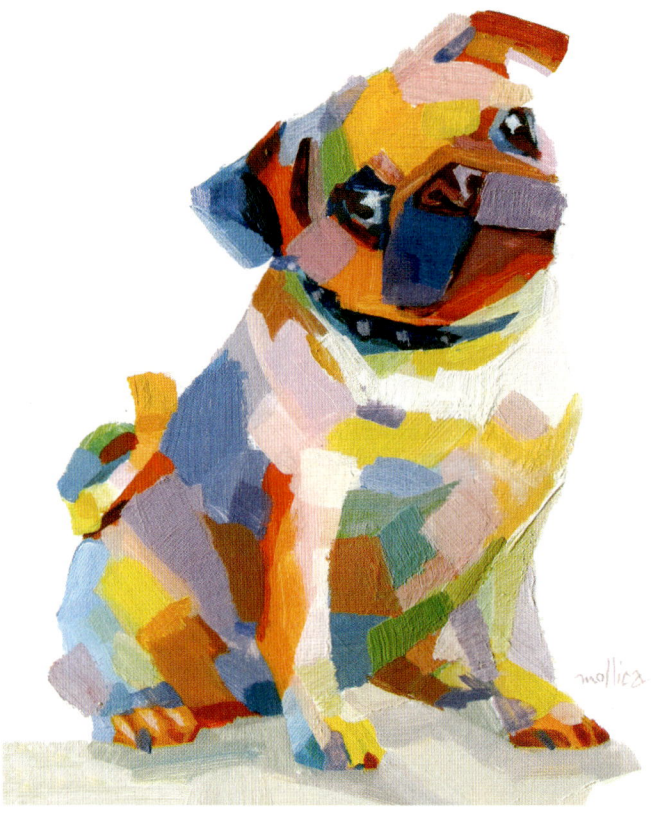

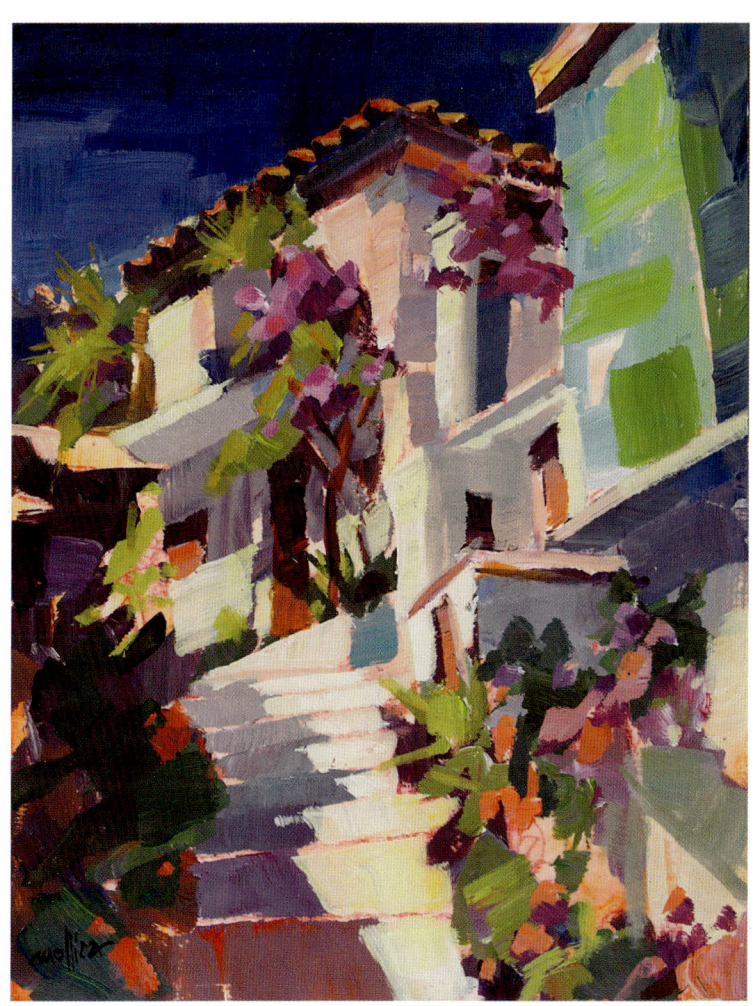

CONTRAST WARM & COOL COLORS

I wanted a warmer look and feel to the overall painting than the reference photo of this hillside home. So I used predominantly warm colors to depict the sunstruck areas, and retained the deep blue sky for some added color contrast.

66 STEPS
Acrylic on panel
12" × 10" (30cm × 25cm)
Private collection

ALTER COLORS FOR MOOD EFFECTS

In reality, urban landscapes are a variety of neutrals, browns and grays, which can leave room for color translation. Street scenes in particular make excellent subjects for altering colors to suggest whatever mood you are going for.

Have fun playing with color and experimenting with your own color schemes—just make sure to get your values right!

GALLERY DISTRICT
Acrylic on panel
8" × 10" (20cm × 25cm)
Private collection

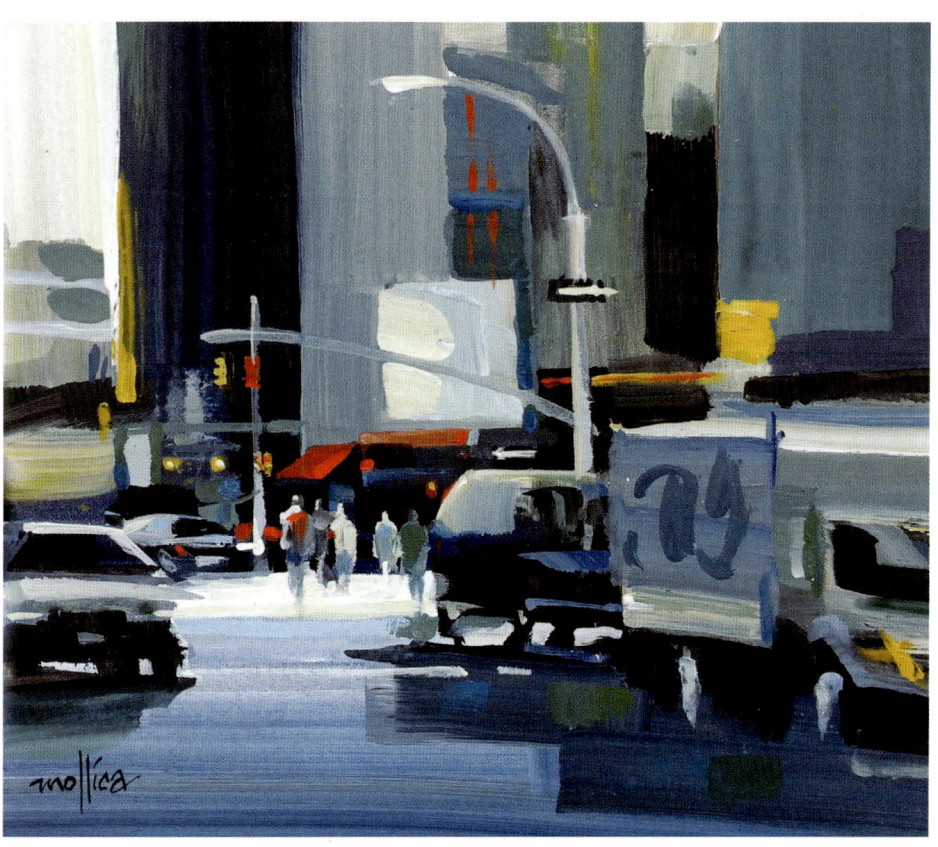

The Color Wheel

The color wheel is a simple visual tool that shows the relationships between different colors. It can help you see how colors are arranged as well as how certain color combinations work together. The most simple color wheel is based on the three primary colors of red, yellow and blue; the three secondary colors of green, purple and orange; and the six tertiary colors of red–orange, red–violet, yellow–orange, yellow–green, blue–violet and blue–green.

Primary colors are so named because they cannot be created by combining any other colors. Secondary colors are formed by mixing two primary colors, and tertiary colors are formed by mixing a primary color with a secondary color. This creates a color wheel with a total of twelve main divisions.

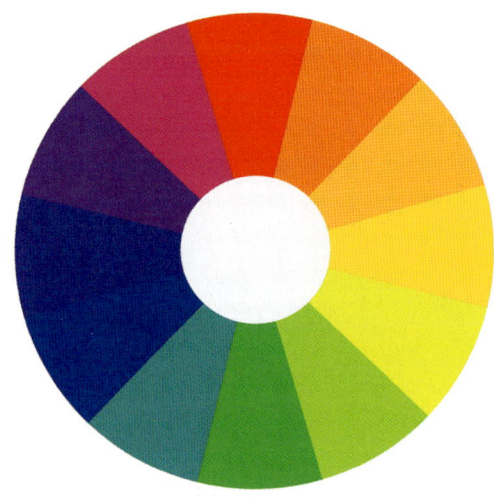

SIMPLIFIED COLOR WHEEL
Often you will see color wheels depicted in a simplistic diagram, only showing the most vibrant hues.

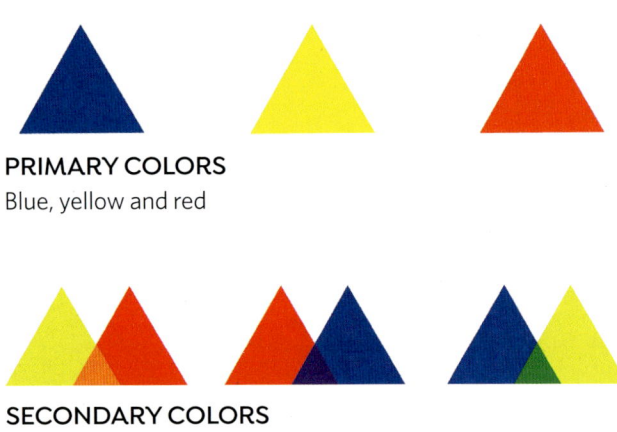

PRIMARY COLORS
Blue, yellow and red

SECONDARY COLORS
Orange, violet and green

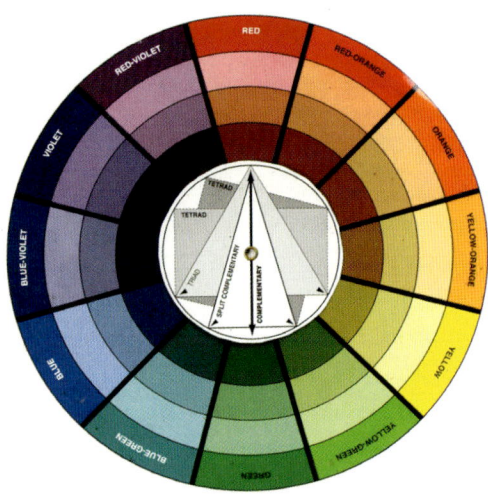

EXPANDED COLOR WHEEL
I recommend using a color wheel with a revolving centerpiece/slider that has all of the common color schemes printed on it. That way you can spin the center wheel around to see the various color combination choices.

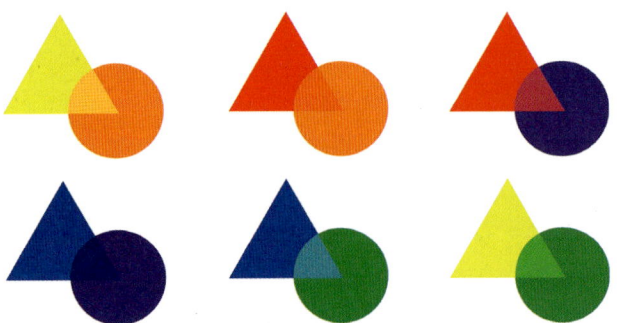

TERTIARY COLORS
Yellow-orange, red-orange, red-violet, blue-violet, blue-green and yellow-green

Harmonic Color Schemes

Although it is enjoyable to experiment with color schemes by choosing colors randomly based on our individual preferences, there are a number of color combinations, known as harmonic color schemes, that are considered especially pleasing. Harmonic color schemes consist of two or more colors on the color wheel that have a specific relationship to each other based on their position and distance from each other. When used together, they create a pleasing contrast and compatibility. Many artists use traditional harmonic color schemes from the color wheel as the basis for successful designs and paintings.

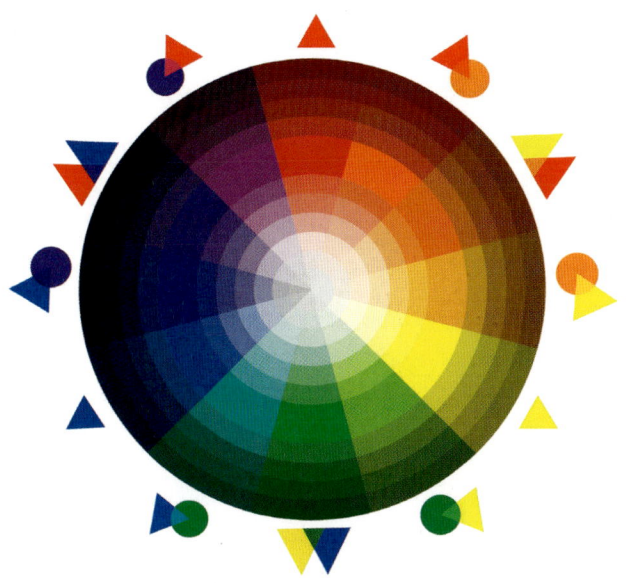

COLOR WHEEL WITH PRIMARY, SECONDARY AND TERTIARY HUES

It's important to realize that when you are working with color schemes, you should consider using each color's extended range. This includes its shades, tints and tones. It will offer the eye some restful colors that have been lightened, darkened or neutralized. These variations also allow the more powerful saturated colors to be used more sparingly for emphasis when needed.

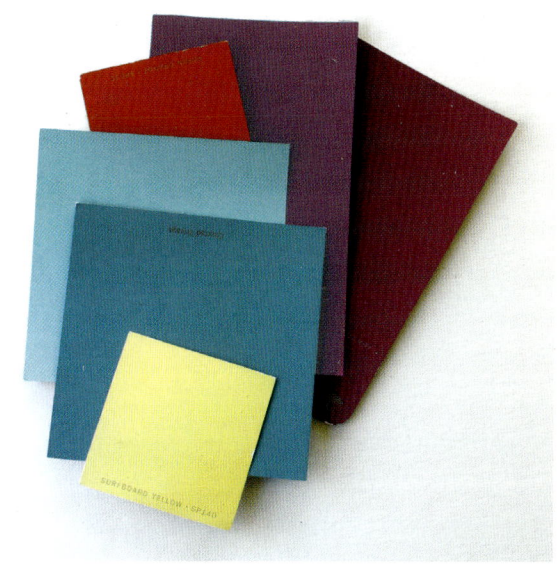

CHOOSE A NONTRADITIONAL COLOR SCHEME

If you want to work with colors of your choice but are not sure how to start, it can be helpful to do some quick color sketches. If you need color inspiration, go to the hardware store and pick up some color chips or swatches in the hues you want to work with. It is useful to see the colors together, and you can easily modify your palette by adding and removing colors to suit your taste.

Once you have made your color palette decisions, mix and blend those colors to create new hues, including beautiful unified grays and other related variations. (For more on color mixing, see Chapter 3.)

Common Color Terms

It helps if you are familiar with some of the most commonly used color terms:

- **Tint:** A color that has been lightened by adding white.
- **Hue:** The color of paint as it appears out of the tube, unmixed.
- **Tone:** A color that been lightened or darkened by adding gray.
- **Shade:** A color that has been darkened by adding black.

Commonly Used Color Schemes

Here are several of the most commonly used color schemes with paintings that were created using those same color schemes.

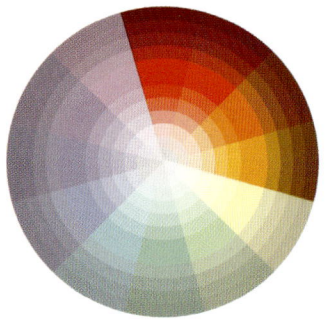

ANALOGOUS COLOR SCHEME

Uses three or more colors that sit next to each other on the color wheel.

HARRY, MO & CURLY
Oil on panel
6" × 6" (15cm × 15cm)
Private collection

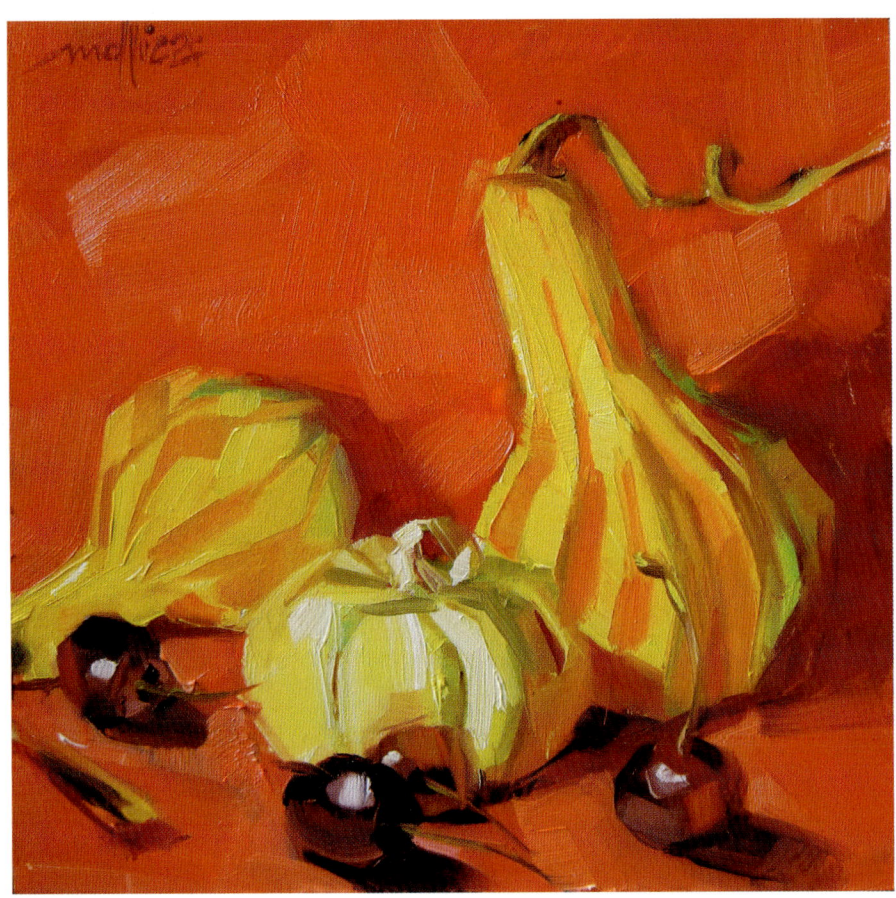

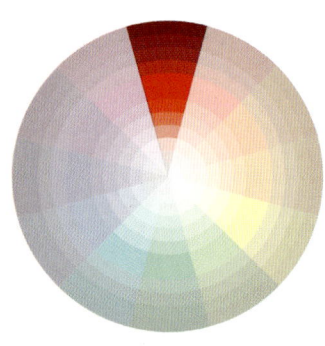

MONOCHROMATIC COLOR SCHEME

Uses tints, tones and shades within the same hue or color family.

BRIDGE VIEW
Oil on panel
10" × 12" (25cm × 30cm)
Private collection

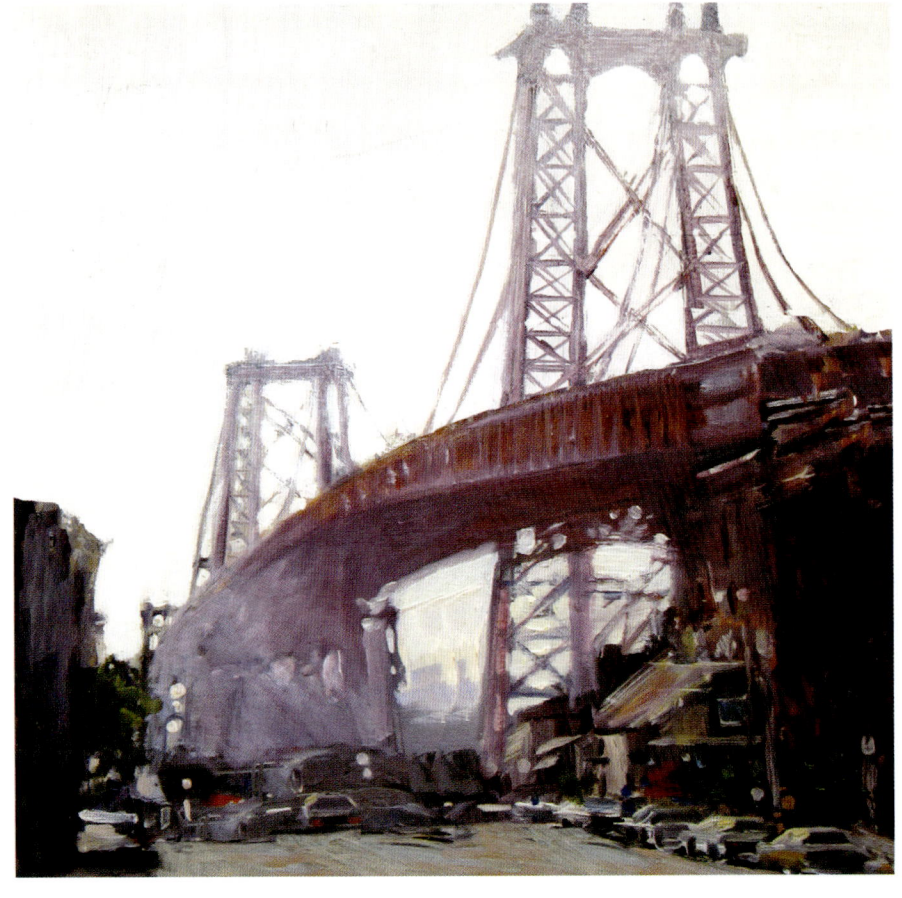

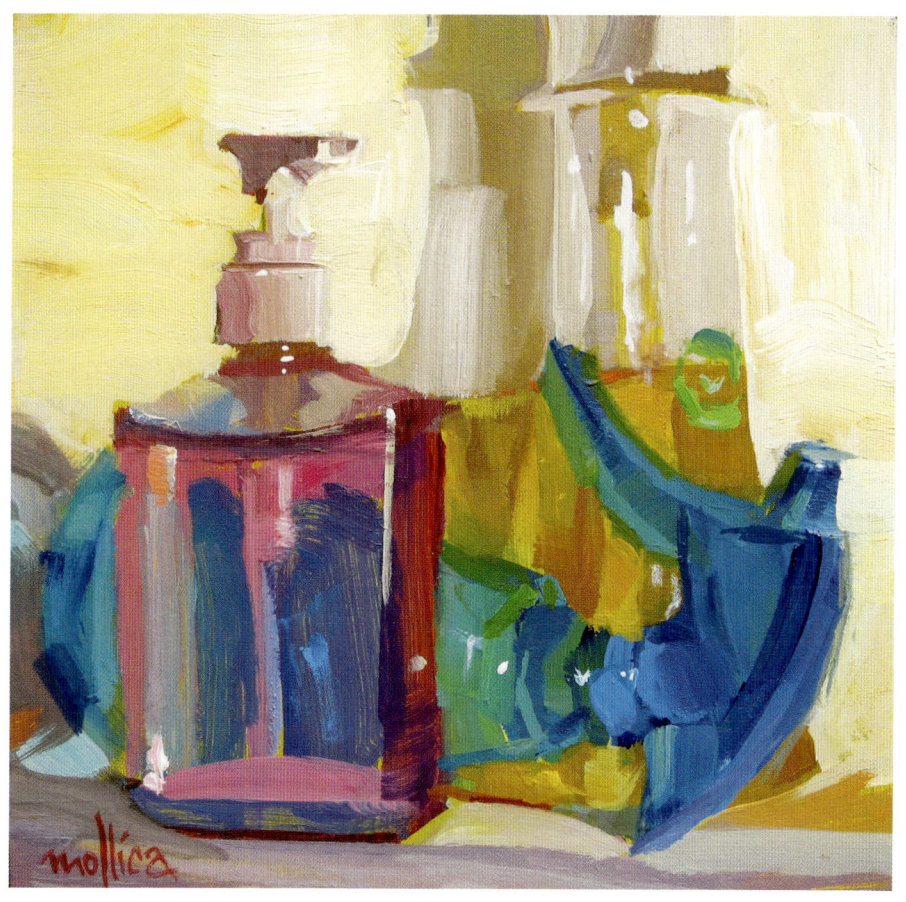

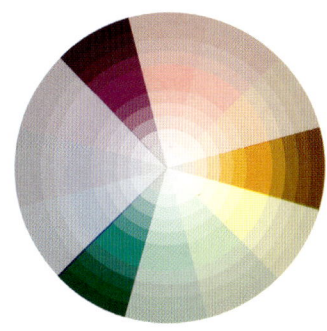

TRIADIC COLOR SCHEME

Uses three colors that are evenly spaced around the color wheel.

ONE SLACKER
Acrylic on panel
6" × 6" (15cm × 15cm)
Private collection

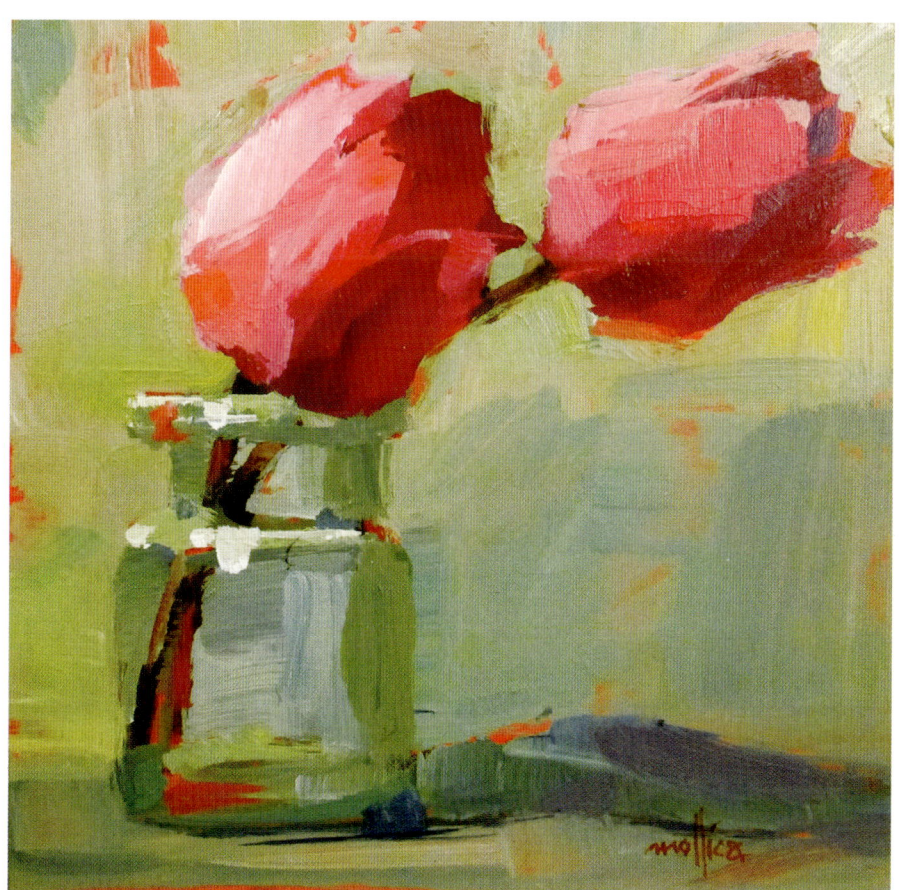

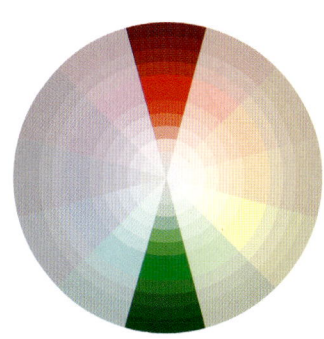

COMPLEMENTARY COLOR SCHEME

Uses colors opposite of each other on the color wheel.

TWO-LIPS
Acrylic on panel
8" × 8" (20cm × 20cm)
Private collection

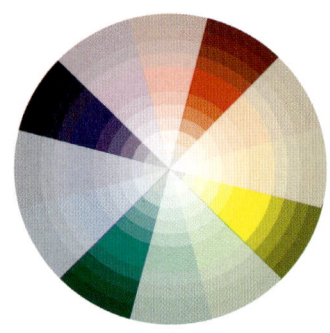

SQUARE COLOR SCHEME

Uses four colors evenly spaced around the color wheel.

UPPER WEST SIDE
Acrylic on canvas
14" × 14" (36cm × 36cm)
Private collection

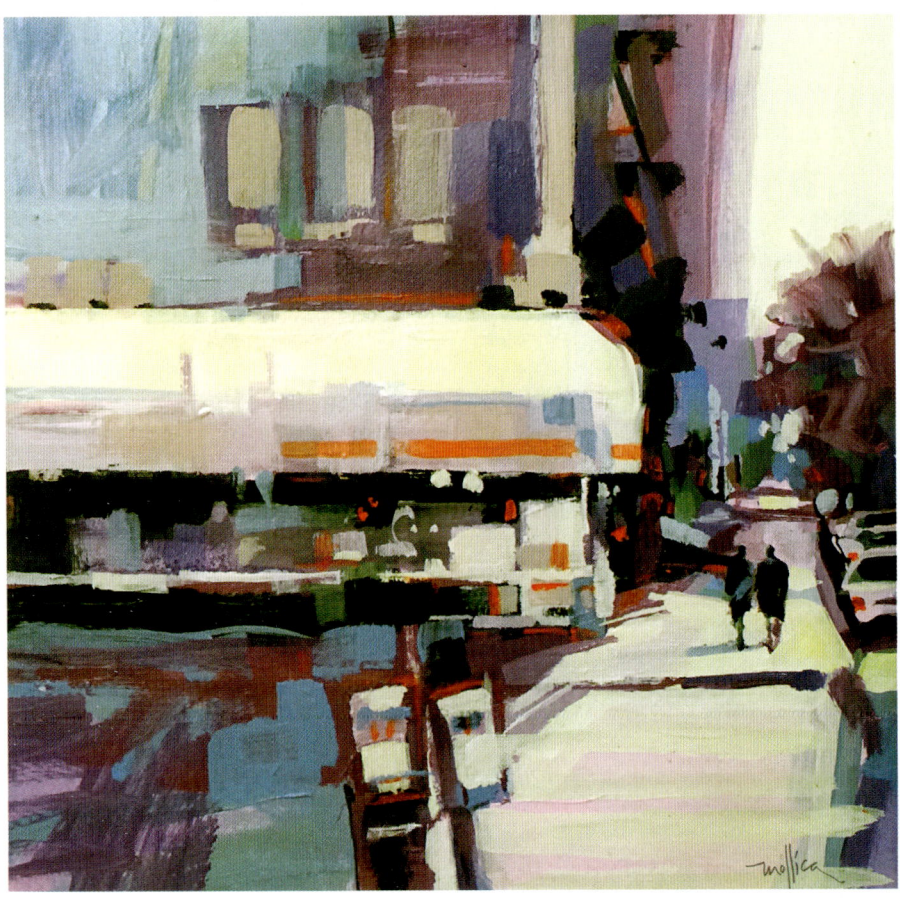

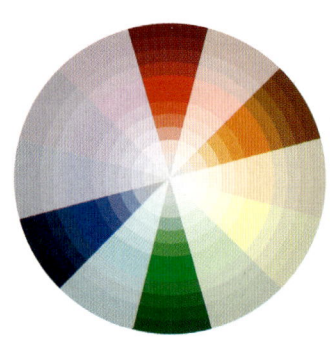

TETRAD (OR RECTANGULAR) COLOR SCHEME

Uses four colors made from two complementary pairs.

CROSSING MADISON
Acrylic on panel
24" × 24" (61cm × 61cm)
Collection of Allison Corey

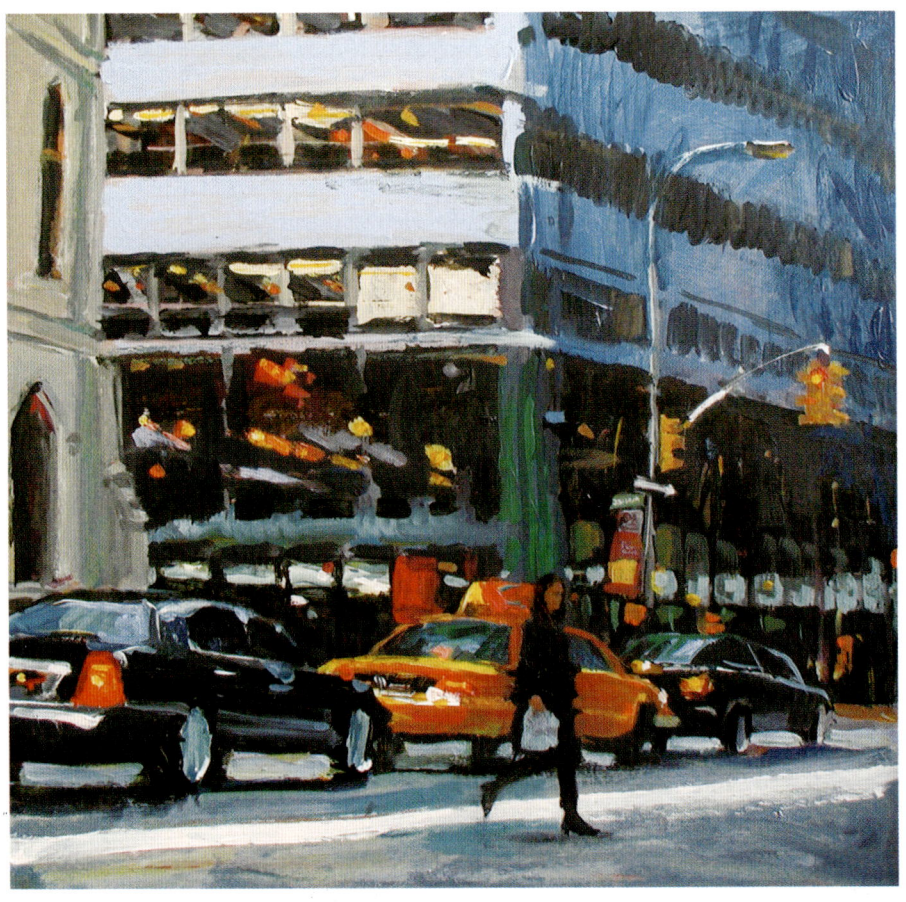

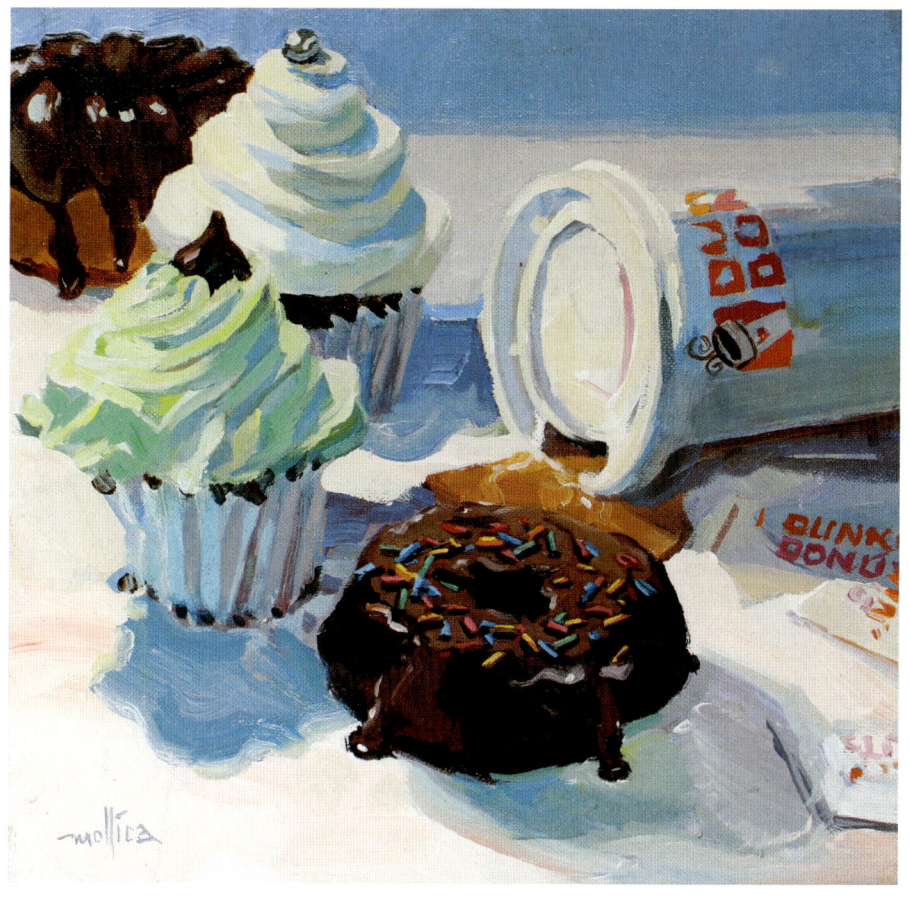

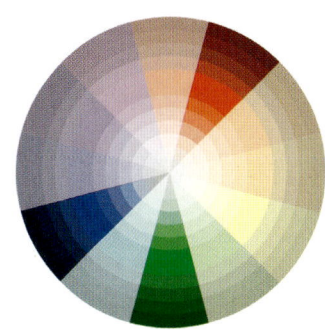

SPLIT COMPLEMENTARY COLOR SCHEME

Uses one root color plus the two colors that are on either side of the root color's complement.

DUNKIN' DONUTS
Acrylic on canvas
12" × 12" (30cm × 30cm)
Private collection

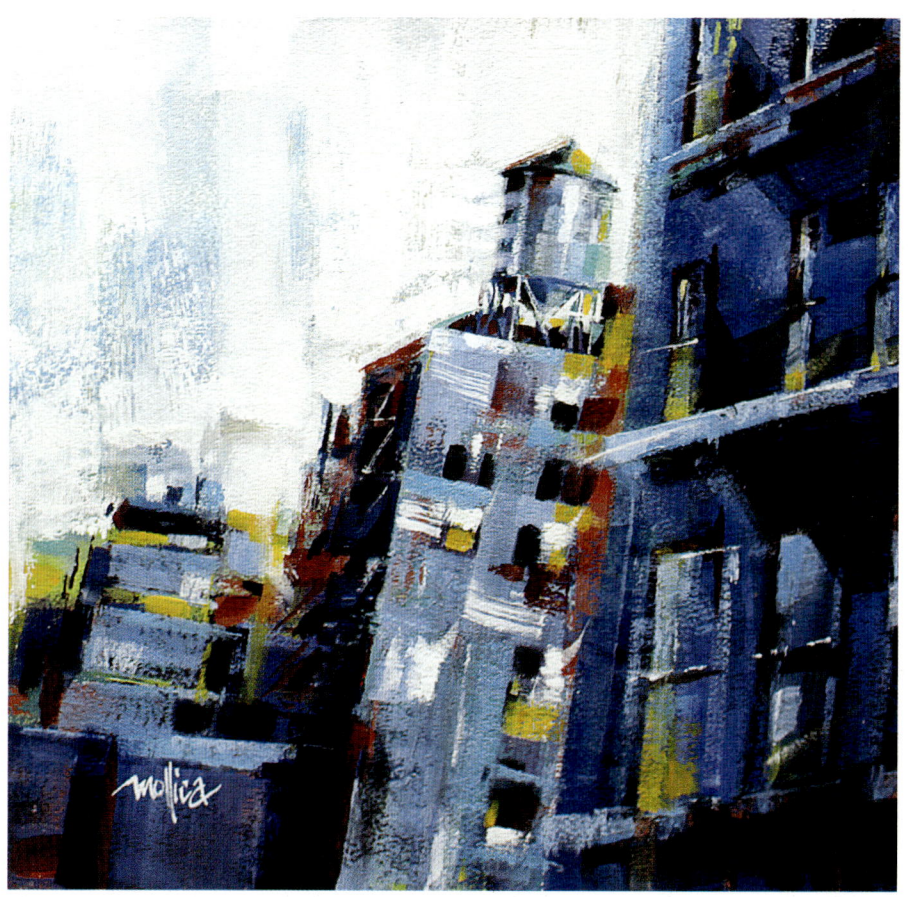

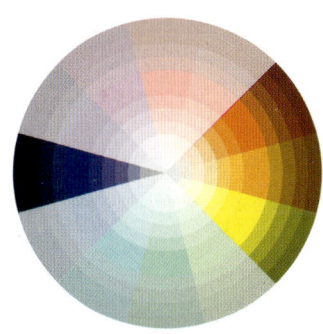

ANALOGOUS COMPLEMENTARY COLOR SCHEME

Uses three analogous colors, plus the complement of the middle analogous color.

LOOKING UPTOWN
Acrylic on panel
14" × 14" (36cm × 36cm)
Collection of William Shortell

Developing a Color Scheme

Let's explore the way a color scheme is developed.

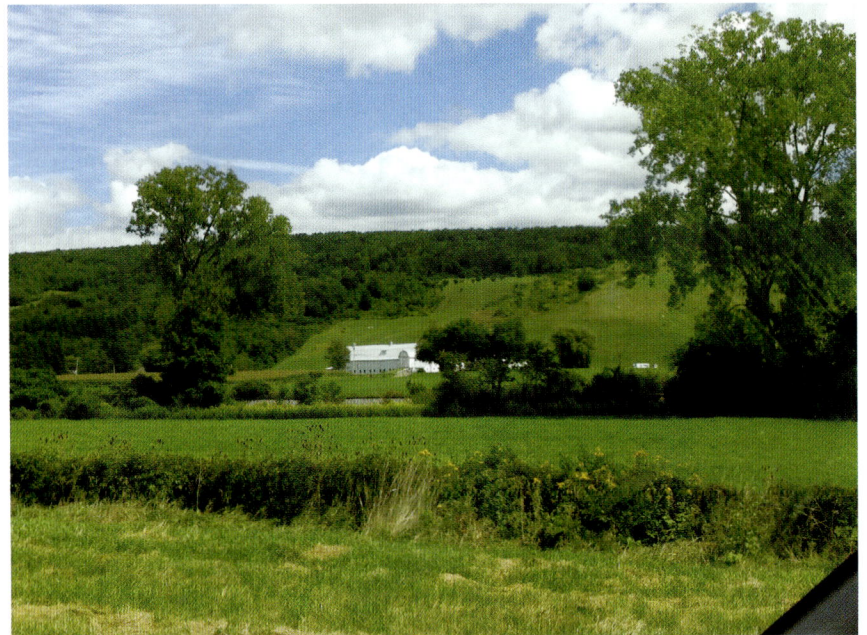

START WITH A REFERENCE PHOTO

Use a reference photo as a springboard to work on the overall design of the image for a more dynamic composition. The most important aspect of a good painting is a good underlying design. If you bypass this step, you will end up simply copying exactly what you see in front of you—and rarely does nature offer the best possible composition for a successful painting. You will often have to move mountains, trees, and anything else that weakens rather than strengthens your composition.

CREATE A THREE-VALUE SKETCH

From the photo, create a three-value sketch and try out some modifications that you feel might enhance the composition. In this case, I wanted the barn to be more prominent so I enlarged it and added a silo. I changed the angle of the hill from a horizontal to a diagonal so that the viewer's eye is led right to the barn, which is the focal point. I brought the height of the hill down because I felt the tree on the left would add an interesting silhouette shape against the sky. The strip of greenery in the foreground felt distracting because it split the foreground into two even areas. So I turned it into a diagonal dark patch to add a more interesting angle to an otherwise very horizontal design.

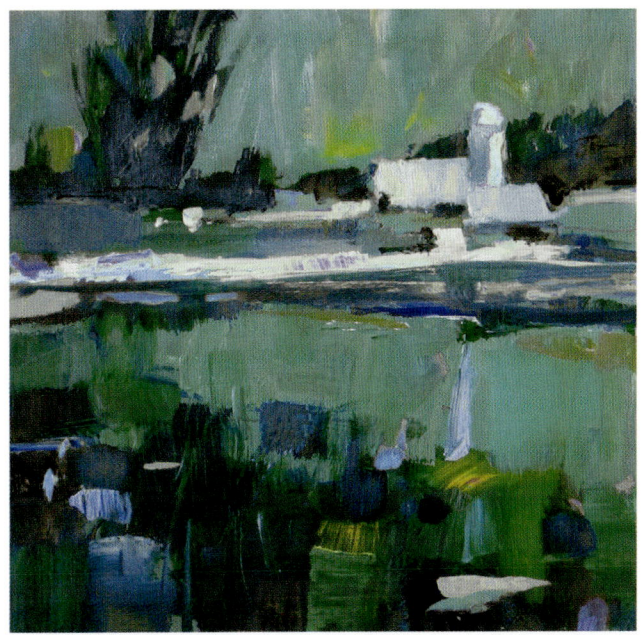
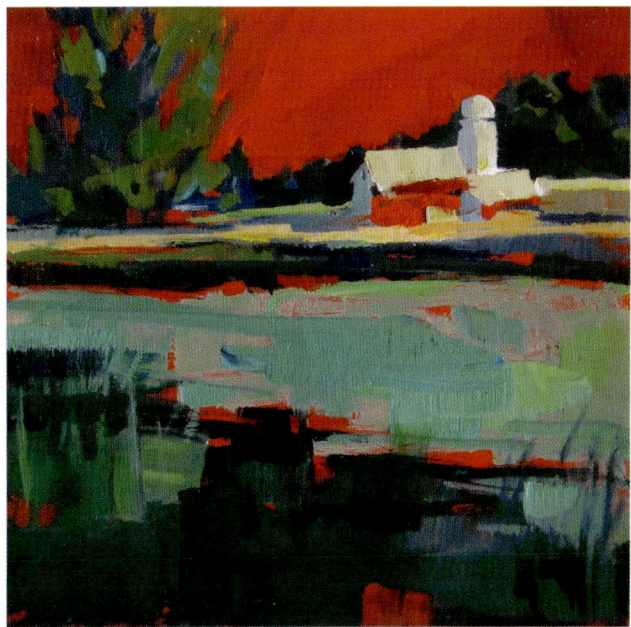
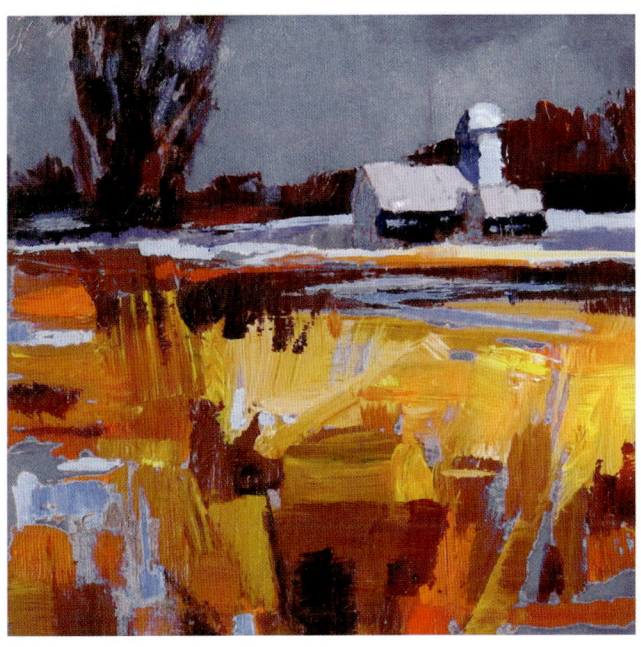
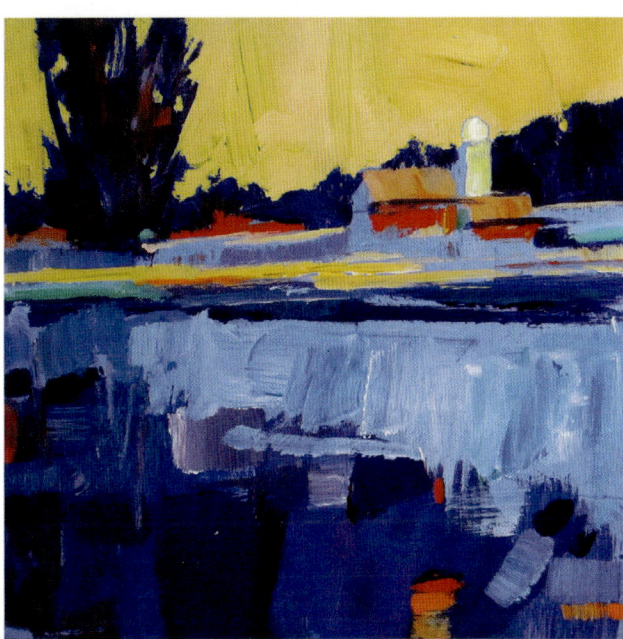

CHOOSE A COLOR SCHEME WITH DOMINANT AND SUBORDINATE COLORS

Once you are satisfied with the value sketch, choose a few color schemes to experiment with. Clockwise from the left are the color schemes I used:

1. Analogous: Greens and blues
2. Complementary: Reds and greens
3. Triad: Primary colors—red, yellow and blue
4. Analogous Complementary: Blues and violets, yellows and oranges

When working with color schemes, whether based on personal preference or any of the traditional schemes from the color wheel relationships, it is best to choose one color as the dominant color and use the rest of the colors as subordinate colors. In other words, colors are more interesting when they are used in unequal amounts.

For example, if you are using a complementary color scheme of red and green, it's best to make either red or green the dominant color, rather than using both colors in equal amounts. This gives the painting an overall mood and feeling. A painting that is 50% red and 50% green will not convey an overall mood as effectively as a painting where one color dominates.

Color Temperature

Artists often refer to a color's "temperature" as being warm or cool. Magentas, reds, yellows and oranges are known as warm colors. Purples, blues and greens are considered cool colors. The warm colors lie on one side of the wheel and the cools on the other.

The temperature of the dominant colors you use is important in determining the overall mood and feeling of your painting. Warm colors are often associated with sunlight, fire, passion and energy, whereas cool colors often depict shadows, coldness, and somber, calm or reserved moods. It should also be noted that colors are perceived very differently between various world cultures.

When choosing colors to depict a mood, temperature can help create a sense of depth in the painting. Warm colors are perceived to advance toward the viewer, and cool colors tend to recede into the distance. It is common for artists to add warm tones to their mixtures in the foreground plane, making that part of the painting feel closer, while adding cool hues to push the background objects and planes further back. This helps create an enhanced sense of depth.

Let's explore some color schemes based on the three characteristics which define color: Hue, saturation and key.

Hue

Hue is the straight color as we see it. Whenever you are working with a complementary color scheme, you are working with a warm/cool palette, since every set of complements is composed of one warm color and one cool color.

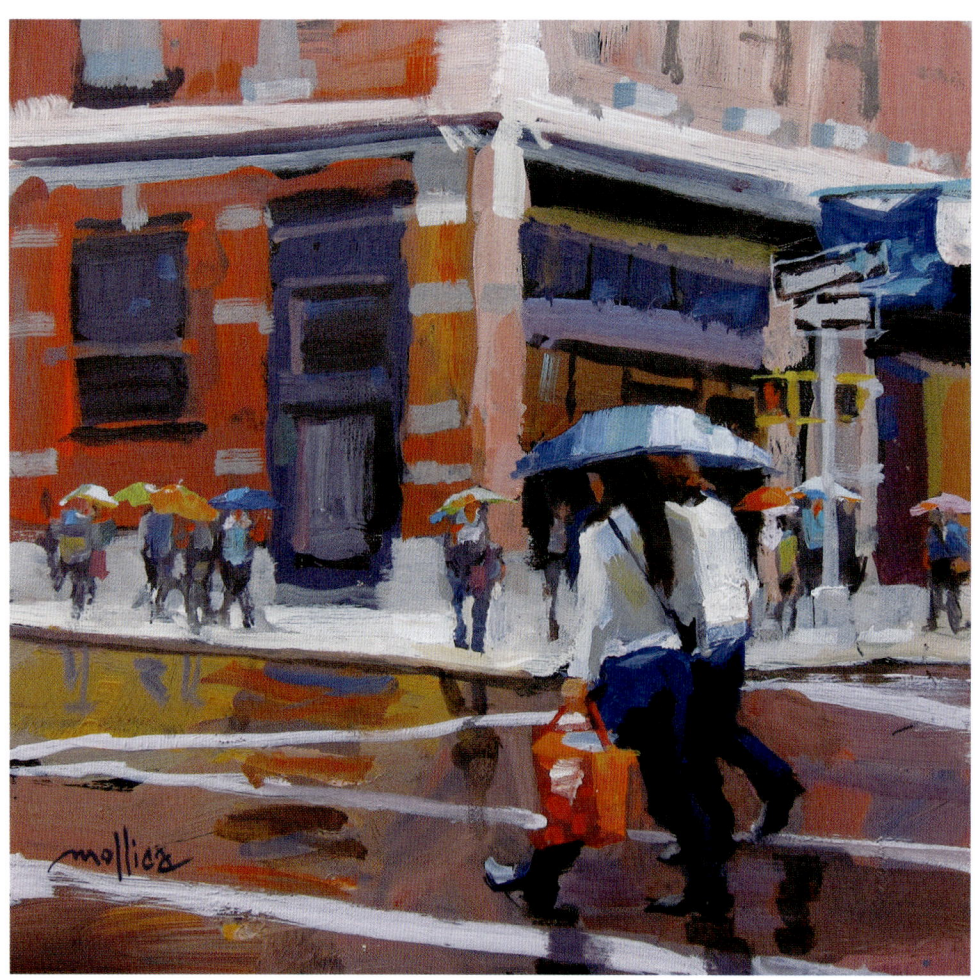

◄ SOHO SHOWERS
Acrylic on panel
8" × 8" (20cm × 20cm)
Private collection

► PINK SUNSET IN TUSCANY
Acrylic on board
12" × 10" (30cm × 25cm)
Private collection

WARM (DOMINANT) / COOL (SUBORDINATE)

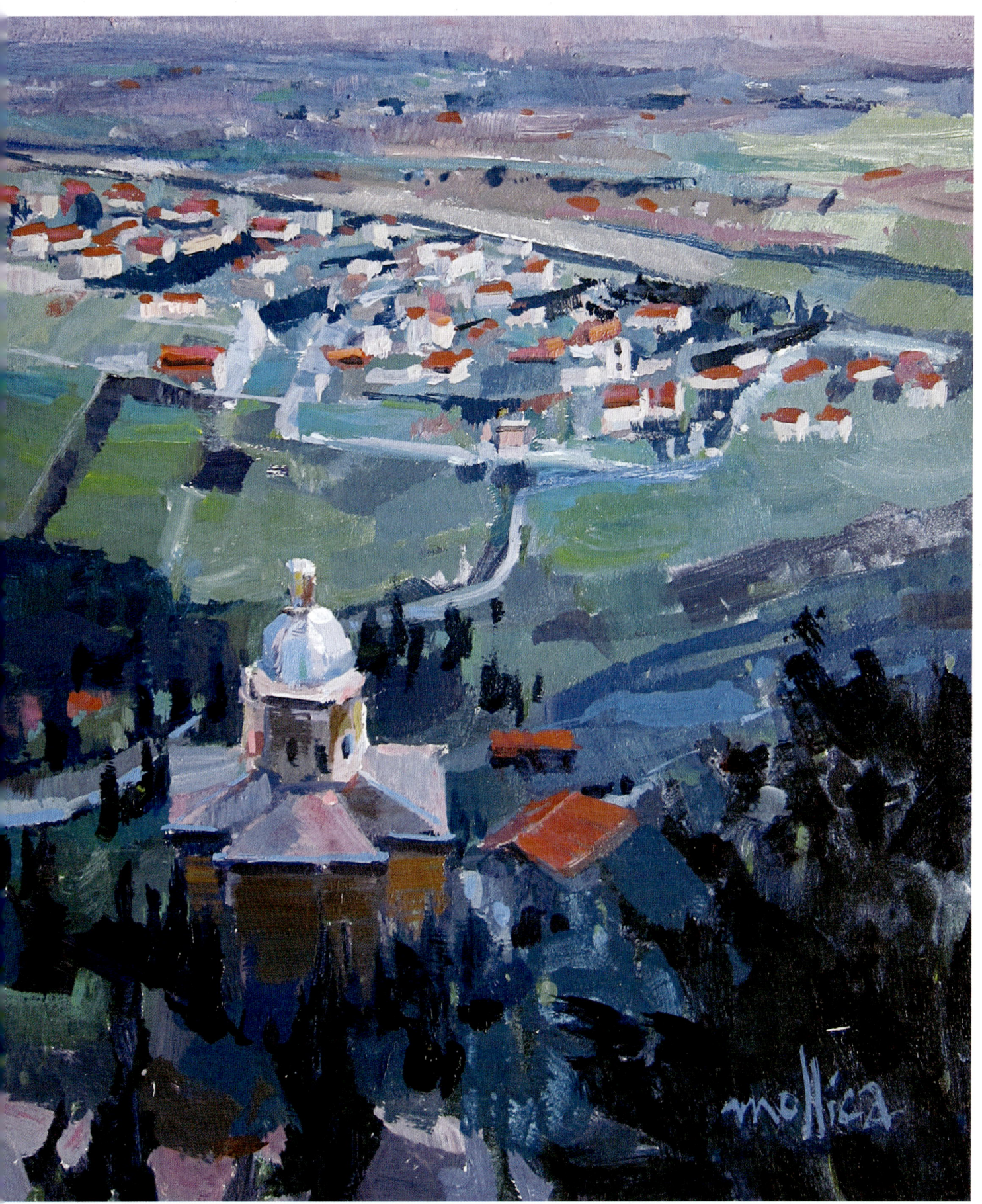

COOL (DOMINANT) / WARM (SUBORDINATE)

Saturation

Saturation is the intensity of a color. If hue refers to the color itself, saturation describes the dominance of the hue within that color.

When you have a dominant color temperature in your paintings it helps to create harmony. You should also be aware of the balance of saturated vs. grayed colors.

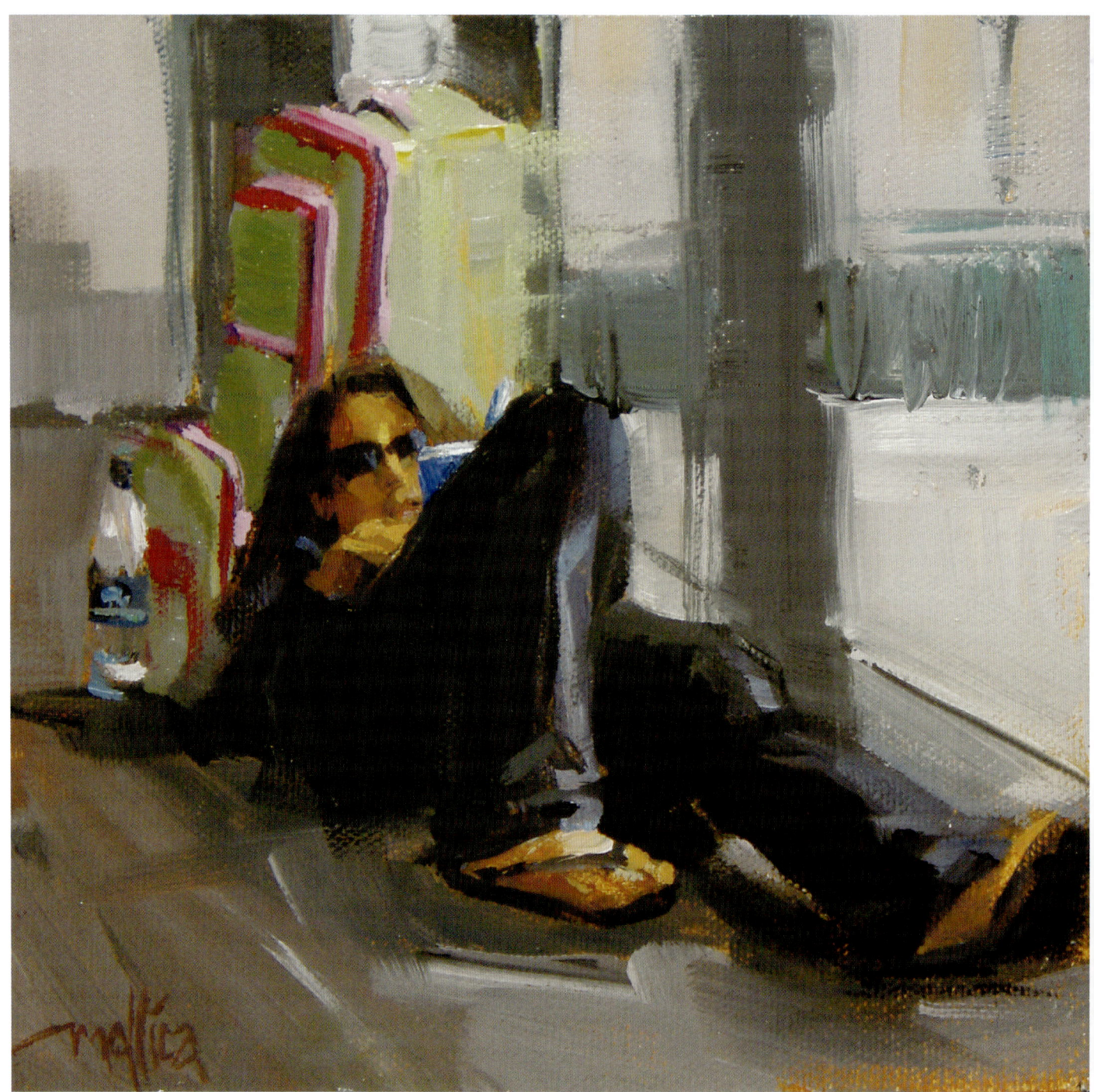

MOSTLY GRAYED/LESS SATURATED
We all love bright vivid color, but too many saturated colors can create chaos rather than unity. If all colors are bright and saturated, they are all competing for attention, much like a movie that is cast with all stars and no supporting actors. Neutrals and grays are important in that they enhance the saturated colors.

BUSTED FLAT
Acrylic on canvas
8" × 8" (20cm × 20cm)
Private collection

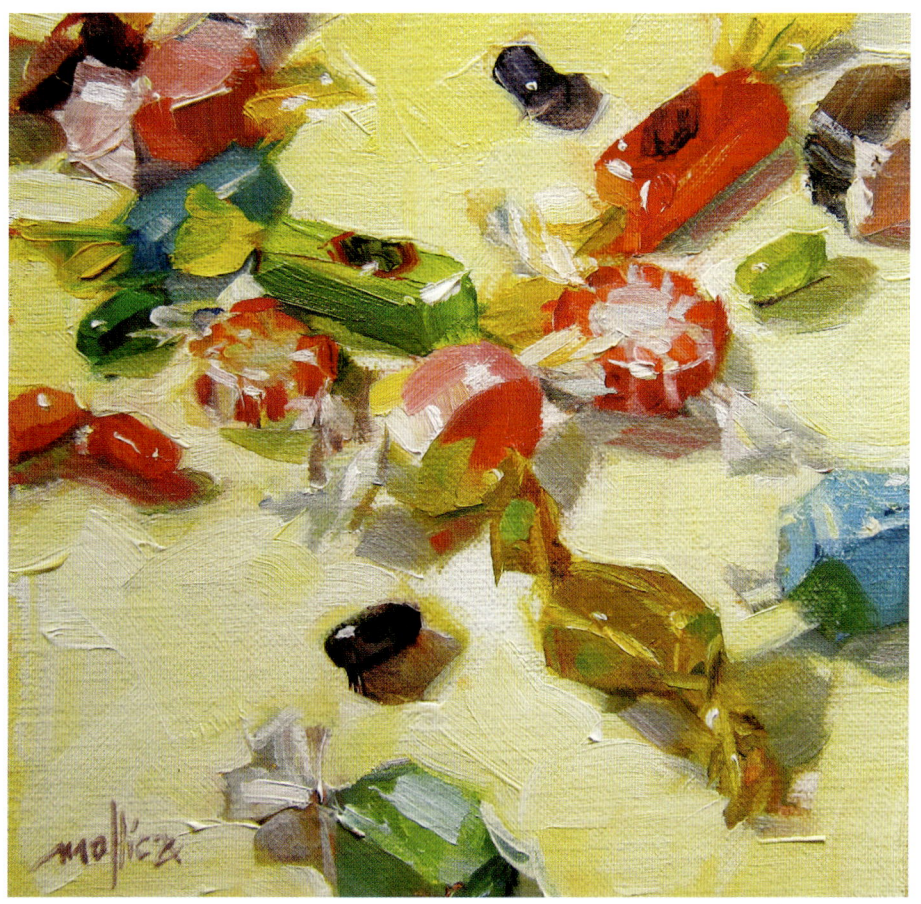

MOSTLY SATURATED/ LESS GRAYED

If your goal is to celebrate color in all its glory, a saturated color palette may be the perfect choice.

EYE CANDY
Oil on canvas
8" × 8" (20cm × 20cm)
Collection of Lily Tajalli

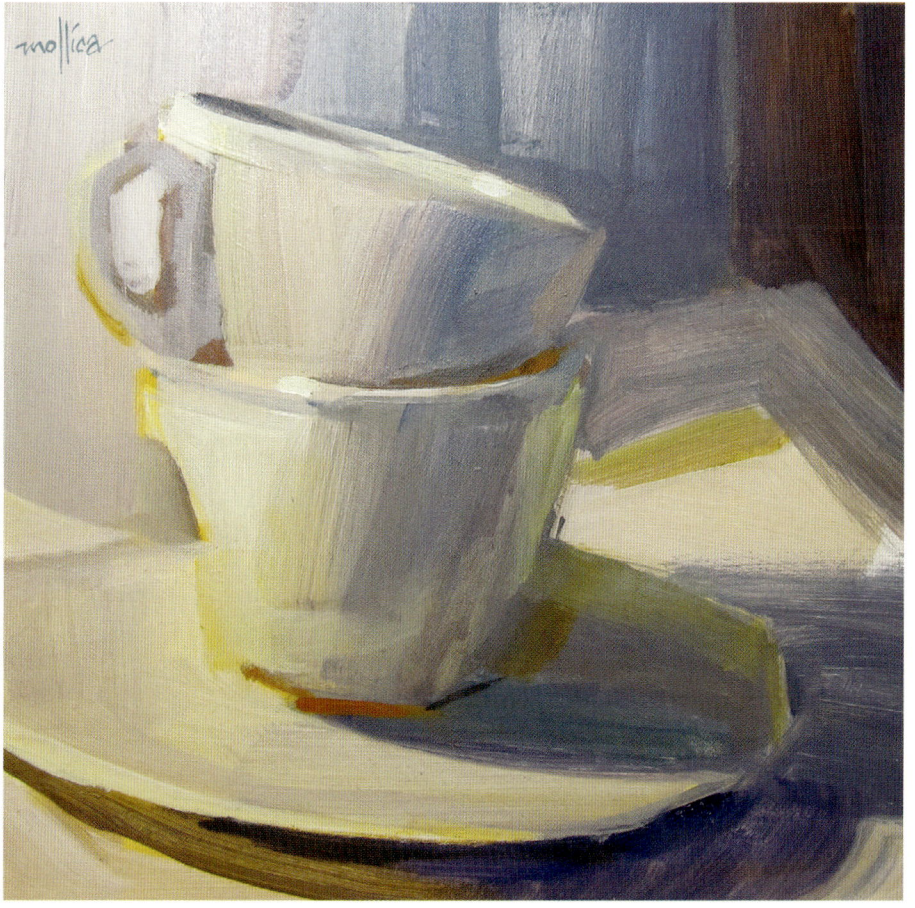

NO SATURATION/ALL GRAYED

A color palette with all neutrals and delicate grays can be just as lovely, but in a different way. This palette has a soothing, calm, understated elegance. The unsaturated color palette will be comprised mostly of neutral colors made from some combination of all three primaries, or complementary colors. There will be few, if any, vivid or saturated colors.

WHITE CUPS
Acrylic on panel
8" × 8" (20cm × 20cm)
Collection of Kathy Fallon Byrne

Key

Key refers to the overall value of a painting. This is important when you want to communicate a mood. Work in the value key that best describes the feeling you want to communicate.

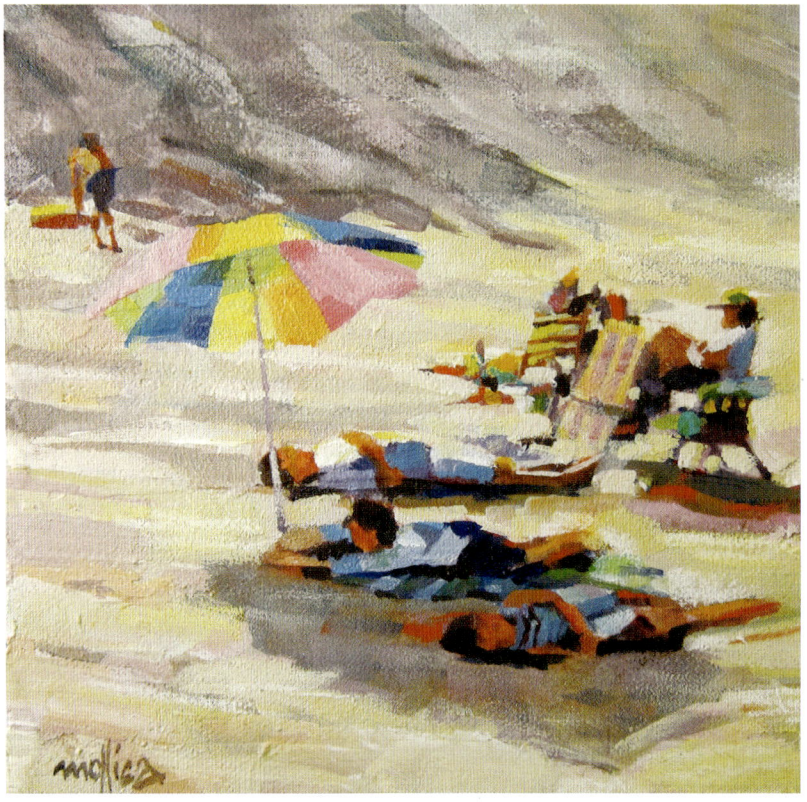

HIGH KEY PAINTING

High key describes mostly lighter values, such as a bright sunny beach scene. Most values in a high-key painting will be concentrated in the light to middle range.

SUNLOGGED
Acrylic on canvas
8" × 8" (20cm × 20cm)
Collection of Annette Proimos

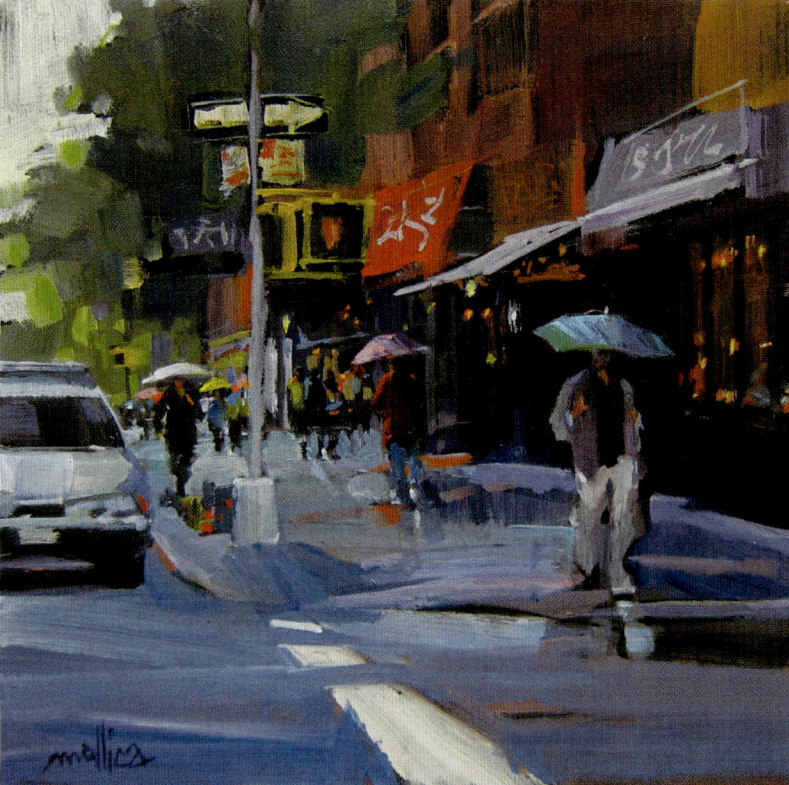

LOW KEY PAINTING

Low key means the painting was created in mostly darker values, such as a night scene. The majority of color values in a low-key range will be from the middle to the dark.

MIDTOWN SHOWERS
Acrylic on panel
8" × 8" (20cm × 20cm)
Collection of Alison Hoffman

Colorful Neutrals

Neutral colors (grays, browns and the hues in between) are the unsung heroes of many successful paintings because they allow the other colors to sing loudly. Experienced painters understand the importance of mixing and using neutrals effectively. These colors are beautiful in their own right and often make up the backbone of a successful painting by contrasting vibrant hues, meant to be used sparsely.

Colorful and nuanced neutrals can be created by working with complements. When you add a bit of a complement to a color, it desaturates or dulls it in direct proportion to the amount of complement used. For instance, in order to dull down a red, you would add a bit of green. If you want to neutralize it completely, add as much green as necessary to achieve the neutral brown or gray.

A mixture of any two primaries will create the complement of the third primary. For example, mixing red and yellow creates orange. The third primary is blue, which is the complement of orange. When all three primaries (plus white) are mixed together in any proportion, they create a neutralized color. Depend-ing on the proportions used, the resulting color can be slightly dulled or completely neutralized. Using more or less white will lighten or darken the value accordingly. Mixing primaries plus white in equal proportions will result in a gray or brownish color.

You can also experiment with mixing two tube colors plus whatever proportion of white you choose to see the array of neutral tones that emerge. Rich and lovely black colors can be created by leaving white out of your mixtures.

The more hands-on knowledge you have about how colors are created, the better you will be at re-creating them at will. Working with primaries to create all your colors is the easiest way to create harmonious colors in your painting. Additionally, your color palette will become much more sophisticated, and you will find yourself using bright tube colors far more strategically.

Practice creating some colorful gray swatches, then try your hand at a painting where all your colors are mixed in the same manner—with all three primary colors plus white. You will be surprised at how colorful a painting can be using just grays.

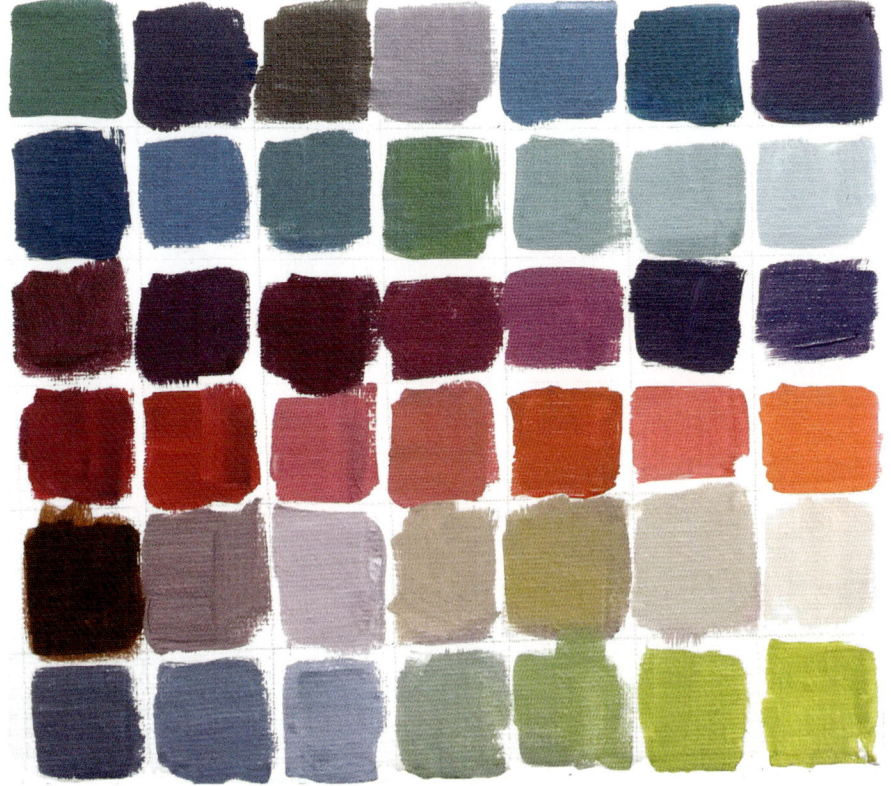

GRAYED COLORS
These swatches of color are harmonious because each one contains the exact same colors (the three primaries plus white), only in varying proportions.

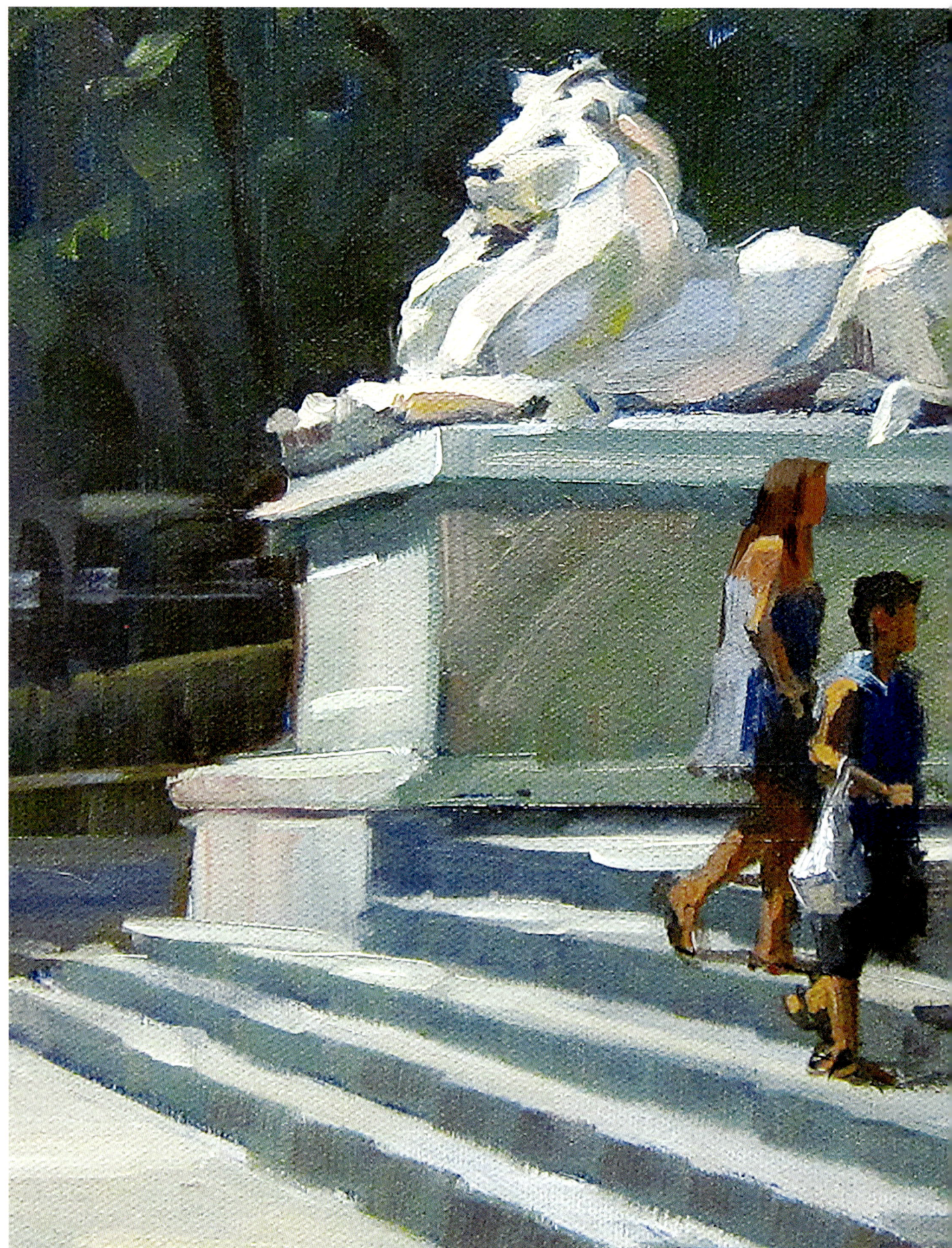

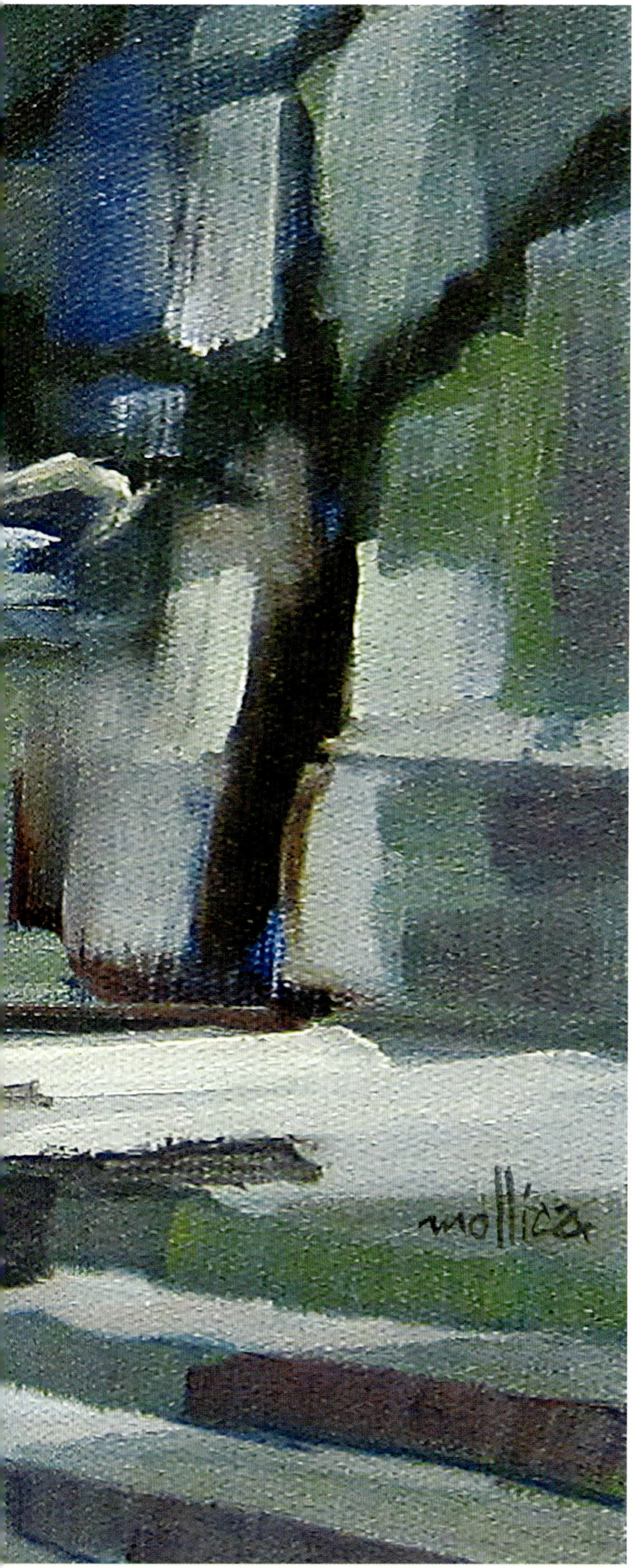

Color Mixing for Unity

Color is usually the first thing that gets noticed in a painting, which makes it a significant factor in a painting's success or failure. Every artist needs some know-how in assuring their colors are unified, harmonious and pleasing. With the huge array of paint colors to choose from, it can be challenging to decide which ones will harmonize and "play" nicely together.

In this chapter we will learn about working with traditional and non-traditional harmonic color schemes, as well as mixing basics that will demonstrate how to mix the colors you envision. We will look at a less-is-more approach using limited color palettes, along with some additional techniques that will result in lovely unified colors.

PATIENCE (THE NEW YORK PUBLIC LIBRARY LION)
Acrylic on canvas
12" × 12" (30cm × 30cm)
Collection of Sally Walsh

Choosing Paints

Walk into the paint section of any art supply store and you will be mesmerized by the spectacular array of colors available. Though you may feel compelled to grab all the colors that make your heart jump, a little understanding of how pigments actually work, and the results they will yield, will go a long way toward helping you make smart choices that are consistent with your artistic goals.

The first thing you want to consider is your painting style. Do you work in layers of translucent glazes, building each successive layer upon the previous ones to create luminous passages resulting from the light source bouncing through and interacting with the layers? Do you work in washes and pours? Or perhaps you work in thick impasto passages that reveal the brushstrokes or choppy action of a lively palette knife application. Having a clear knowledge of your artistic style and your intentions is the key to choosing the correct colors as well as viscosity of paint.

In its most simplistic definition, paint consists of binder and pigment. The binder is what adheres the paint to your substrate, i.e. canvas, panels, paper, wood, etc. The binder also is the vehicle that holds the colored pigment particles. The binder for oil paints is linseed oil. Acrylic binder is called polymer dispersion, and for watercolors it's gum arabic. Although the binders for various mediums are different, the pigments are the same. Pigments are derived from two main sources: mineral or modern.

Mineral Pigments

Mineral pigments have earth-based origins such as ground-up rocks and decayed plant and animal matter. They have names that imply their earthy origins such as siennas, cadmiums, ochres, umbers, cobalts, oxides and more. In most cases, they are very opaque, make weak mixing colors, are not considered vivid hues, and have dull sheens. Think of a pulverized rock—no matter how small the size of the particles, the particles are still rock and thus very opaque.

MINERAL VS. MODERN PIGMENT HUE COMPARISON

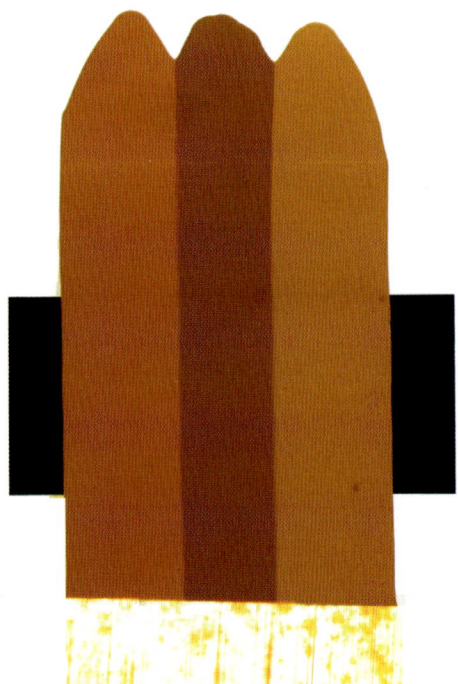

Mineral Pigments: Ochre, Raw Sienna, Yellow Ochre

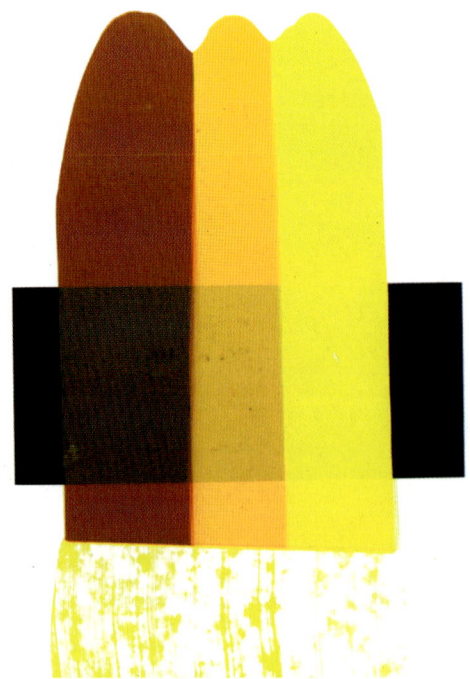

Modern Pigments: Nickel Azo Yellow, Hansa Yellow Medium, Hansa Yellow Light

Some common mineral pigments are:

- Cerulean Blue
- Chromium Oxide Green
- Cadmium Yellow
- Yellow Ochre
- Cadmium Orange
- Cadmium Red
- Burnt Umber
- Titanium White

Modern Pigments

In the mid 1950s, chemists discovered how to make colored pigment particles from experiments conducted in a laboratory setting. What resulted was a classification of pigments that offered exciting new characteristics when used in paint. These new modern pigments have names that hint at their chemical origins such as dioxazine, anthraquinone, phthalocyanine, quinacridone, naphthol, azo, hansa and more. If viewed under a microscope, they appear like jagged shards of stained glass—very translucent with brilliant saturated hues and an inherently glossy sheen.

Some common modern pigments are:

- Anthraquinone Blue
- Phthalo Green
- Hansa Yellow
- Nickel Azo Yellow
- Pyrrole Orange
- Naphthol Red
- Quinacridone Crimson
- Dioxazine Purple

Blending Mineral and Modern Pigments

Although the origins are different, it is perfectly fine to blend mineral colors with modern colors to achieve the best of both worlds. Use a mineral color if you need opacity and coverage. Add a brilliant modern counterpart to your mixture if you want add some zing to the hue.

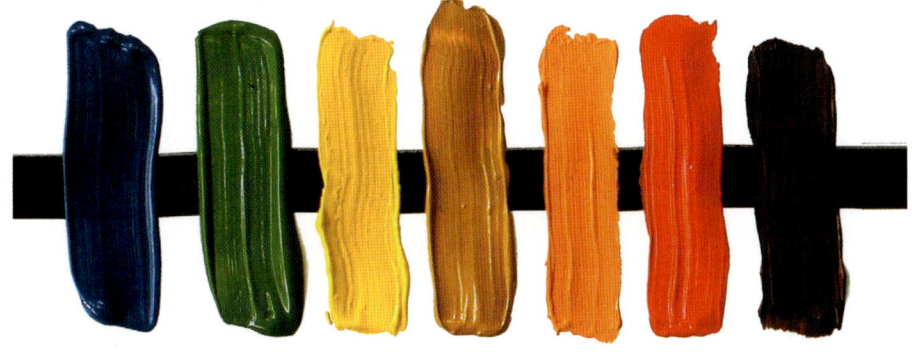

MINERAL PIGMENTS

These colors have excellent covering ability and are a perfect choice for underpaintings and base colors. Conversely, they are poor choices for translucent glazing techniques. If you paint in a direct style that does not rely on building up translucent layers of color, you will want to use paints made from pigments that have their chemical basis from mineral origins.

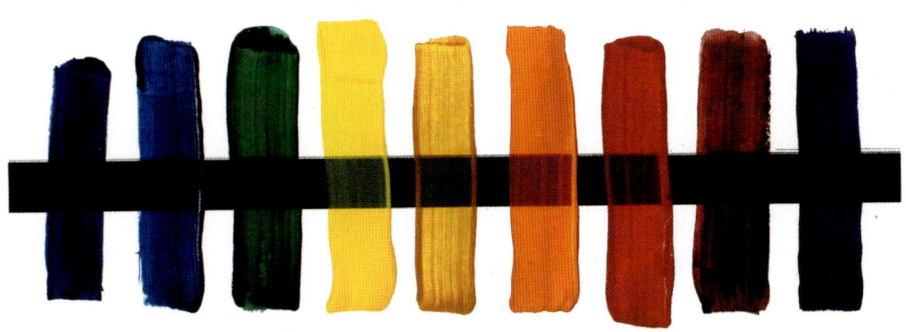

MODERN PIGMENTS

This classification of pigments is made of powerful colors as well as strong mixing colors. In other words, a little goes a very long way.

Modern pigments are perfect for glazing in multiple sheer layers because their translucent nature allows light waves to pass through and blend two or more colors optically.

Paint Viscosity

Another consideration in choosing which paint to buy is viscosity. Viscosity refers to the consistency, the thickness or thinness of the paint. You may have noticed that paint is available in consistencies ranging from drip-like and pourable like heavy cream, to soft and spreadable like soft butter, to stiff and firm like peanut butter.

In my observation there are many more viscosities offered in acrylic paint than in oil paint, but it is possible to buy additives for oil paint that will alter its viscosity to a thinner or thicker variation. The point is to choose your paint viscosity according to your style. The thinner viscosity will self-level and provide long, uniform strokes. Low viscosity paints require less medium to create washes, glazes and more transparent passages.

If you want to work in thin layers you can always use a heavier viscosity paint and add water or acrylic medium (for acrylic), or turps (for oils), to thin it down, but you will be extending the pigment load of your mixture and lose depth of color. The same is true for painters that work in a textural impasto style. You would want to buy heavy, full-bodied paint to achieve volume, texture and dimension.

Again, you could always buy a low viscosity paint, often called "fluid" or "soft body" and add a stiffer heavy gel to give it volume, but in doing so, you are diluting the concentration of pigment in your passages, thus creating a translucent effect that may not give you the coverage or opacity you need. All the additives that are available to change the viscosity of your paint become transparent when they dry, and therefore will weaken the saturation and depth of your color. So, buy the viscosity that suits your needs.

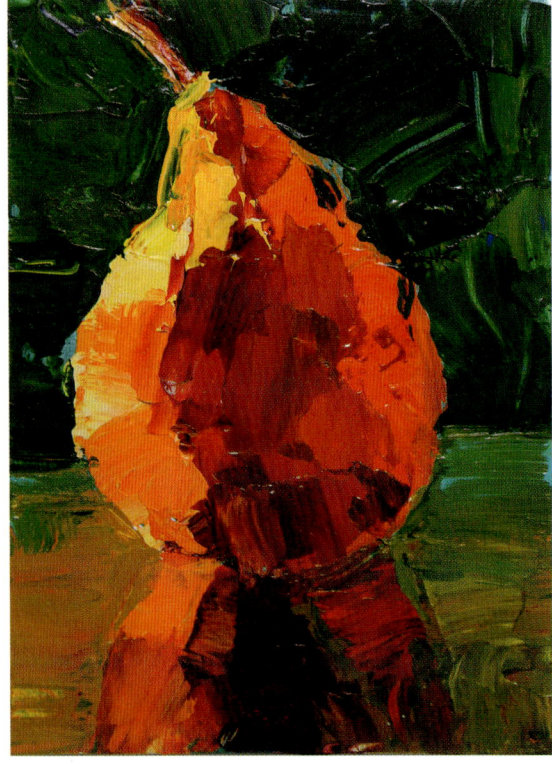
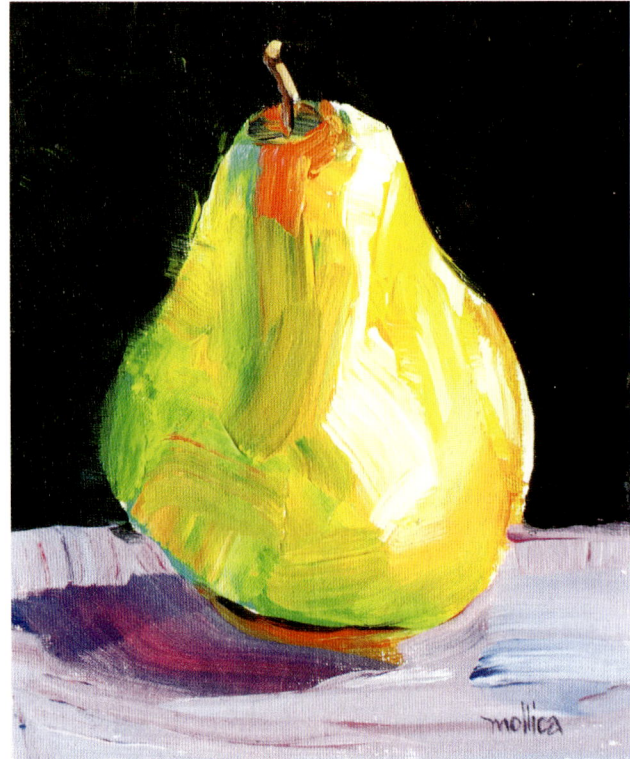

HEAVY BODY VS. FLUID PAINTS
Choose the viscosity paint that suits the style you work in. Here are two popular acrylic viscosities—heavy body applied with a palette knife, and fluid applied with a brush. Both will yield different results in your painting.

Mixing Colors

Let's talk about basic color mixing and how to mix the colors you want. First you must consider the three characteristics that define color: hue, saturation and value. Hue is also often referred to as color. For instance if you were to describe the hue of a tree, you would say green. All variations of that green—lime green, emerald green, gray green, etc.—are still considered part of the green family hue.

All the hues (colors) that are perceptible to the human eye originate exclusively from some combination of the three primary colors. To review, when each of the primaries is mixed with another primary, the resulting color is called a secondary color. The secondary colors are: orange (red+yellow), green (yellow+blue) and purple (red+blue).

Saturation

The next aspect of color mixing is saturation, or chroma, which is defined as the purity or intensity of color. Colors with a high chroma are vibrant and bright. An artist needs to be able to mix colors in both high and low chroma. Simply mixing any primary color may not yield the correct chroma of the secondary color you have in mind. This is why it is necessary to understand the primaries and their hue properties.

Each primary color has a tendency to be biased toward a warmer or cooler hue. There are no completely neutral primary colors that will result in creating all vibrant secondary mixtures. For instance, there is no "true" red that will result in a vivid purple *and* a brilliant orange. For this reason, many artists use what is called a split primary palette.

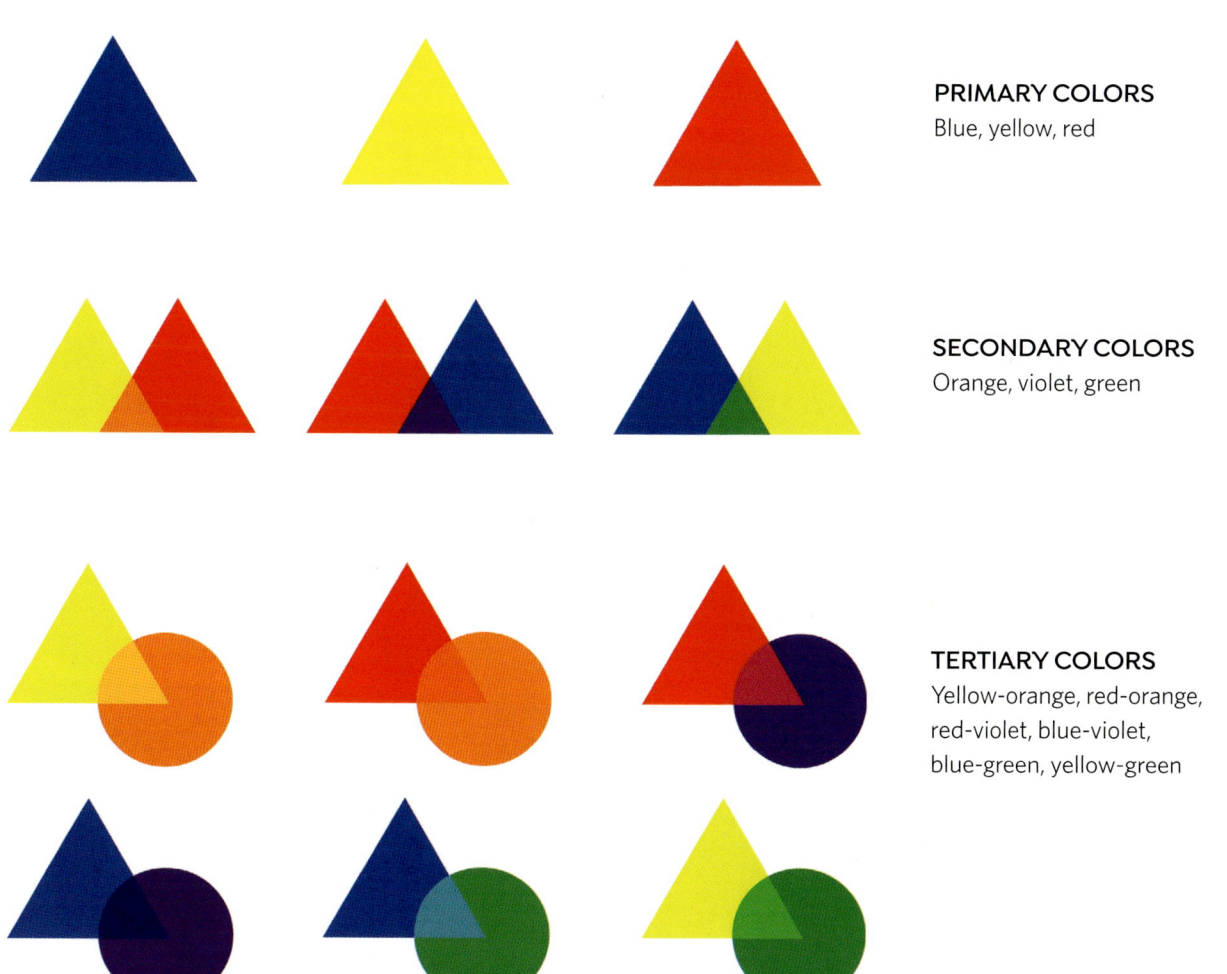

PRIMARY COLORS
Blue, yellow, red

SECONDARY COLORS
Orange, violet, green

TERTIARY COLORS
Yellow-orange, red-orange, red-violet, blue-violet, blue-green, yellow-green

Split Primary Palette

To create the most saturated secondary colors possible, your split primary palette must consist of two of each primary color—one with a warm bias and one with a cool bias. Avoid muddy colors by mixing primaries that lean toward each other, meaning they have bits of that color already in them. The chart below shows two of each primary color along with the way the colors lean. For instance, Cadmium Red Medium has some yellow in it.

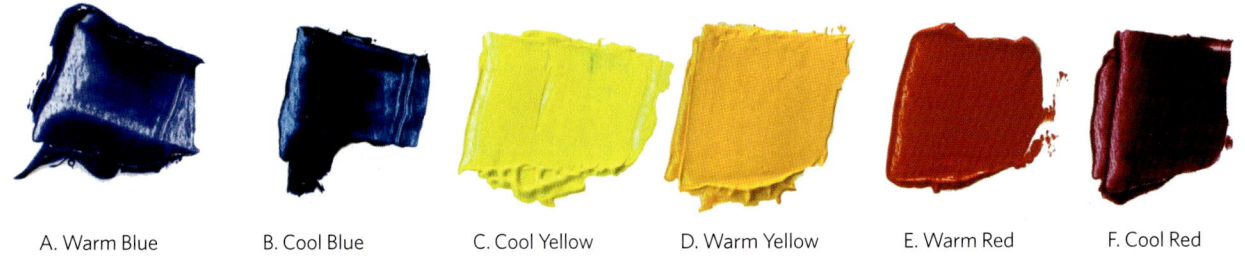

| A. Warm Blue | B. Cool Blue | C. Cool Yellow | D. Warm Yellow | E. Warm Red | F. Cool Red |

SPLIT PRIMARY PALETTE

This example shows two variations of each primary color.

A. Ultramarine Blue leans red.
B. Phthalo Blue leans yellow.
C. Cadmium Lemon Yellow leans blue.
D. Cadmium Yellow Medium leans red.
E. Cadmium Red Medium leans yellow.
F. Alizarin Crimson leans blue.

MIXING VIBRANT AND DULL COLORS

Sometimes it helps to look at the hues in relation to each other on the color wheel. In order to mix a vibrant orange for example, you would mix red and yellow. To dull that orange, you would mix in a bit of the color that sits opposite from it on the color wheel (blue). So if you are mixing a red (that has blue in it) with a yellow (that also has blue in it), you're adding a lot of blue into your orange. This mixture will result in a dull, earthy orange. In order to keep your secondary mixtures as clean as possible, keep its complementary color (or the third primary) out of your mixtures!

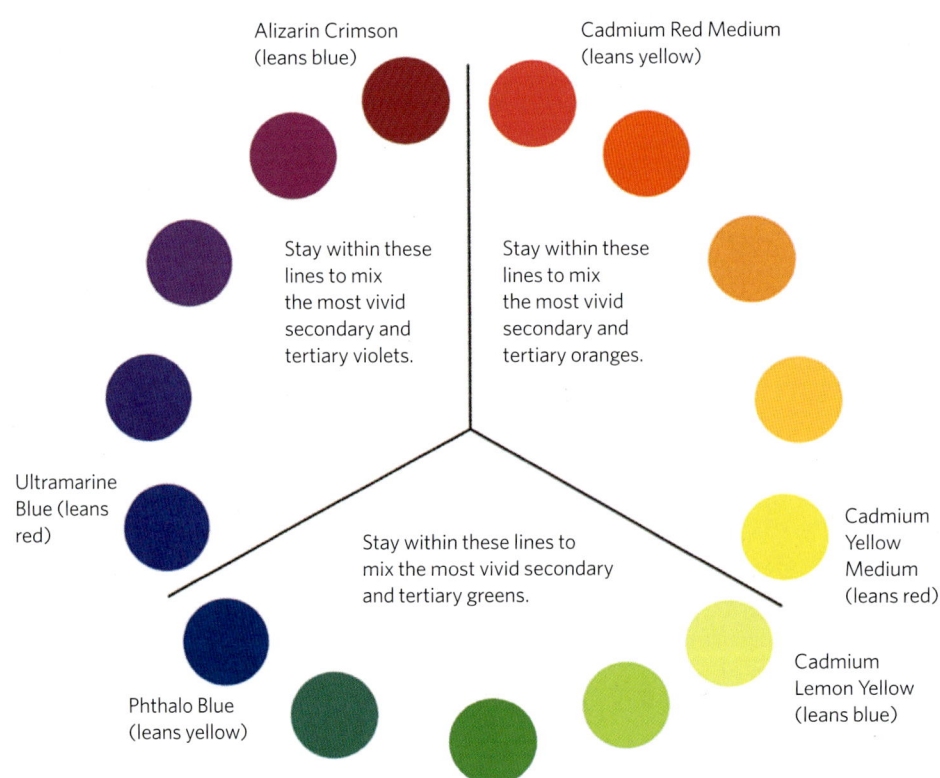

Alizarin Crimson (leans blue)

Cadmium Red Medium (leans yellow)

Stay within these lines to mix the most vivid secondary and tertiary violets.

Stay within these lines to mix the most vivid secondary and tertiary oranges.

Ultramarine Blue (leans red)

Stay within these lines to mix the most vivid secondary and tertiary greens.

Cadmium Yellow Medium (leans red)

Cadmium Lemon Yellow (leans blue)

Phthalo Blue (leans yellow)

VIBRANT SECONDARY COLOR MIXTURES

These are the best mixtures for creating vibrant secondary colors.

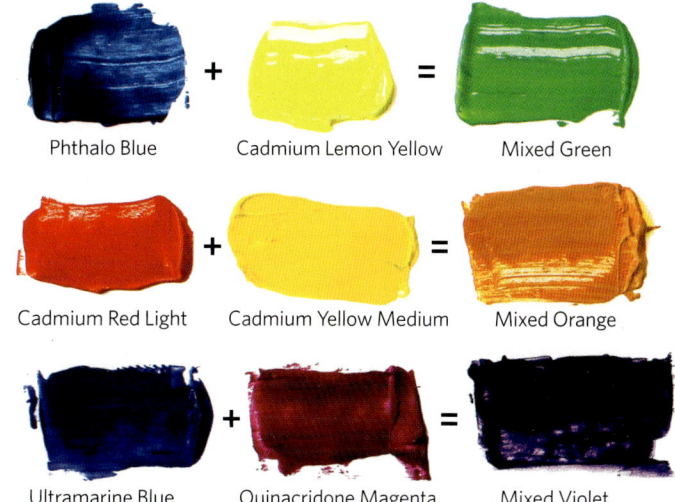

Phthalo Blue + Cadmium Lemon Yellow = Mixed Green

Cadmium Red Light + Cadmium Yellow Medium = Mixed Orange

Ultramarine Blue + Quinacridone Magenta = Mixed Violet

VIBRANT TERTIARY COLOR MIXTURES

Here are the best mixtures for creating vibrant tertiary colors.

What's in a (Paint) Name?

When learning how to mix colors, it is important to experiment for yourself rather than rely on printed charts. Each paint manufacturer names and creates their colors differently, so there is a lack of uniformity of colors even if they have the same name. Acrylic formulas will not only differ from oils, but also from other acrylic brands.

For instance, when using a certain brand of oil paints, the Cadmium Red Medium mixed with Cadmium Yellow Medium makes a beautiful, brilliant orange. However, those same colors mixed in acrylics result in a much duller orange. Experimentation is the best way to learn.

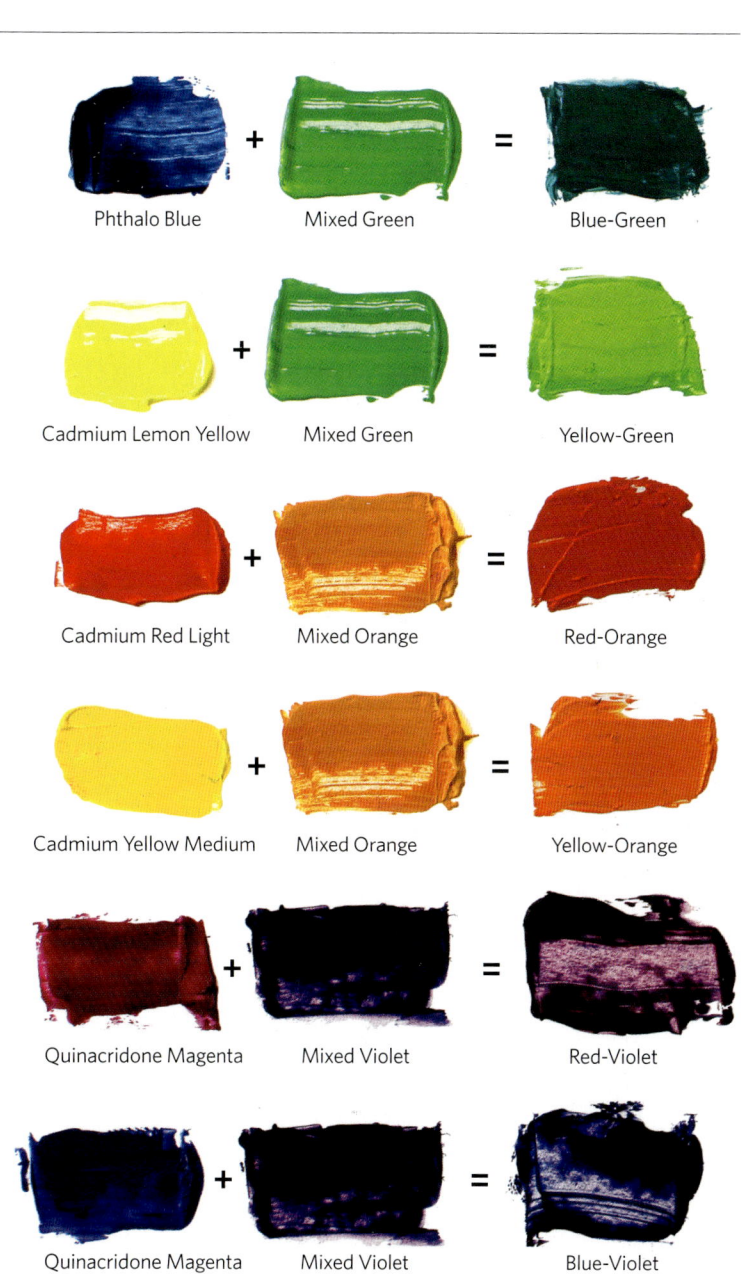

Phthalo Blue + Mixed Green = Blue-Green

Cadmium Lemon Yellow + Mixed Green = Yellow-Green

Cadmium Red Light + Mixed Orange = Red-Orange

Cadmium Yellow Medium + Mixed Orange = Yellow-Orange

Quinacridone Magenta + Mixed Violet = Red-Violet

Quinacridone Magenta + Mixed Violet = Blue-Violet

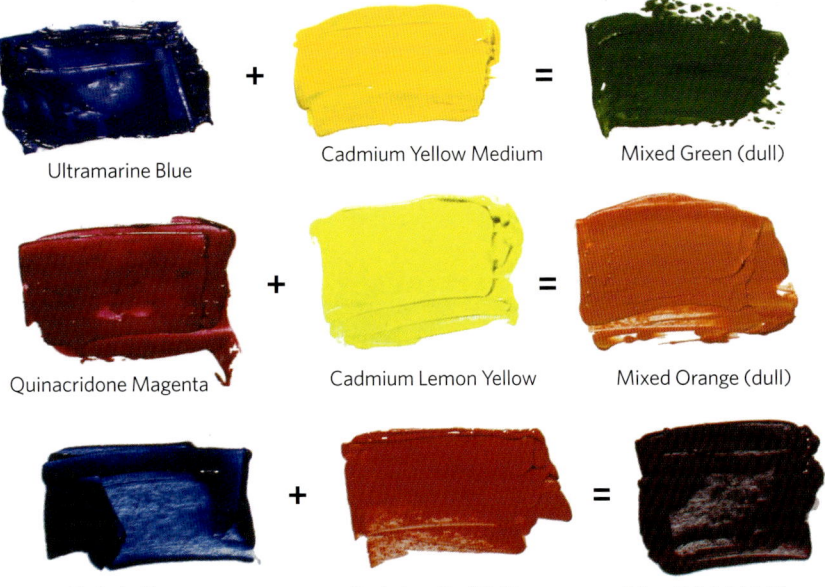

Ultramarine Blue + Cadmium Yellow Medium = Mixed Green (dull)

Quinacridone Magenta + Cadmium Lemon Yellow = Mixed Orange (dull)

Phthalo Blue + Cadmium Red Light = Mixed Violet (dull)

LOW CHROMA SECONDARIES

Creating toned-down color mixtures is important for the unity of your painting. For instance if you mix Cadmium Yellow Medium (leans red) with Ultramarine Blue (leans red), you will create a green that is a far more natural and believable foliage color than if you mixed Phthalo Blue with Cadmium Lemon Yellow.

Consider the duller variations of your secondary and tertiary colors if you want a painting that has selective areas of bright color, especially around the focal point. If you are strategic and selective in your use of vivid colors, your painting will have more impact.

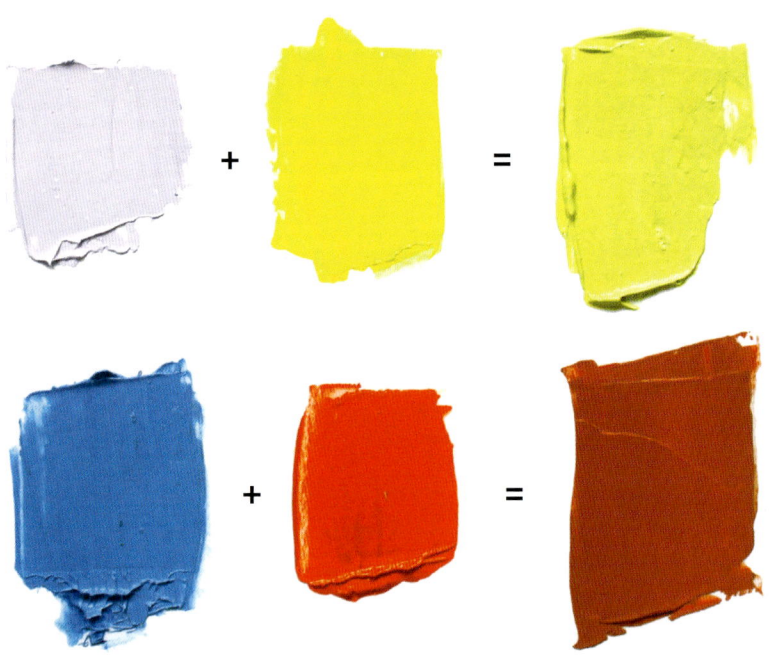

ALTER SATURATION, MAINTAIN VALUE

We have already discussed that the best way to neutralize or desaturate a color is by adding a bit of the complementary color. But since each of the colors have different values, it's important to be able to control the chroma, or saturation, while maintaining its value. Whenever you add a dark value color to a light value color, or vice versa, you will changing its value. For instance, if you wanted to gray down a bright yellow by adding violet, you would darken it as well. The easiest way to keep the value consistent while toning it down is to make the complementary color the *same value* as the color you are trying to alter. Add plenty of white into the violet so that it is the same value as the yellow. Then simply add it to your yellow and the chroma will lower with no value change. You can use this method for any of your colors when you need to change the saturation, but not the value.

Changing the Value of Color Mixtures

When beginner painters want to lighten or darken their mixtures, the obvious solution is to reach for the white or black paint. While some white is often necessary to lighten or black to darken, the resulting mixture will likely not communicate a wide spectrum of colors represented by the effects of various light sources.

Light sources can be warm or cool. For instance, when the light from the sun is striking an object, it is bathed in warm light, such as yellow, pink or orange, depending on the time of day. This object will cast a cool shadow where the warm temperature of the sunlight is blocked, and the blue of the sky will be reflected on it. When trying to realistically portray this dynamic light effect, simply using white and black will not be a convincing representation of all the colors on display.

Many artists feel that adding black will "deaden" the color. Personally I think that black can be used effectively to achieve beautiful, subtle, subdued and also rich color mixtures. Again, experimentation is the best way to decide what works best for you. Don't automatically eliminate black from your palette just because that is what you have heard secondhand.

From a chromatic point of view, there are more colorful ways to lighten and darken your mixtures. By working around the color wheel and using the colors that lie next to or near to the color you want to adjust (analogous colors) you can change its value easily.

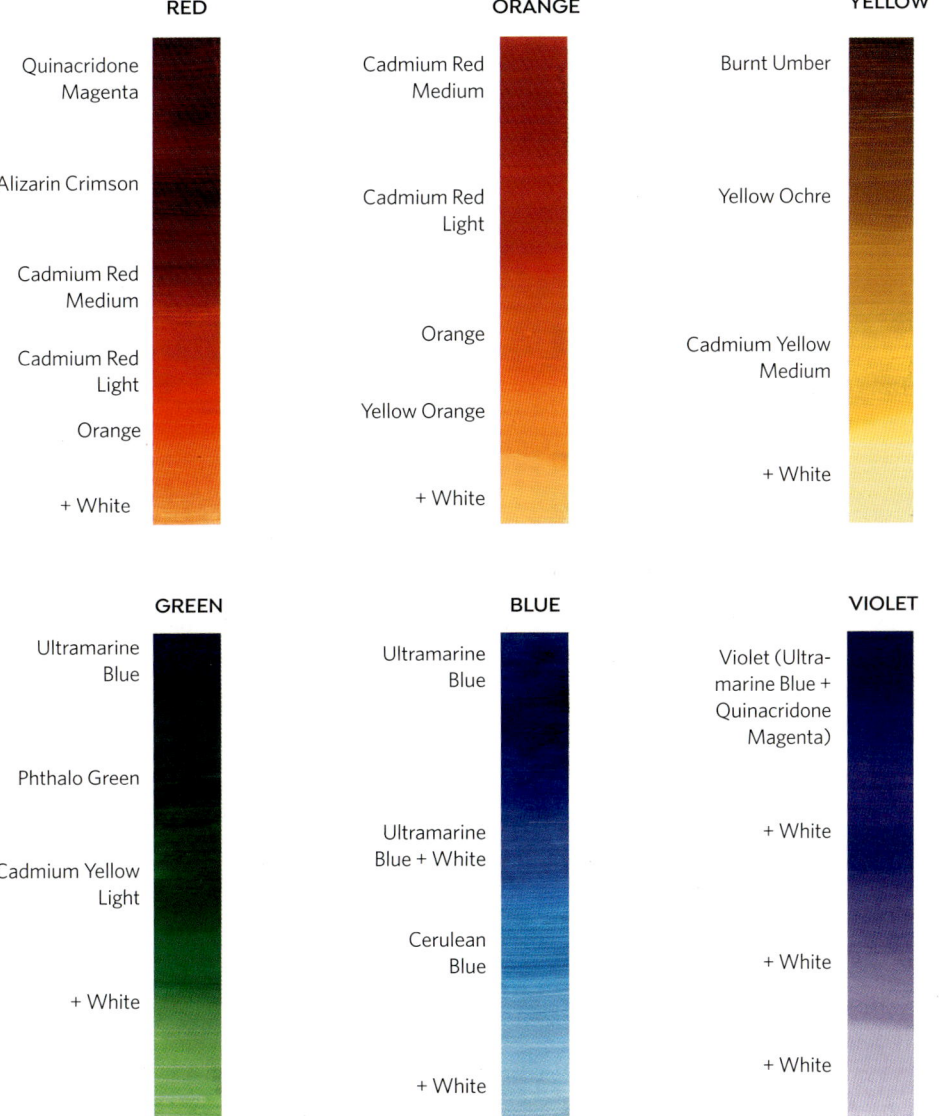

RED
- Quinacridone Magenta
- Alizarin Crimson
- Cadmium Red Medium
- Cadmium Red Light
- Orange
- + White

ORANGE
- Cadmium Red Medium
- Cadmium Red Light
- Orange
- Yellow Orange
- + White

YELLOW
- Burnt Umber
- Yellow Ochre
- Cadmium Yellow Medium
- + White

GREEN
- Ultramarine Blue
- Phthalo Green
- Cadmium Yellow Light
- + White

BLUE
- Ultramarine Blue
- Ultramarine Blue + White
- Cerulean Blue
- + White

VIOLET
- Violet (Ultramarine Blue + Quinacridone Magenta)
- + White
- + White
- + White

DARKENING VALUES

In each example here, I've lightened or darkened the middle value by adding its analogous color on either side of the color wheel. I used tube colors to lighten and darken, however you can also use your split palette colors to create color mixtures to simulate tube colors. This is where experimentation will come in handy. If you are a beginner and this feels too daunting, simply purchase darker versions of your lighter value colors.

Altering Hues With Earth Tones

It is easier to lighten dark colors than it is to darken light colors. To lighten violet, for example, you can simply add white plus a little blue if you want it cooler, or magenta if you want it warmer. But how do you darken yellow? If you add black, you will get an acid green, not a warm gold.

Earth tones, such as Burnt Umber, Burnt Sienna, Raw Sienna and Yellow Ochre can be used effectively to darken yellows as well as other warm hues like red and orange.

Earth tones can also be used with darker cool colors to modify their saturation, often in landscape paintings where a wide range of greens are required.

Since the earth tones are basically dark value reds, oranges and yellows, when you add them to your cool hues, you will desaturate them. If you add Burnt Umber to Ultramarine Blue, you will desaturate the blue without altering its value. Many artists use the dark earth tones for this purpose.

BURNT UMBER
A dark and warm brown that can be mixed with other warm colors for earthier, duller variations. If you do not want your dark reds to go too violet, add some Burnt Umber.

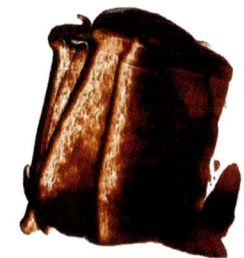

BURNT SIENNA
Think of Burnt Sienna as a dark version of orange. If you want a dark orange that does not veer into dark red, add some Burnt Sienna for an earthier, duller hue.

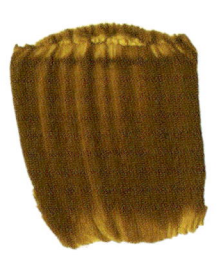

RAW SIENNA
Raw Sienna can be used to darken yellow effectively. For more variations of dark yellow, or gold, experiment with adding bits of other earth tones as well.

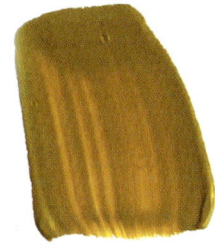

YELLOW OCHRE
Yellow Ochre is a middle value, unsaturated yellow with a gold hue.

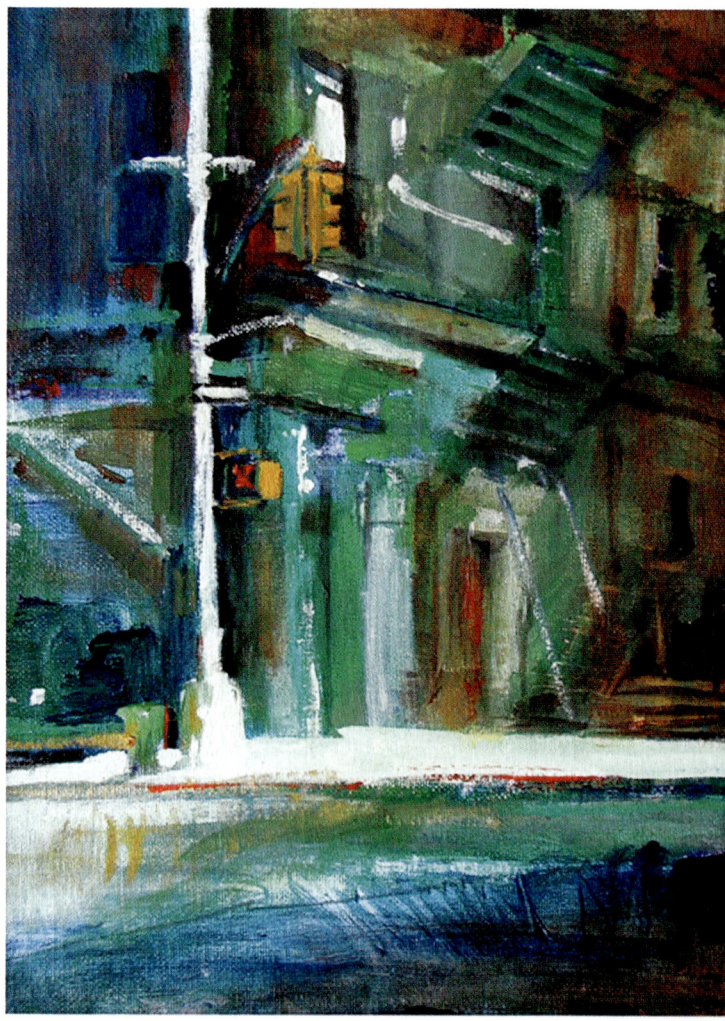

LOST AND FOUND
Acrylic on canvas
14" × 11" (36cm × 28cm)
Collection of Herbert Gastgeir

Mixing Greens

Many artists derive their inspiration from natural landscapes lush with brilliant and subtle greens and rich complementary earth tones. Mixing realistic greens that communicate hue variations can be challenging for both beginner and experienced landscape painters. One of the most obvious signs of a beginner is their use of greens, which are typically far too vibrant. Beginners often use Phthalo Green right out of the tube, mixing it with white and black to simulate realistic foliage colors. Unfortunately this looks very simplistic.

There are several ways to mix greens using blues, yellows and even black that will provide realistic results. Although some artists refuse to have black on their palette because it can have a color-deadening effect, using black to create realistic greens is an exception. Additionally, mixing greens with a variety of common yellows will produce lovely realistic effects with plenty of cool/warm variations to please the eye.

If you prefer to work with commercially prepared tube greens such as Phthalo Green or Viridian, you will need to mix in a bit of complementary colors—variations of reds or browns—to neutralize them so they do not appear artificial. To give my tube greens a more earthy effect, I often mix in a bit of Burnt Sienna, Burnt Umber, Cadmium Red Light, Cadmium Orange or even Alizarin Crimson.

Experiment and see for yourself how many lovely green variations you can mix from a limited palette— you will be pleasantly surprised.

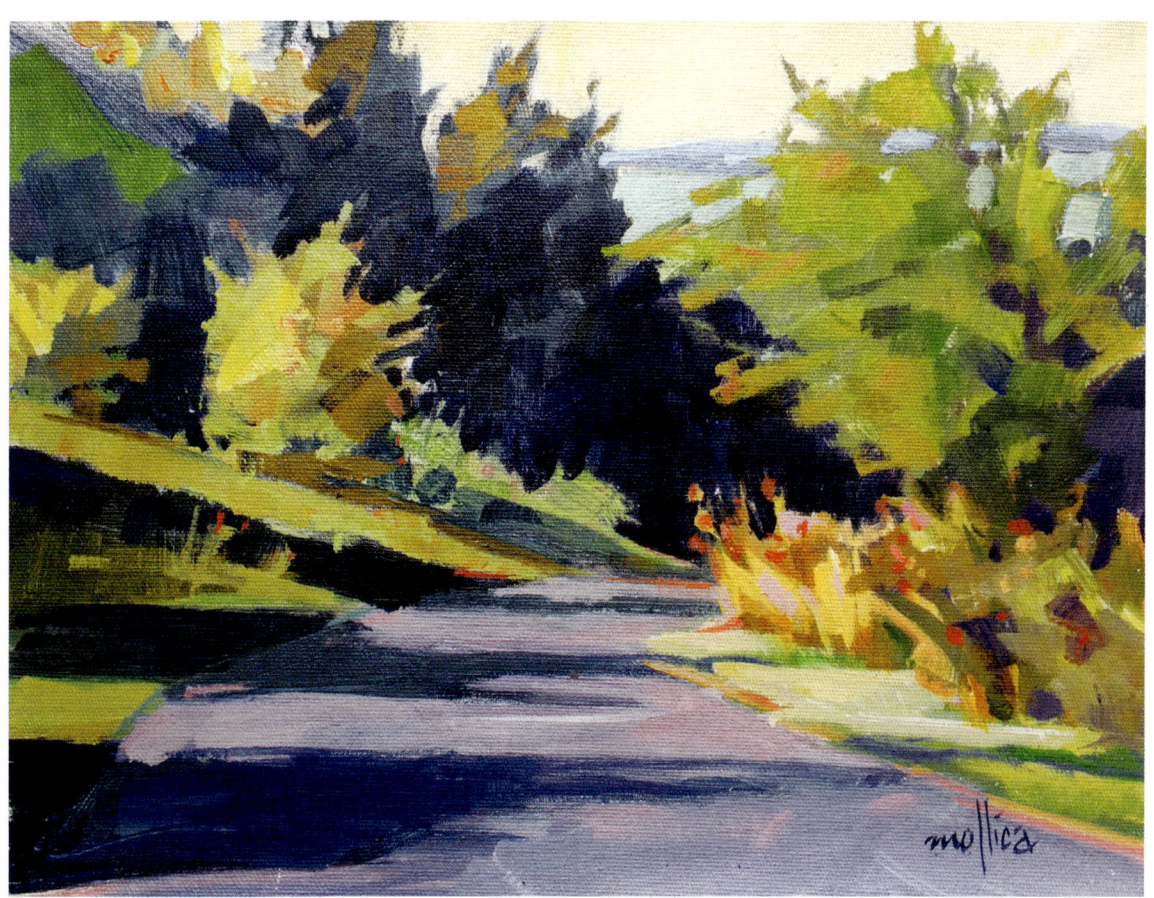

MIXING GREENS FROM A LIMITED PALETTE
When painting in plein air it is advantageous to keep your materials as pared down as possible. Using just two yellows, two blues and one black and one white (to lighten) will offer you many excellent choices and save you from having to drag along a variety of tube greens.

GREEN LAKES PARK
Acrylic on canvas
11" × 14" (28cm × 36cm)

TUBE GREENS (PLUS WHITE)

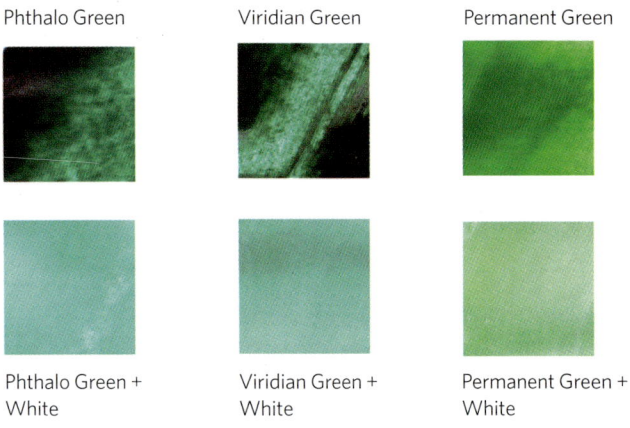

Phthalo Green	Viridian Green	Permanent Green

Phthalo Green + White	Viridian Green + White	Permanent Green + White

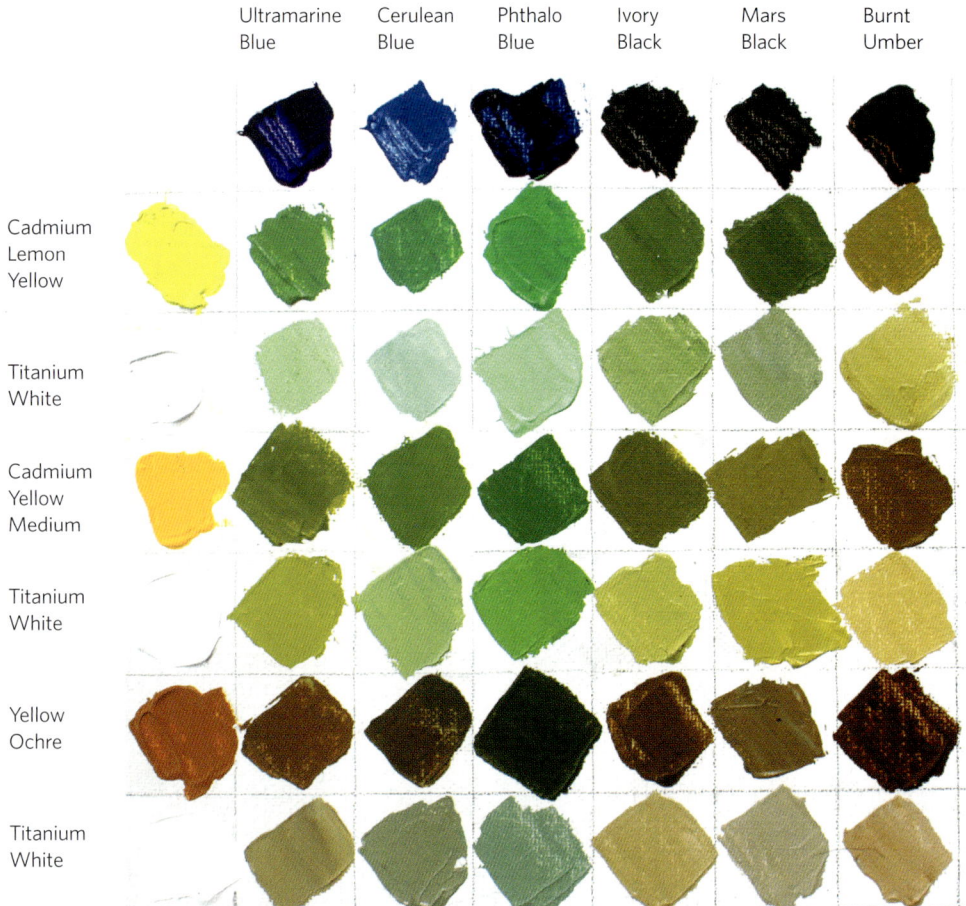

	Ultramarine Blue	Cerulean Blue	Phthalo Blue	Ivory Black	Mars Black	Burnt Umber
Cadmium Lemon Yellow						
Titanium White						
Cadmium Yellow Medium						
Titanium White						
Yellow Ochre						
Titanium White						

REALISTIC, EARTHY GREEN MIXTURES

One of the most common misuses of tube greens involves using them to create foliage colors. Believable landscape colors and color unity come from mixing related colors. Notice the tube colors (with white added) compared to the earthy greens which were all created from a limited split-primary palette, and mixed using two or more colors. (You can choose which black you like best; it's not necessary to have both.) There are many more possible variations than what is shown here, simply by adjusting the proportion of colors.

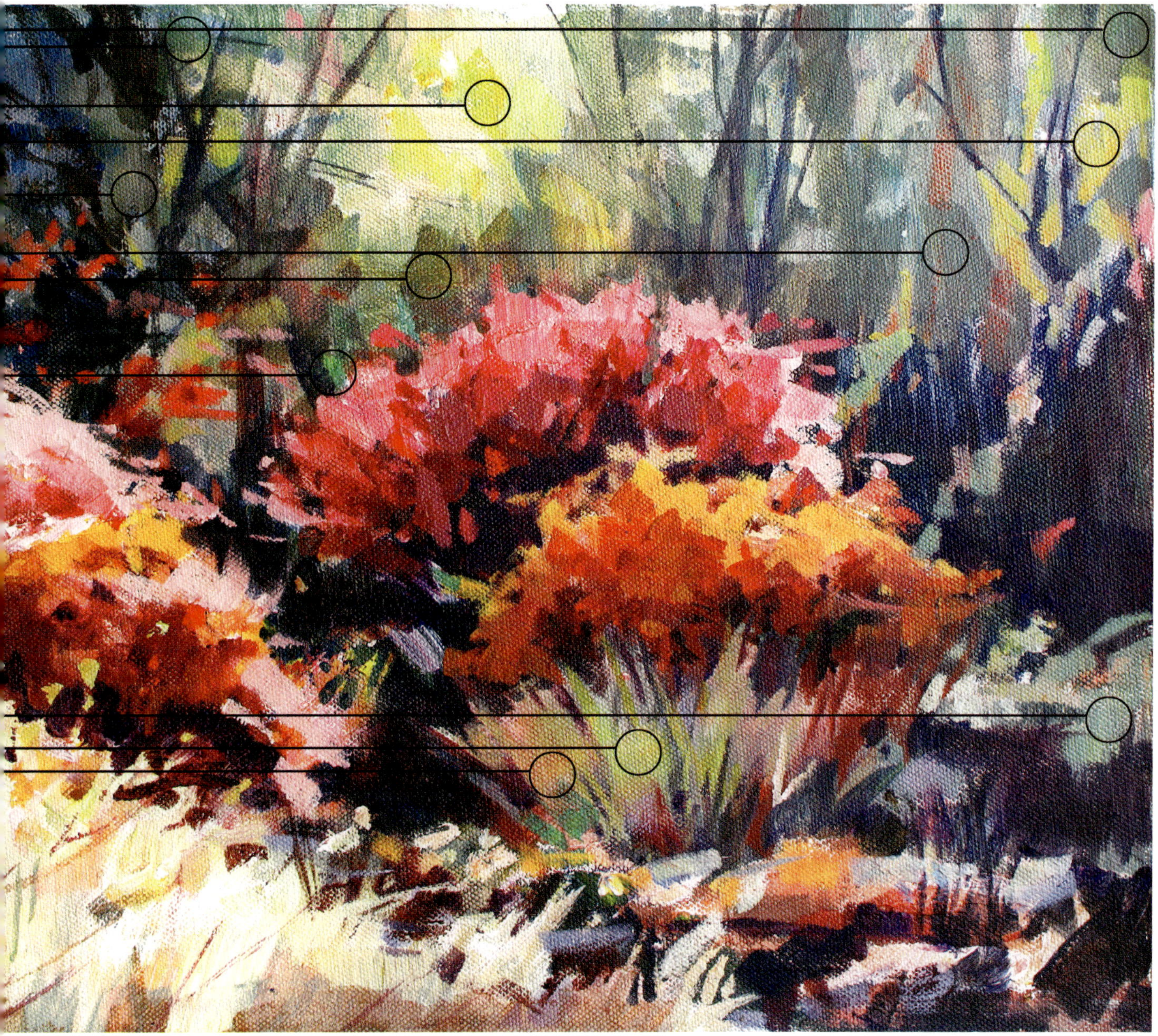

GRAYED GREENS

Most of the green mixtures in this painting are actually variations of color-ful grays. The most vivid greens (the small flecks of color around the pink tree) are used very sparingly. Although this color may look bright in the context of the painting, it's not as highly satu-rated as you might think. (See its actual placement on the color swatch to the right.)

Mixing Blacks & Grays

Although many artists will not use a tube black on their palette as a general rule, we still need the dark values in order to create realistic paintings. Many artists create their blacks from mixing complements or near complements, resulting in colors that appear black, but really lean toward a warmer or cooler hue. These mixtures are not true black, but that is the purpose. Think of them as more colorful blacks, just like the colorful grays we discussed.

Complementary Blacks

Lovely blacks can be created from complementary or near complementary colors. Be aware that you will need to mix the darkest versions from both color families. You can achieve a perfectly neutral black or gray simply by mixing Ultramarine Blue and Burnt Sienna + white.

Whites

Both Titanium White and Zinc White are mineral colors, however Zinc White has a translucency not typical of the mineral pigments we discussed earlier. Titanium White is very opaque and dense, and when added to any color will tint it down substantially. Zinc White creates less of an "Easter egg hue" when mixed with the color families.

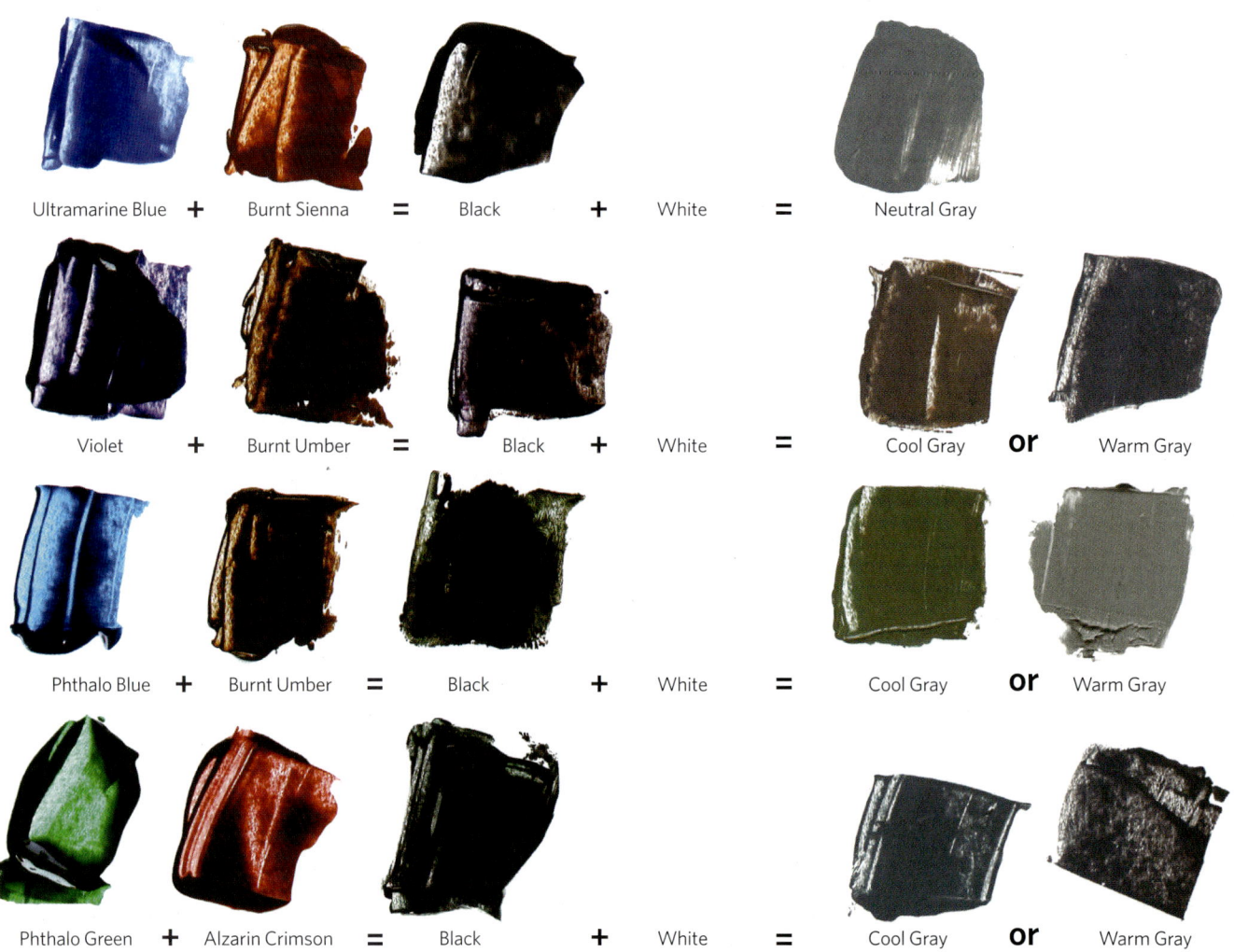

Ultramarine Blue **+** Burnt Sienna **=** Black **+** White **=** Neutral Gray

Violet **+** Burnt Umber **=** Black **+** White **=** Cool Gray **or** Warm Gray

Phthalo Blue **+** Burnt Umber **=** Black **+** White **=** Cool Gray **or** Warm Gray

Phthalo Green **+** Alzarin Crimson **=** Black **+** White **=** Cool Gray **or** Warm Gray

COLOR COMBINATIONS FOR DARKS
Here are a few color combinations that will give you rich, jewel-like darks.

Color Unity

Color unity plays an important role in the success of a painting. In order for colors to feel united, they must have a relationship to one another. In a painting that has unified color or a strong sense of color harmony, all the colors seem to exist under the same lighting conditions and have a believable chromatic relationship to each other.

However, many beginners struggle with mixing and assembling colors that work well together. In their efforts to create brilliant, vibrant colors, they commonly use simple, childlike color palettes. Despite each individual color being attractive on its own, the overall effect lacks a pleasing consensus.

This is most likely because many beginners work with colors straight out of the tube since they are not familiar with the basics of color mixing. As a work-around, they often buy an excessive number of paint tubes in every variation imaginable. Unfortunately, this can lead to poor color unity, because the palette is a collection of predictable, generic hues that lack nuance and sophistication. Tube colors are typically highly saturated, and therefore need some adjustment before making their mark on a canvas.

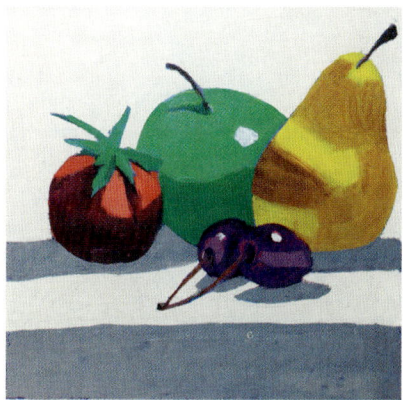

TUBE COLORS VS. MIXED COLORS
Believable colors, and color unity, come from mixing colors that are related. The image on the left was done using mostly tube colors, while the image on the right used mixed colors created from a limited palette. Notice how the tube colors (with white added) look saturated and stylized in the example on the left. Compare the more realistic earth tones—all mixed from two or more colors—used in the example on the right.

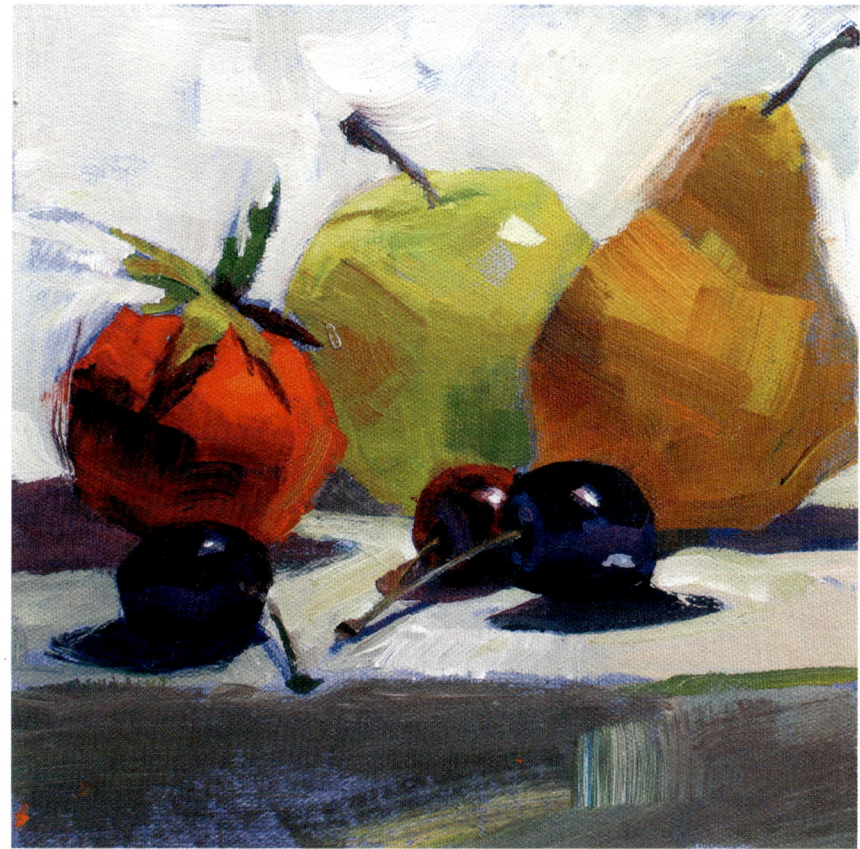

FRUIT GANG
Acrylic on canvas
8" × 8" (20cm × 20cm)
Collection of Allison Darrow

Limited Palettes for Color Harmony

One of the best ways to achieve color harmony in your paintings, is to reduce the number of tube colors you use to create your color mixtures. When less colors are used, the resulting mixtures are all related because they contain the same base colors. Working with fewer colors does mean more mixing, however, you will learn more about color than any book or video could ever teach you. There are no shortcuts for learning how to mix colors—experimentation is your best bet, and working with a limited palette is an effective key to understanding color.

The most obvious choices for a limited palette will include a red, a yellow and a blue, since the primary colors can create all the secondary and tertiary colors. But which red, which yellow and which blue? It is a matter of personal preference, because each primary color will yield different results. The following diagrams show a few simplified color palettes. Note that the charts do not show shades, tints or tones—only the highest possible chroma offered by mixing the tube colors together.

These palettes are just a few of the hundreds of possible color combinations you can work with. If you are familiar with using primary colors, I encourage you to stretch your boundaries. Try using other warm and cool colors as your primaries such as Payne's Gray as your blue, Burnt Sienna as your red or Raw Sienna as your yellow. Or simply try some of your favorite non-primary colors to see what mixtures they yield. This is a great way to personalize your palette and keep your color harmony intact at the same time.

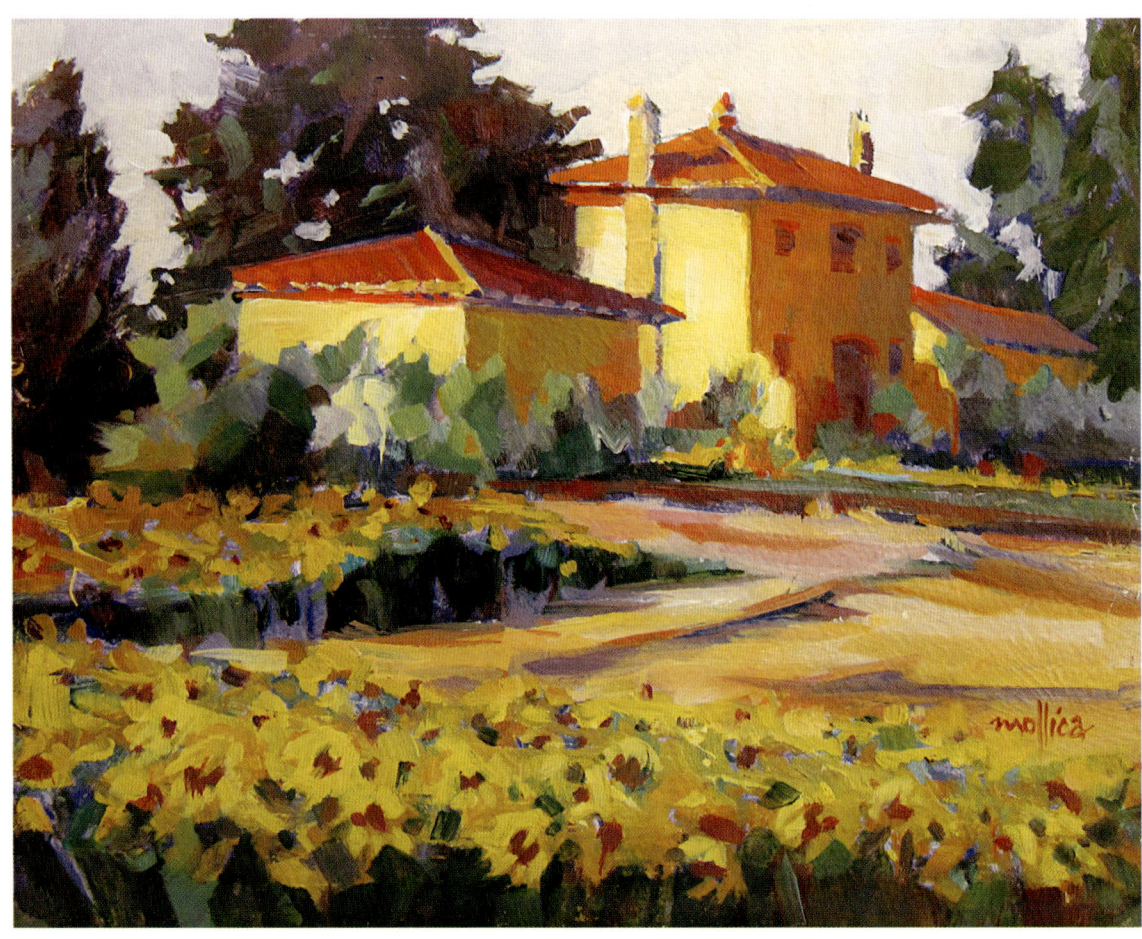

TUSCAN SUNFLOWER FIELD
Acrylic on panel
11" × 14" (28cm × 36cm)
Collection of Lori Wiseman

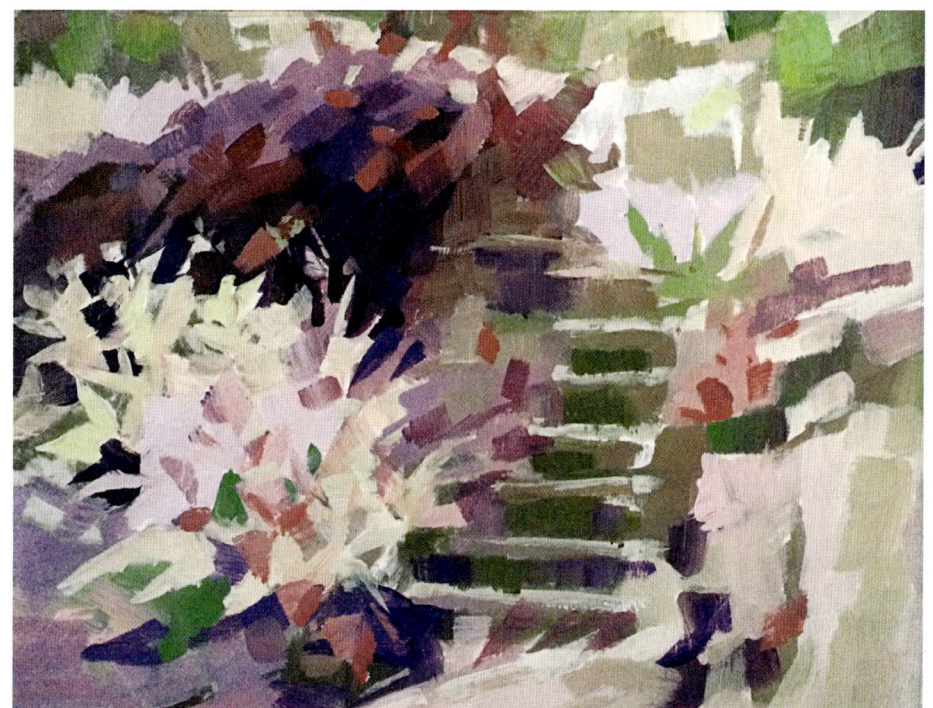

EXPERIMENT WITH NON-PRIMARY COLOR MIXTURES

Both this painting and the one on the previous page were created with a limited palette of purple, green, yellow, red and white. Try playing with some of your favorite non-primary colors to see what mixtures they yield.

SYRACUSE WINTER
Acrylic on panel
6" × 6" (15cm × 15cm)
Private collection

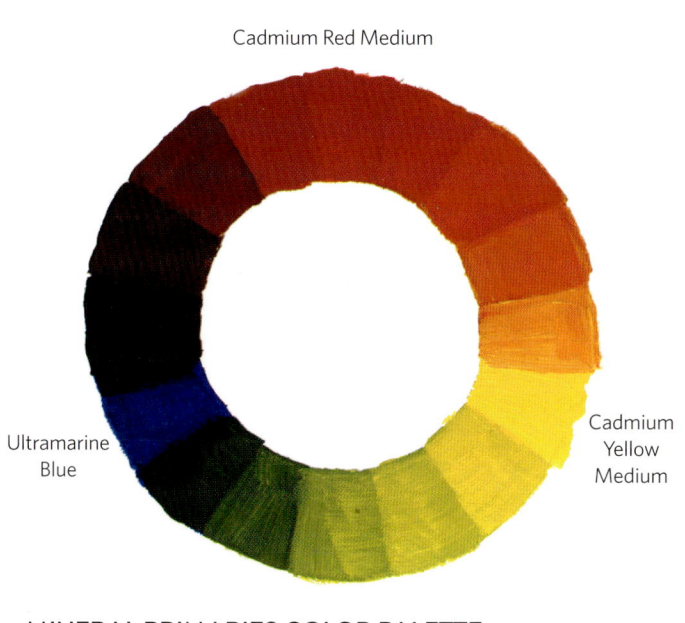

Cadmium Red Medium

Ultramarine Blue

Cadmium Yellow Medium

MINERAL PRIMARIES COLOR PALETTE

These color mixtures are lower chroma and lean on the warm side:
- Cadmium Red Medium
- Cadmium Yellow Medium
- Ultramarine Blue

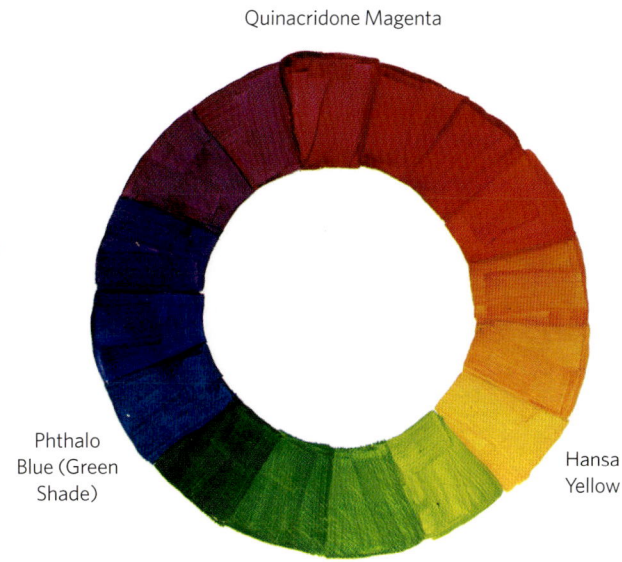

Quinacridone Magenta

Phthalo Blue (Green Shade)

Hansa Yellow

MODERN PRIMARIES COLOR PALETTE

This color palette will yield the most vibrant array of hues:
- Quinacridone Magenta (or Permanent Rose)
- Cadmium Yellow Light (or Cadmium Yellow Primrose or Hansa Yellow Light)
- Phthalo Blue (Green Shade)

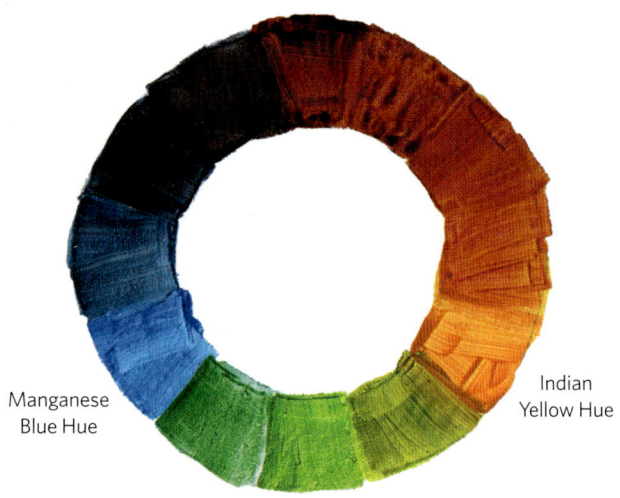

Alizarin Crimson Hue

Manganese Blue Hue

Indian Yellow Hue

HISTORICAL COLOR PALETTE (TRANSPARENT PRIMARIES)

Historical colors are re-creations of the traditional colors used by our past artistic masters who did not have the formulations we have today. These colors were originally derived from elements such as berries, bones and roots. They are labeled "hues," meaning they were created by mixing contemporary (or modern) pigments that have the added benefit of being lightfast. This color palette uses historical, transparent hues for more saturated mixtures:

- Alizarin Crimson Hue
- Indian Yellow Hue
- Manganese Blue Hue

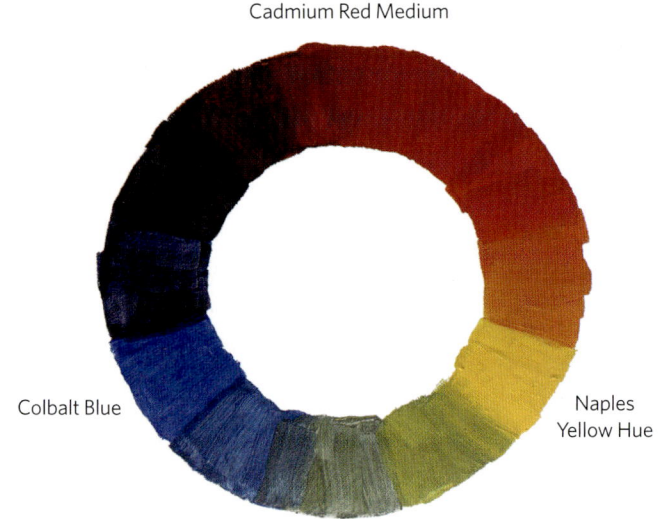

Cadmium Red Medium

Colbalt Blue

Naples Yellow Hue

HISTORICAL COLOR PALETTE (MINERAL PRIMARIES)

This color palette yields low chroma, earthy colors:

- Cadmium Red Medium
- Naples Yellow Hue
- Cobalt Blue

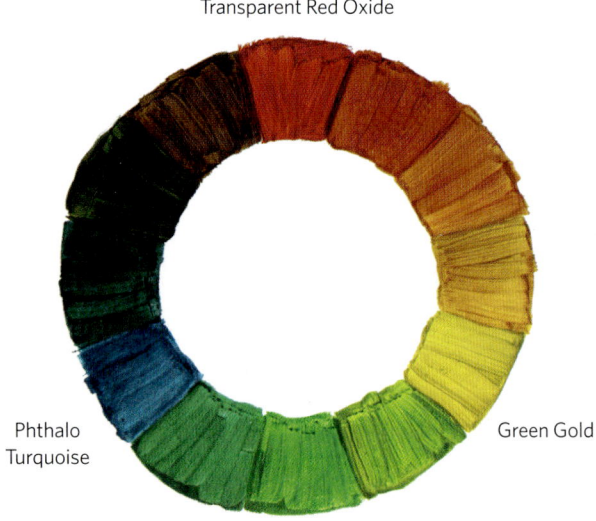

Transparent Red Oxide

Phthalo Turquoise

Green Gold

ALTERNATE MODERN COLOR PALETTE (NONTRADITIONAL PRIMARIES)

Another interesting palette using:

- Transparent Red Oxide
- Green Gold
- Phthalo Turquoise

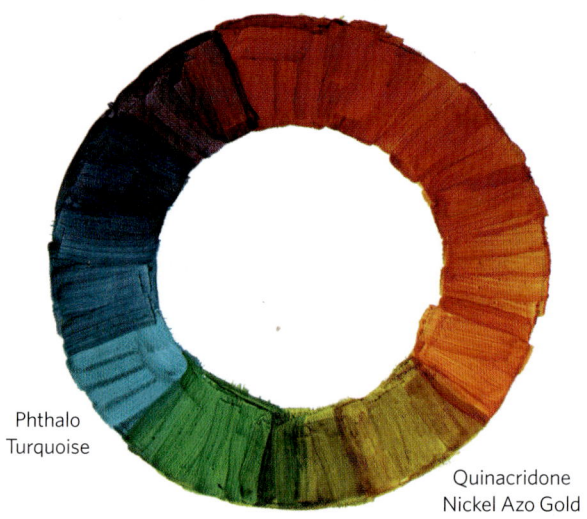

Quinacridone Crimson

Phthalo Turquoise

Quinacridone Nickel Azo Gold

MODERN COLOR PALETTE (NONTRADITIONAL PRIMARIES)

Interesting unified color palettes can be achieved using colors that are not standard traditional Red/Yellow/Blue.

- Quinacridone Crimson
- Quinacridone Nickel Azo Gold
- Phthalo Turquoise

Tonal Values and Limited Palettes

When working with a limited palette based on a few colors of your choice, it's important to use a full range of tonal values. Explore using black and white to lighten and darken whatever colors you have chosen as one alternative, but if you find that your colors are lacking vibrancy, work analogously to create more a saturated range.

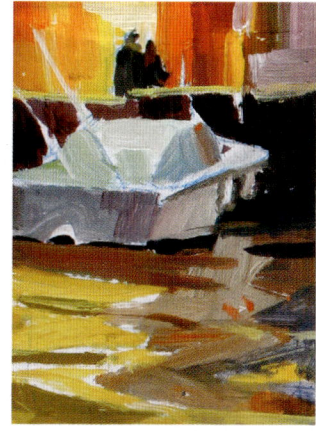 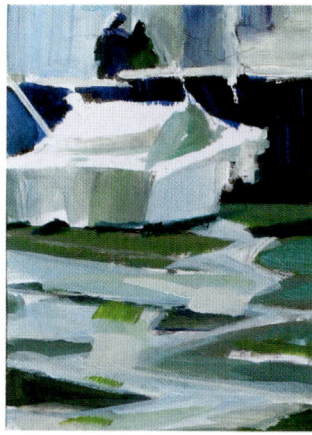 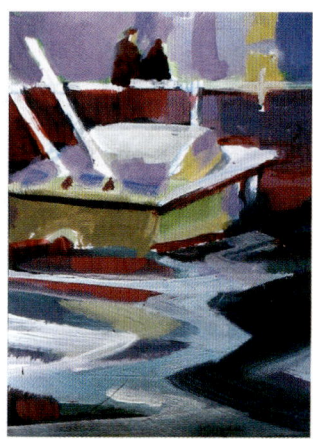

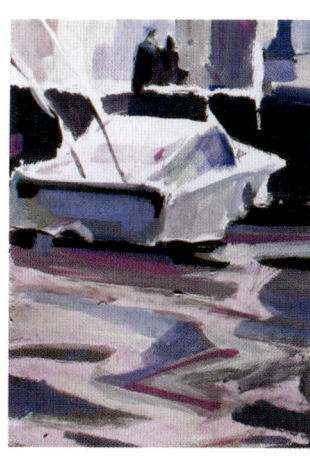 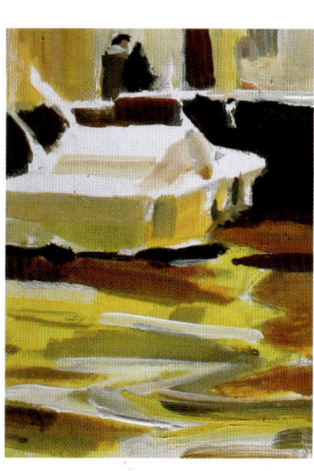 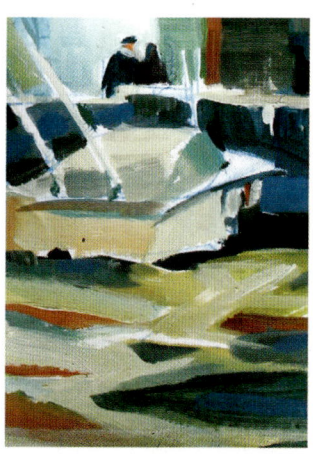

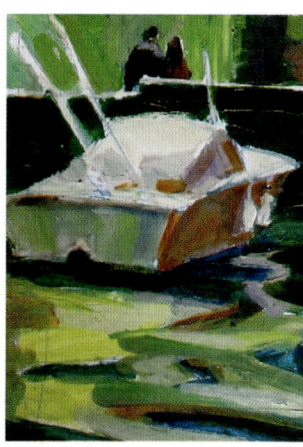 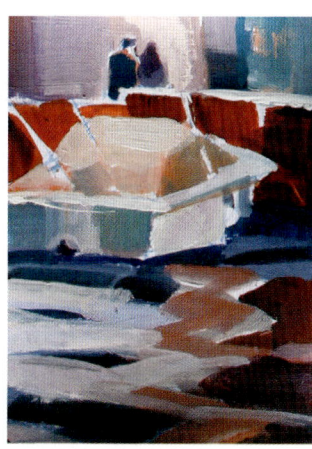 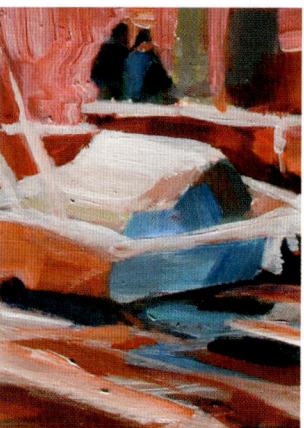

LIMITED PALETTES, MULTIPLE POSSIBILITIES

Here are some quick studies using limited palettes consisting of two to four colors plus white. The differences between them are striking, yet no matter which color scheme you prefer, they each have a sense of harmony.

Limited Palette Color Study

Explore the possibilities inherent in a limited palette of four colors by following the steps below. I intentionally chose an atypical color combination to emphasize how easily colors can work together.

MATERIALS

Surface
white mat board

Pigments
Diarylide Yellow, Payne's Gray, Permanent Violet Dark, Titanium White

Brushes
small flat

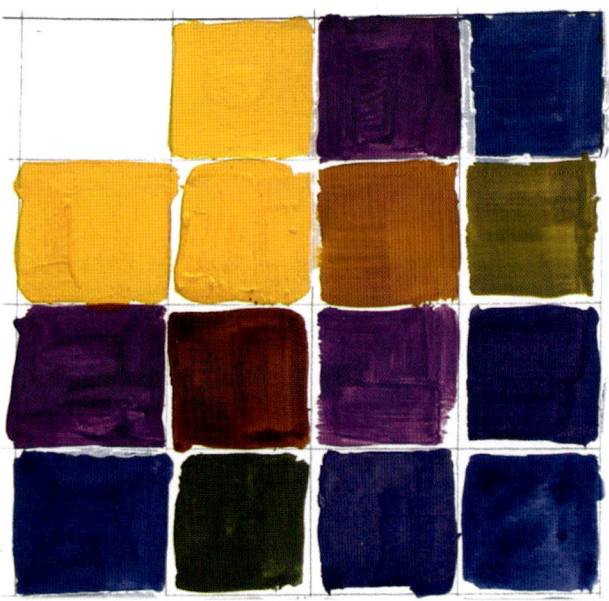

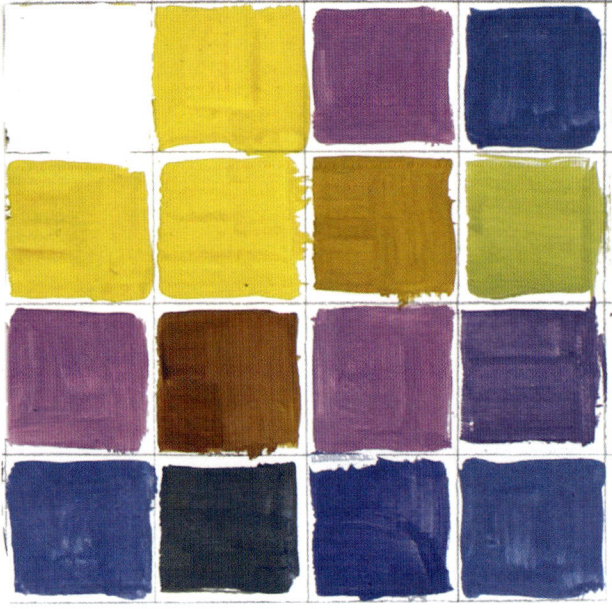

1 CREATE A COLOR GRID

Create a color grid of four squares across and four squares down using three tube colors (Diarylide Yellow, Payne's Gray and Permanent Violet Dark). Leaving the first block blank, fill in your three colors across the top and vertically along the left side. If the colors are too dark, add a little bit of white. (These same colors will also appear in a diagonal since you're mixing the same colors together.) Mix every color along the top row with every color in the left column. Keep the proportion of one to another in a 30/70 ratio: 30% on the top row of colors to 70% on the left column colors. This will skew your colors to be predominantly influenced by the left side.

2 ADD WHITE

In the next grid, add some white to all your tube colors, both the top row and left column. Use these tints for all mixtures. Fill in the boxes in the same manner as step 1.

In all subsequent charts, keep the 70/30 proportion to ensure the resulting mixture will maintain its predominant hue identity with the colors on the left.

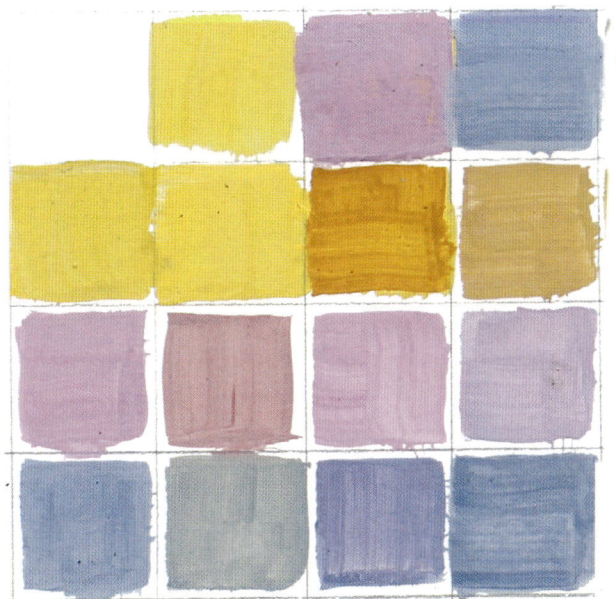

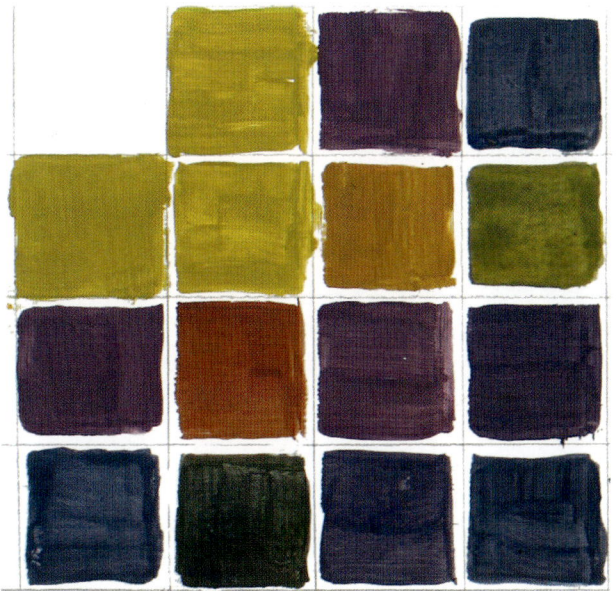

3 CONTINUE MIXING IN WHITE
In the next grid, add additional white so all your mixtures are very light in value.

4 GRAY IT DOWN
In the last grid, add a middle-value gray (mixed from white + black) to all tube colors. If you want to experiment further, make another chart using a 50/50 percent proportion.

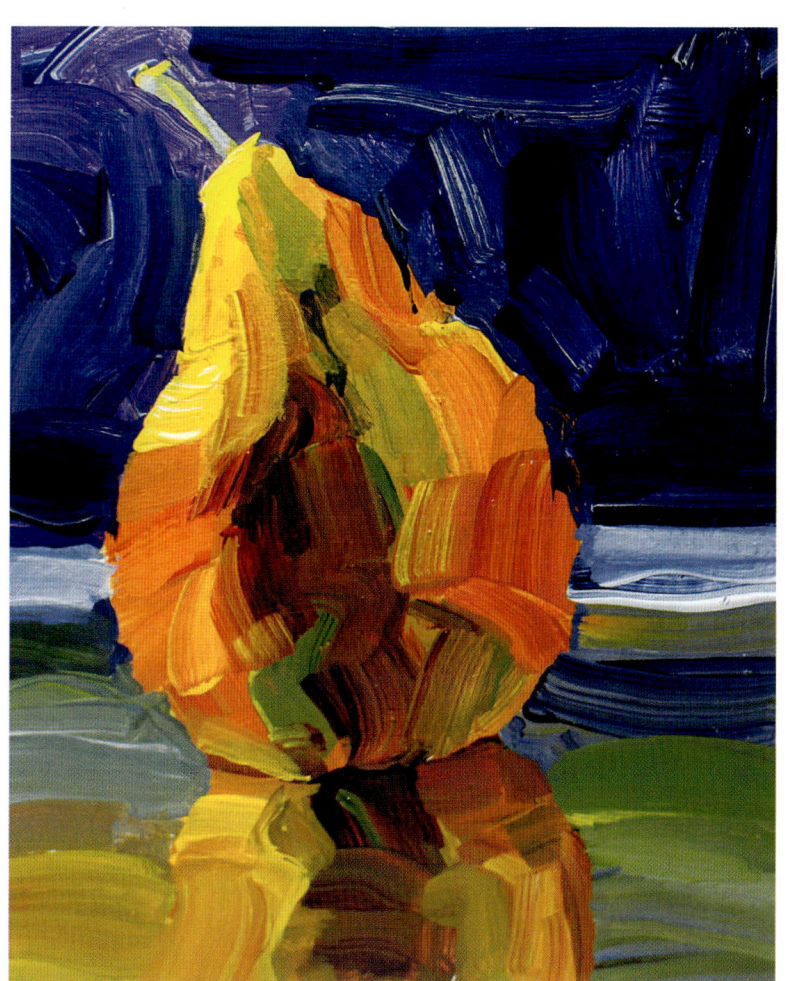

SAMPLE COLOR STUDY
All of the colors in this sample study were created from the mixtures in the exercise, using the same four hues. Notice how much color variety is present, and how lovely and understated the colors are. The use of so few colors guarantees that every one of your mixtures will harmonize because each one is mixed with the other. There are no clashing colors—every color plays nicely with the others!

Mother Color

Another method of ensuring color unity employs using what is known as a "mother color" in all color mixtures, including white. This method dictates there must be a common color present in all mixtures, which will serve as the unifying factor. Andrew Loomis, author of *Creative Illustration* (1947), suggests that a mother color works successfully when it is the dominant color in a painting.

The most common use of a mother color is to use a single gray, or several warm and cool grays, to tone down most of the mixtures. This allows you to use saturated colors more strategically where necessary. Many artists keep a few warm and cool grays handy during a painting session for this very purpose.

Mother Color

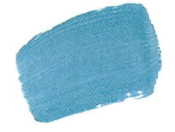 + 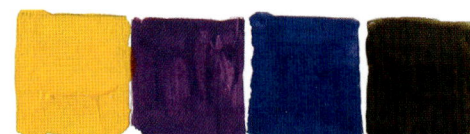 =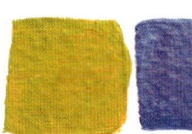

MOTHER COLOR AS A UNIFYING FACTOR
Let's take the same four tube colors used in the previous exercise and add another random color to each. Here, Cobalt Teal was used as the mother color and added to each of the tube colors. See how the addition of one common color can unify an otherwise haphazard palette.

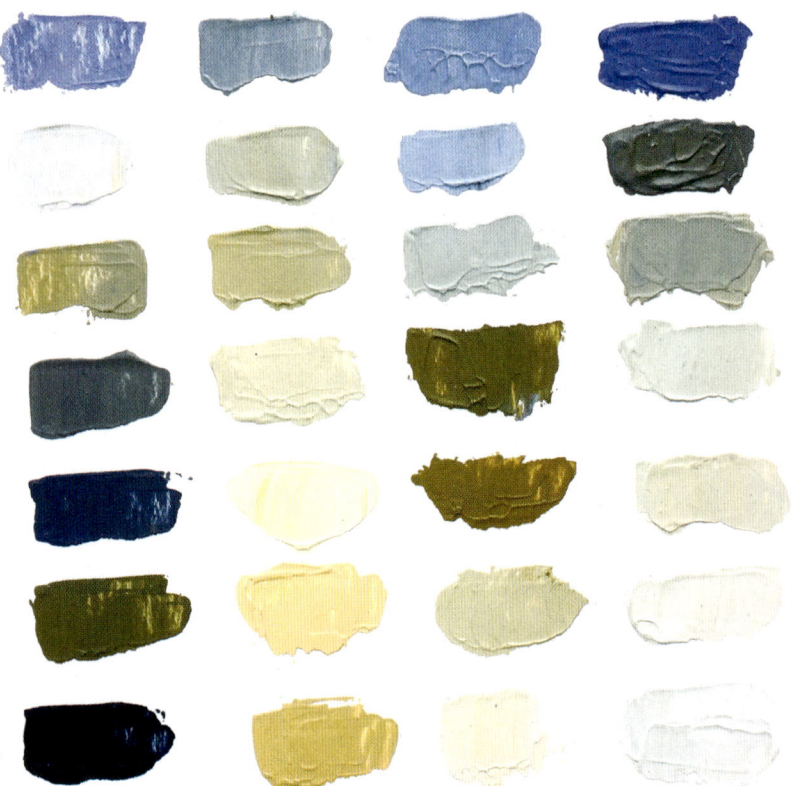

MOTHER COLOR MIXTURES WITH WHITE/BLACK ADDED
Every swatch in this example includes two mother colors—Ultramarine Blue and Yellow Ochre—in various proportions. Notice the variety of tints, tones and shades that are possible, and how well they all unify when white and black are added.

TUBE COLORS

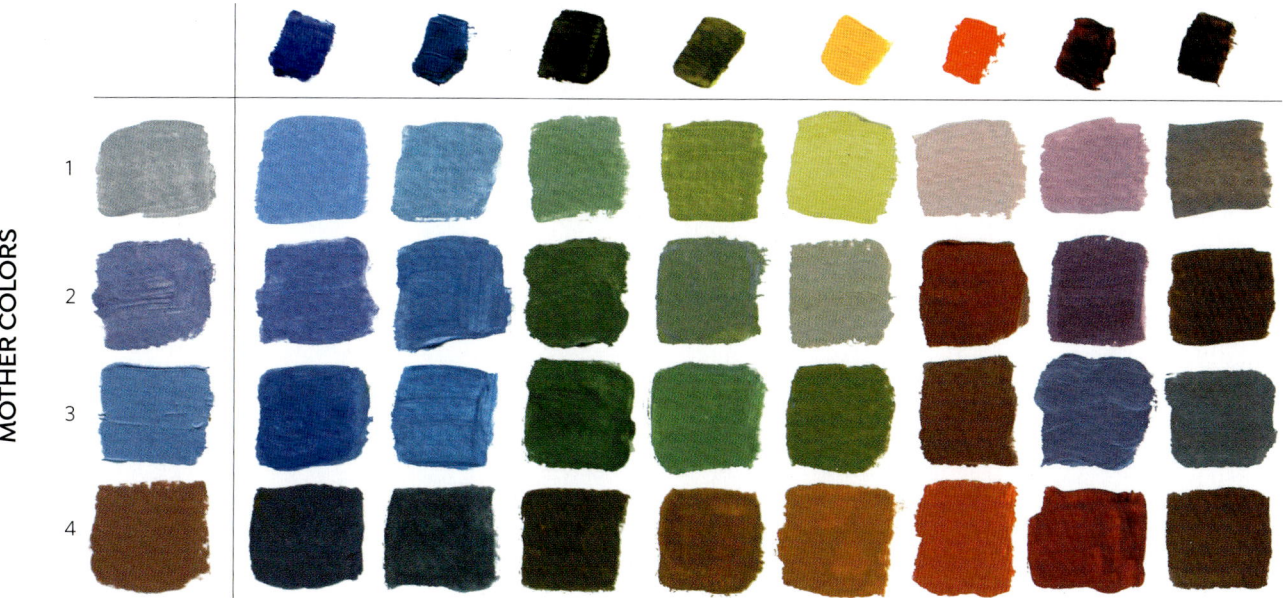

MOTHER COLORS

1

2

3

4

UNIFYING COLOR MIXTURES WITH GRAY AS THE MOTHER COLOR

You can see the influence of several grays (the four colors in the far-left column) mixed with a selection of tube colors:

1. Neutral Gray (Ultramarine + Burnt Sienna + White)
2. Violet Gray (Ultramarine + Alizarin + Neutral Gray)
3. Blue Gray (Ultramarine + Cerulean + Neutral Gray)
4. Warm Gray (Burnt Sienna + Neutral Gray)

What a beautiful palette of colors—all neutralized by a few warm and cool grays; all harmonized and working together like a charm!

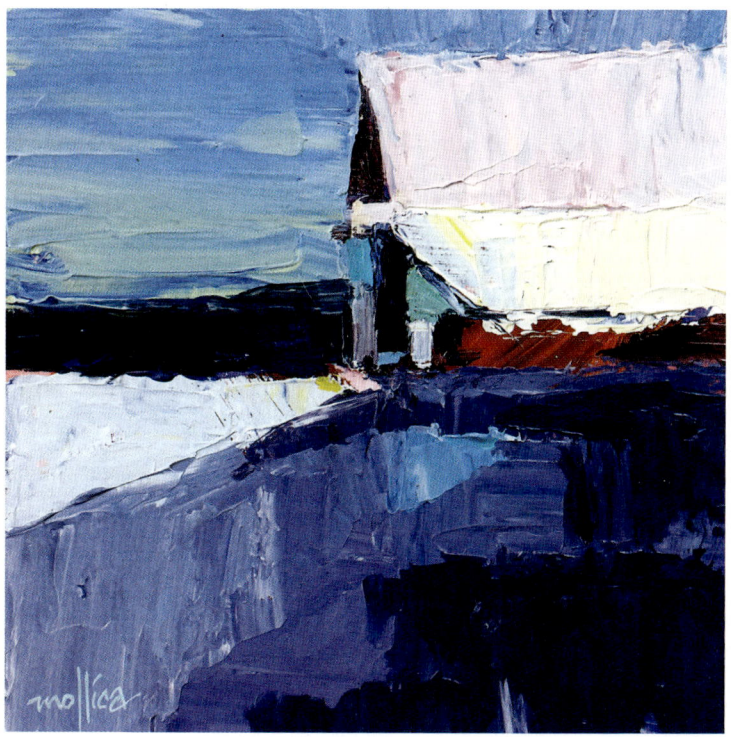

TONING DOWN SATURATION

A common practice after a painting session is to scrape up all the color mixtures left on the palette and blend them into one pile of gray, or "mud," to be saved for use in future paintings. However, by starting with a pile of neutral gray paint (made by mixing black and white, or complementary colors such as Ultramarine Blue and Burnt Sienna plus white), you can easily make a neutral gray and tint it with other colors as a shortcut to toning down the saturation level. A small amount of neutral gray was added into each of the color mixtures used in this painting to tone down the saturation and harmonize the hues.

VERMONT BARN
Acrylic on panel
8" × 8" (20cm × 20cm)
Private collection

Toning the Canvas

Another popular way of unifying colors is to tone the canvas before you begin painting. If you know in advance what your dominant color will be, tone the canvas in a contrasting or complementary color. This offers several advantages. The bright white of a primed canvas can be intimidating, so toning the canvas first can help break the ice in starting the painting process. Additionally, if there are places in your painting where the brushstrokes don't overlap, the background color of the toned canvas will peek out between the adjacent colors, often in unexpected places, and help create an overall optical unity.

There is no hard and fast rule about which color to tone the canvas—it all depends on what your goals are. Sometimes I tone the canvas strategically, but I often tone with spontaneous color choices. Sometimes I tone in neutrals such as a middle gray or Burnt Umber. Other times I use black. And sometimes I don't tone the background at all. However, when I do, I try to envision what color might look interesting as a small accent, and then I proceed accordingly. Experiment to see what works best for you. Regardless of what color you choose, your background color will have a unifying effect on your painting.

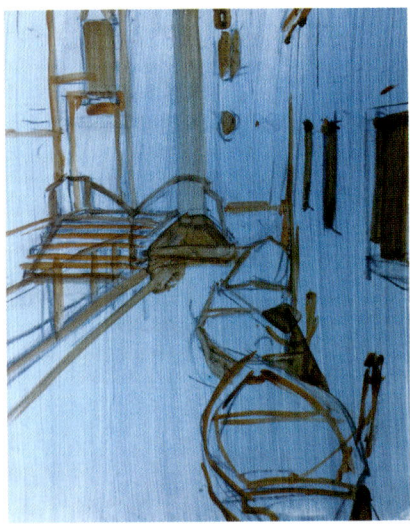

TONING WITH CONTRASTING COLORS

In this example, I toned my canvas with a cool medium value blue. Since I would be using cool tones in many other areas of the painting, it blended nicely and I did not feel compelled to cover up every bit of the canvas. The small bits of blue peeking through added unifying and harmonious accents.

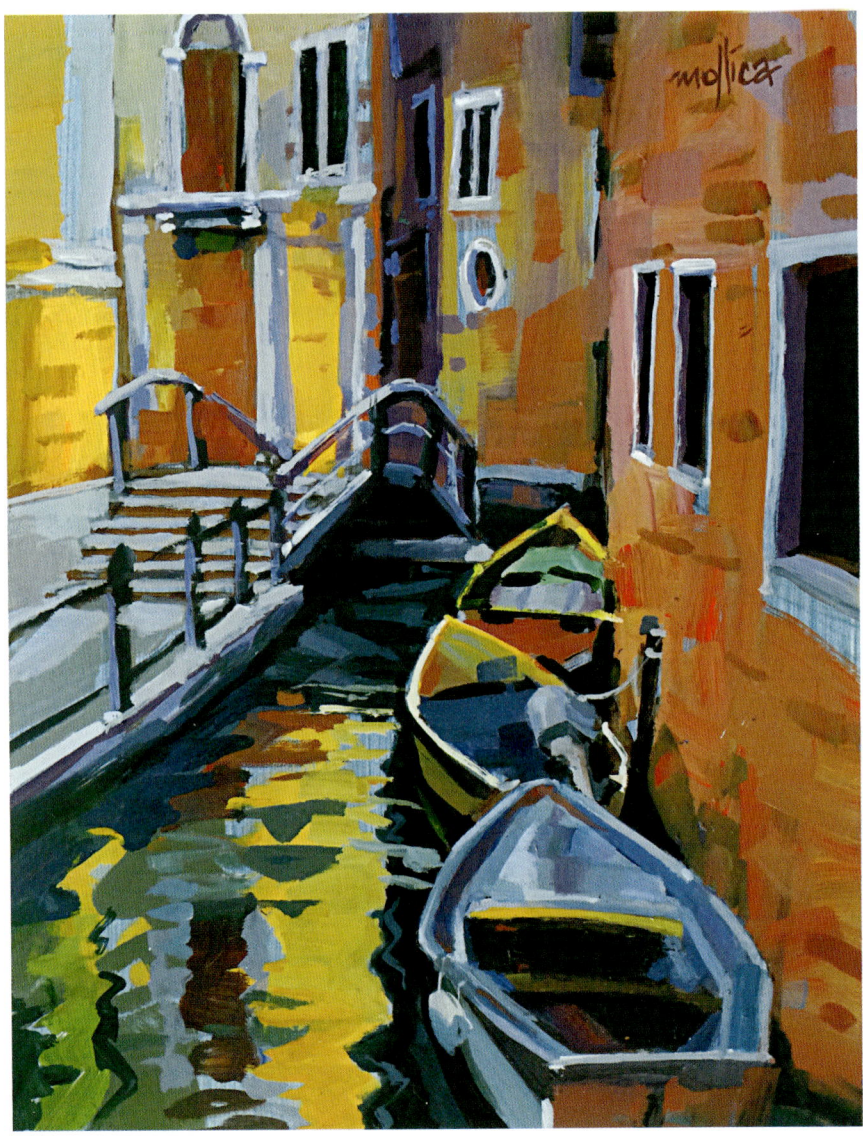

VENICE CANAL
Acrylic on panel
16" × 12" (41cm × 30cm)
Private collection

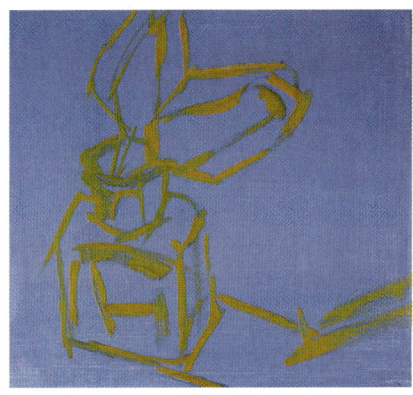

TONING WITH COMPLEMENTARY COLORS

In this example, I decided beforehand that my dominant color would be yellow. I chose to tone the canvas a shade of lavender so that the bits and pieces of that color would show through and provide some supplementary accent color throughout the piece. You can see small bits of the toned background showing through, which helps to integrate that color into the focal point.

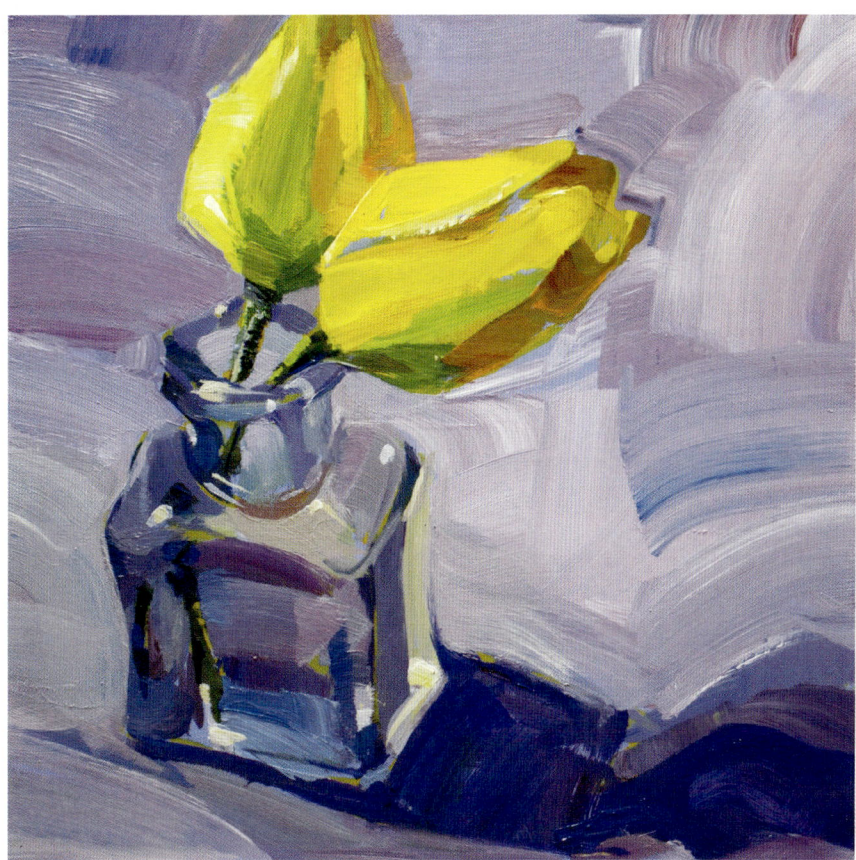

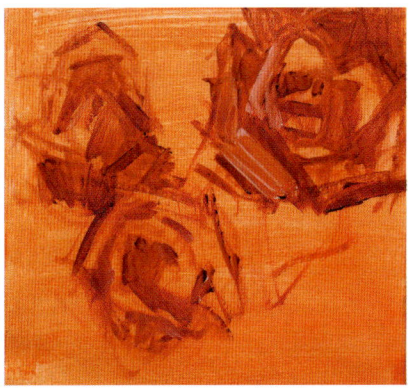

TONING WITH ANALOGOUS COLORS

Sometimes I tone the canvas with a similar, analogous color to my focal point. It can be disorienting to start this way because there is little color contrast to guide you while you are painting the focal point. However, about midway through the painting process it all starts to fall into place.

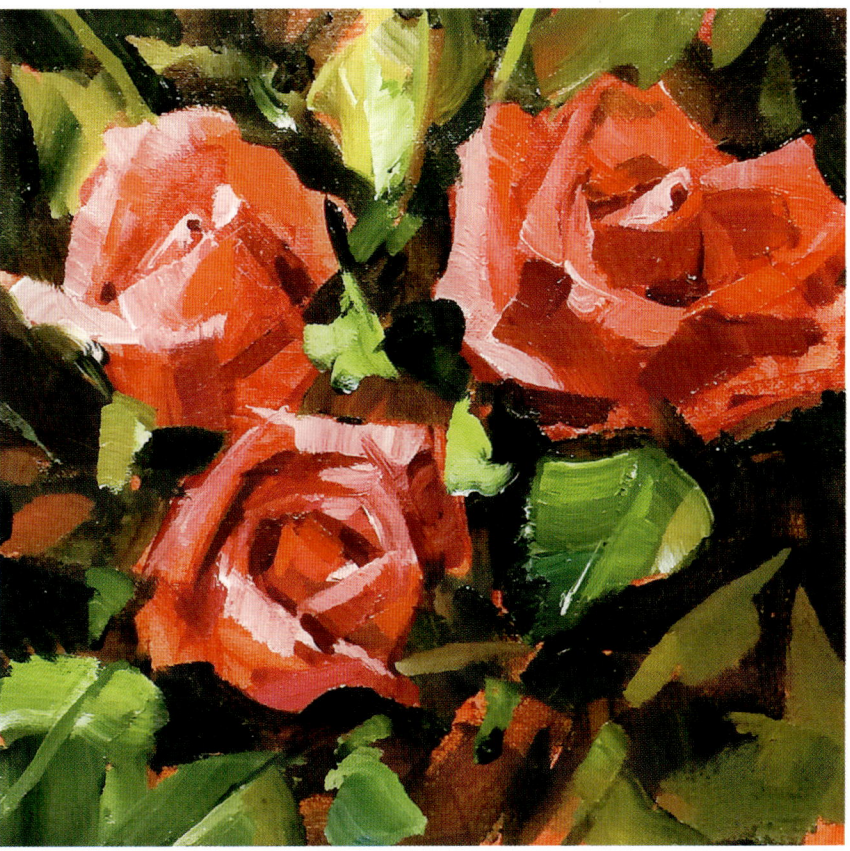

Glazing

A glaze is a thin, transparent or semitransparent layer of paint that is applied on top of an opaque, dry passage of paint for the purpose of modifying the appearance or color of the underlying layer. Glazes can lighten or darken, depending on the pigment used. Glazes can also shift the chroma, value and hue of an underlying passage on a painting. Because they are semitransparent, light travels through the glaze and is reflected back off of the opaque layer below.

The glaze color can be thought of like a sheer thin piece of colored glass, or colored film, laid on top of a painting. It is made of a very small amount of pigment in proportion to a substantial amount of clear medium. Glazes can be applied one on top of another to build up depth and richness in a painting. Each layer must be allowed to dry before the next application.

Glazing is similar to using a mother color except rather than adding the mother color to each palette color, the glaze is applied over the entire piece, or in specific sections of the painting as needed. A glaze of color over an entire painting creates a unifying appearance because each color of the underlying painting is now influenced by the glaze color, and all colors now have a common denominator.

The influence of a glaze color is that it will enhance colors that are similar (analogous) and subdue colors that are opposite on the color wheel (complementary). Notice in the painting example with the blue glaze, the pink becomes more purple, and the greens become more cool. The Sap Green glaze will enhance the greens and subdue the pinks/reds. The gold glaze actually enhances the warm reds since both red and green contain yellow.

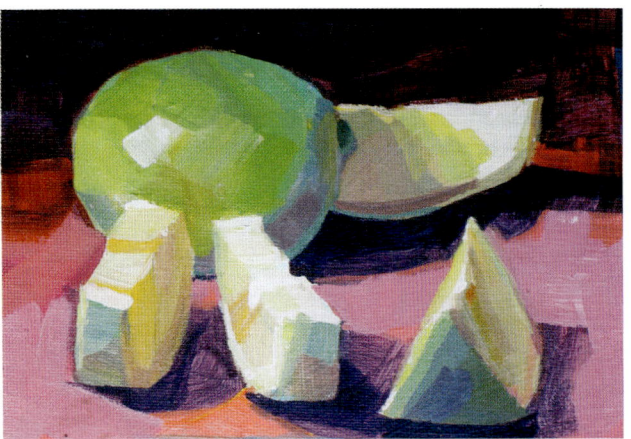

NO GLAZE

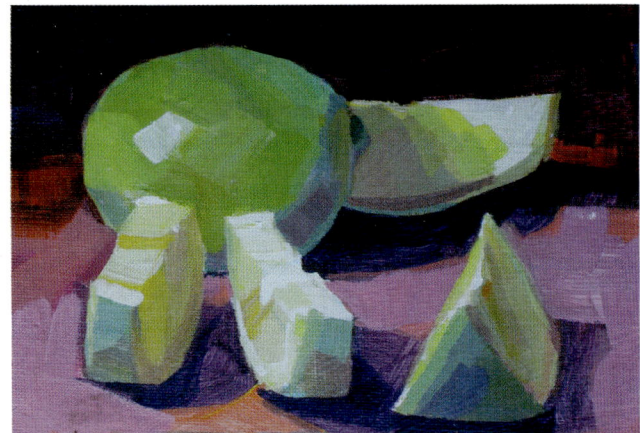

MANGANESE BLUE HUE GLAZE

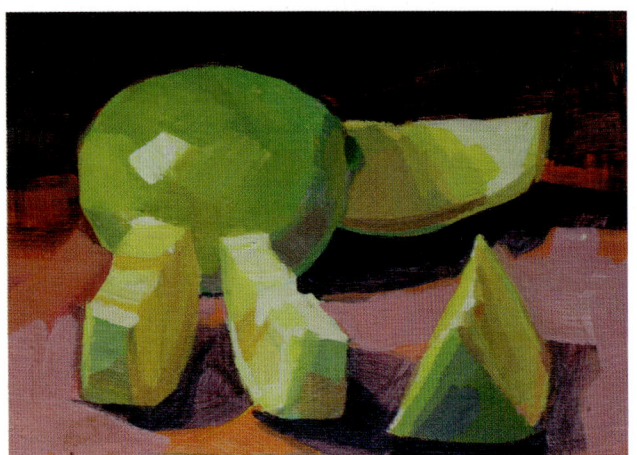

SAP GREEN GLAZE

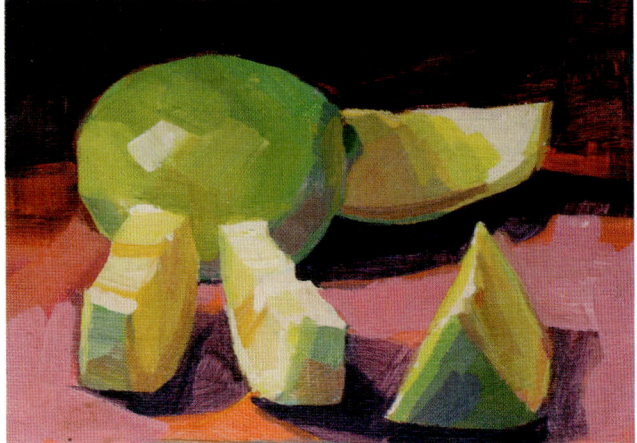

QUINACRIDONE NICKEL AZO GOLD GLAZE

Making a Glaze

Regardless of what medium you are working in, a glaze is a small amount of pigment dispersed in a much larger proportion of binder. Typically the ratio is 1:10 pigment to binder, but that ratio is subjective depending on the strength of the pigment and whether you want a more subtle or stronger color shift. When working with acrylics, I use Golden's Acrylic Glazing Liquid, which is available in gloss and satin finishes. (All acrylic mediums are milky when wet, but will dry clear.) For a very transparent glaze, I mix 1 part paint to 10 parts glazing liquid. I adjust accordingly if a stronger glaze color is needed. For oils I use linseed oil or an oil painting medium.

When making a glaze, it's best to start out conservatively with color and add more if needed. It is much easier to add color incrementally than to start off with too much. Make sure each layer is completely dry before adding additional layers. Be aware that each time you apply a colored glaze on your painting or a previous glaze, it will darken and the color will shift.

You do not have to apply one color glaze over the entire painting although that is the most efficient way to unify all the various colors. If you want to subdue, enhance or modify specific parts of the painting, only apply the colored glazes in the areas that need adjustments. Use a common color in all your glazes to keep the harmony throughout.

Use translucent (modern) colors for glazing such as Quinacridones, Phthalos and Hansas as described in chapter 3. The goal is to let the underlying color show through. If you are working with mineral pigments such as Cadmiums, which are opaque, the underneath layer will be obscured. If you need to lighten with white, Zinc White has a translucent quality even though it is a mineral pigment. Do not use Titanium White, which is opaque.

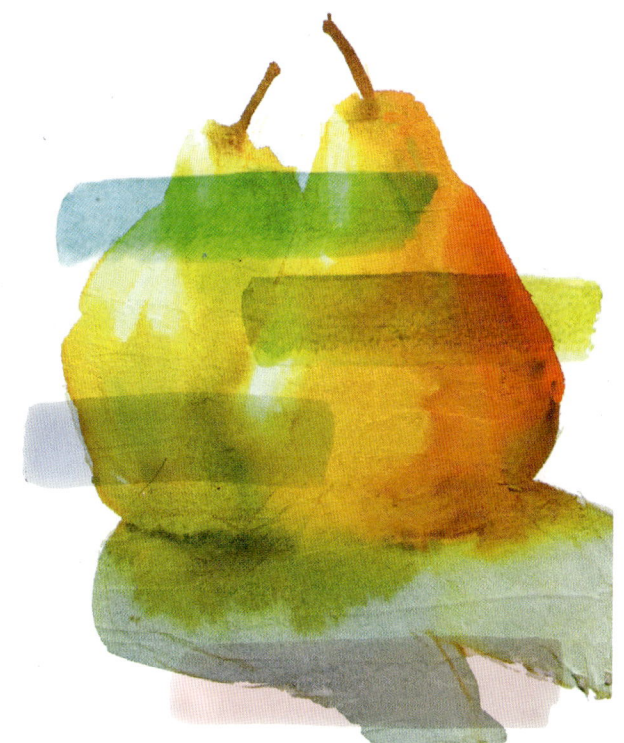

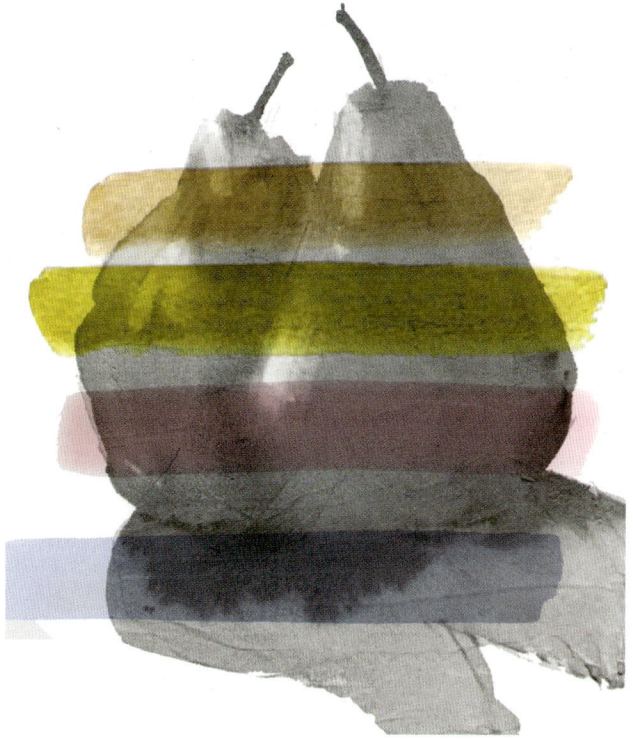

LAYERED GLAZES

Here we see colored glazes applied over a colored pear and grayscale pear. You can use layered glazes to gradually build up the color from a monochromatic or grayscale painting. Many of the Old Masters such as Vermeer and Leonardo da Vinci worked in this way as well. It allowed the foundational tonal painting (called a grisaille) to be worked out in completion before adding color.

Brushwork

Brushwork is similar to a signature in that it is a natural expression of the way you wield the paintbrush with your own particular way of creating marks and strokes. Many great painters such as Vincent van Gogh, John Singer Sargent, Joaquín Sorolla and Franz Kline are celebrated for their unique and uninhibited brushwork—it is simply an extension of their personality and artistic vision.

Just as every signature evolves by itself after years of repetition, each artist's response to mark-making follows the same natural course. There is no way to teach an artist how to conjure up a unique brushwork style because each individual's style will make itself apparent over time.

If you feel that your brushwork is not expressing your vision, the most important thing to do is be patient and give yourself time to allow your style to develop. It is a process that will fall into place the more you paint.

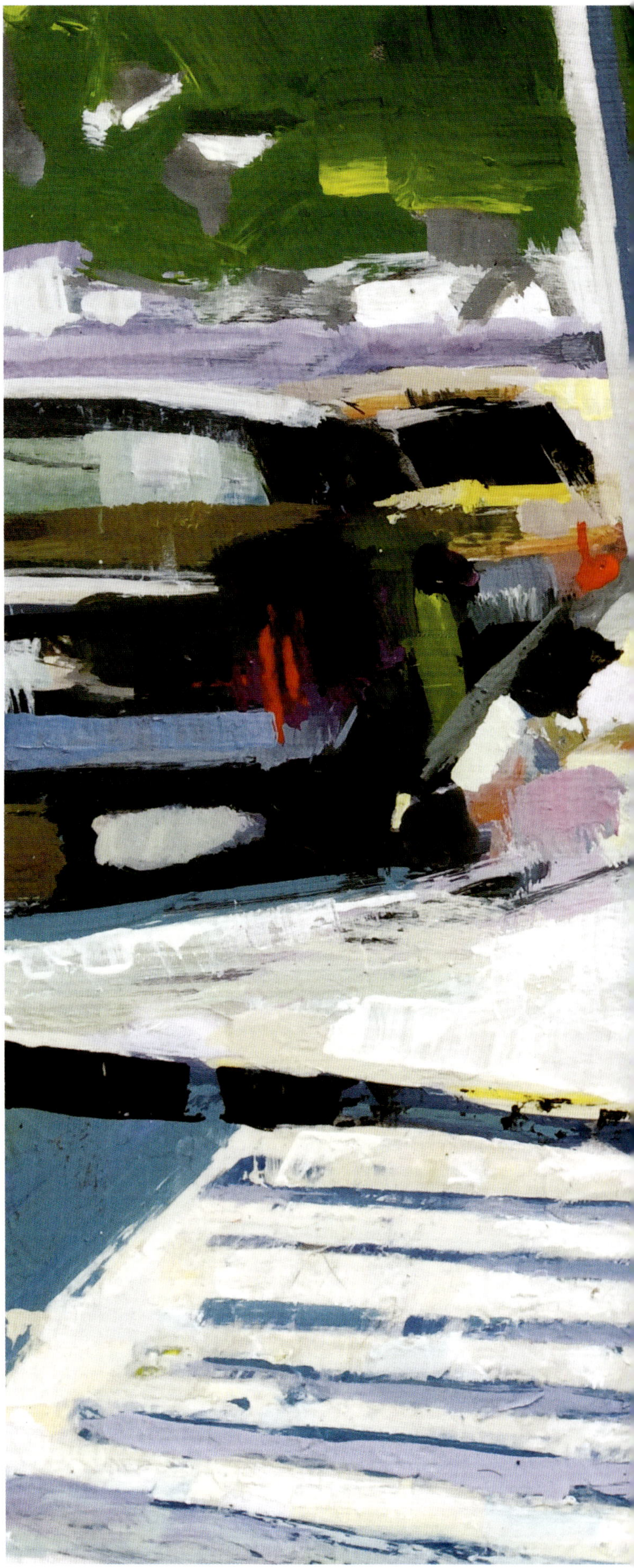

WEST VILLAGE WALK
Acrylic on panel
9" × 12" (23cm × 30cm)
Private collection

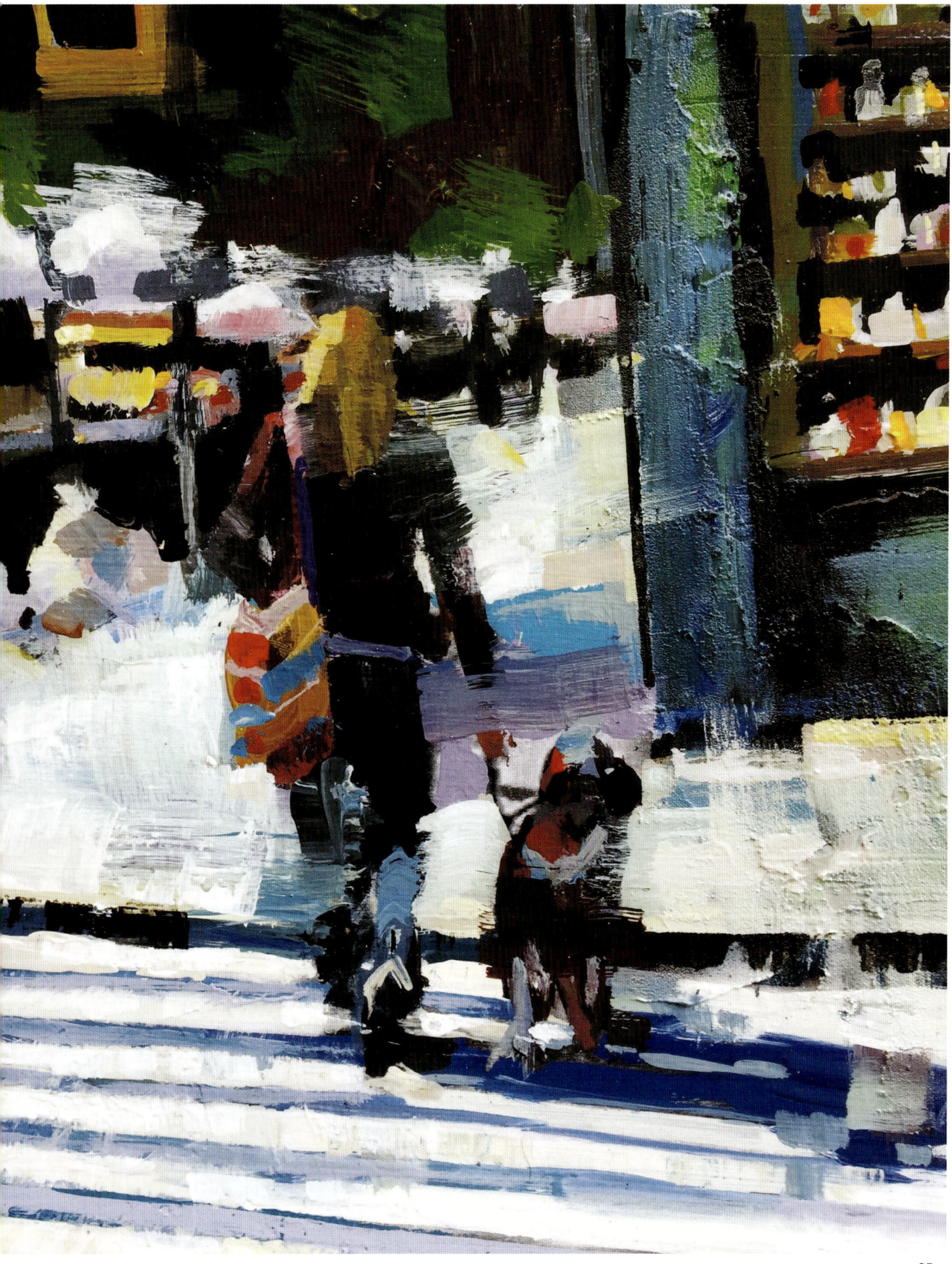

Developing Your Style

It is more challenging to master brushwork than other aspects of painting such as color mixing, value simplification and composition. However, the more you know about brush fundamentals, the easier it will be to use that knowledge to develop a look that best expresses your personal vision.

Some teachers will push a certain brush shape or grip method on their students, which may not be right or comfortable for them. My feeling is that it's much harder to unlearn a bad habit than it is to experiment and discover what feels comfortable and natural from the start. I have spent many years unlearning certain habits that were imposed on me by well meaning teachers. It is for this reason that I'd like to introduce some important considerations that will yield various effects in your brushwork.

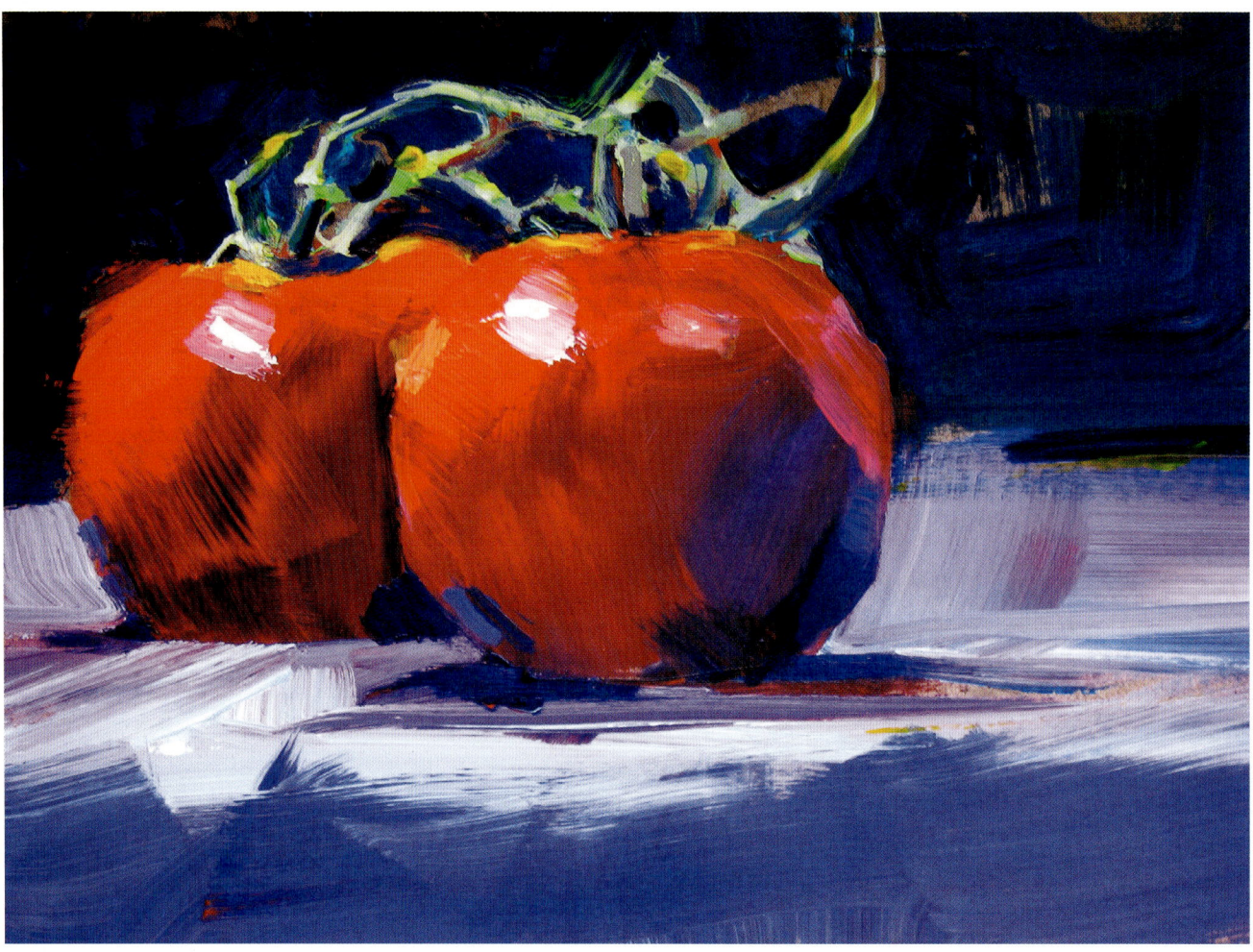

GESTURAL PAINTING

Gestural painting is a style of painting distinguished by energetic, expressive brushstrokes that convey the movement of the artist's arm in broad sweeps of lively expression. I feel there is a beauty in seeing the hand of the artist in their strokes. It allows the viewer to sense the physical act of painting.

Gestural painting is the term best used to describe my style of painting. I did not choose this style; it chose me. My style developed as an authentic response to my very busy schedule and lifestyle. I simply had precious little time to paint, so my brushstrokes became direct and definitive, with little or no fussing.

TWO MATERS
Acrylic on panel
10" × 12" (25cm × 30cm)
Private collection

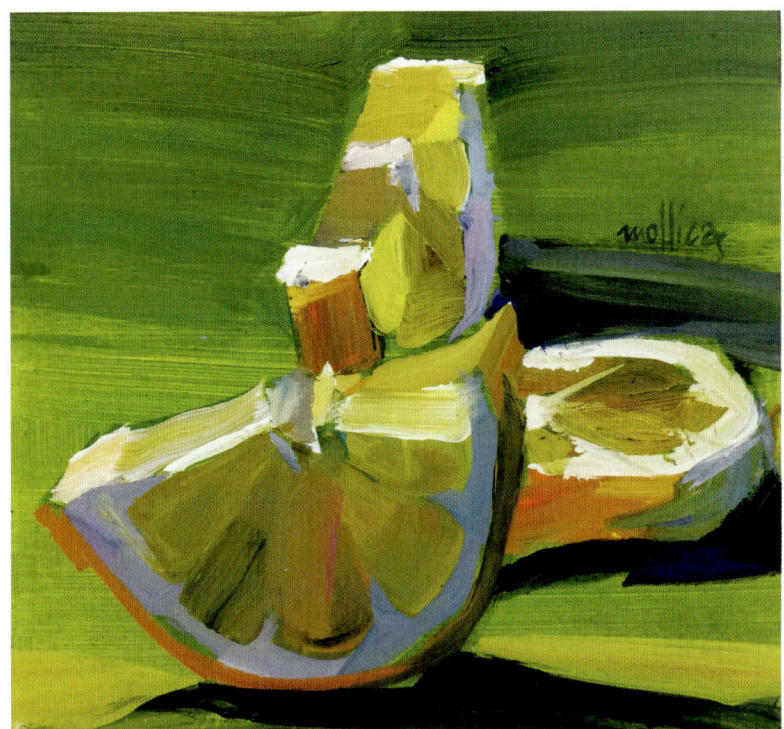

LOAD UP THAT PALETTE

Many beginners sabotage their efforts simply by not using enough paint. In order to have a painterly application, you must use enough paint to create a sweeping brushstroke. It is important to put large dollops of paint on your palette, rather than dime-sized spots of color. Although it may seem economical to conserve your colors as much as possible, there is just no way to substitute for lack of paint in a composition. If the cost of paint is prohibitive for you, the best solution is to buy cheaper student-grade paints and practice with those before moving on to higher-grade paints.

LEMON SLICES
Acrylic on panel
8" × 8" (20cm × 20cm)
Collection of Colleen Ulrich

USE LIMITED STROKES AND A MINDFUL APPROACH

A common culprit in flat, tedious brushwork is dabbing too many brushstrokes when only one is required. This is the result of not being sure of what you're doing, as you do it. It is best to take a mindful approach. The overall process will go much faster if you think before you lay down each stroke.

Consider the values, colors and shapes you are placing on the canvas before you actually place them. If you are clear about those three attributes, you can lay down your paint with complete confidence in one expressive stroke. This may seem the antithesis of the concept of expressive painting, but the results speak for themselves.

Energetic, painterly brushwork is accomplished by using ample paint, applying your stroke and then leaving it alone. It is far more interesting to have one luscious, energetic mark that may be a bit sloppy or imperfect than to have every stroke dabbed into oblivion.

BLUE CUP
Acrylic on panel
10" × 8" (25cm × 20cm)
Collection of Andrea McLaughlin

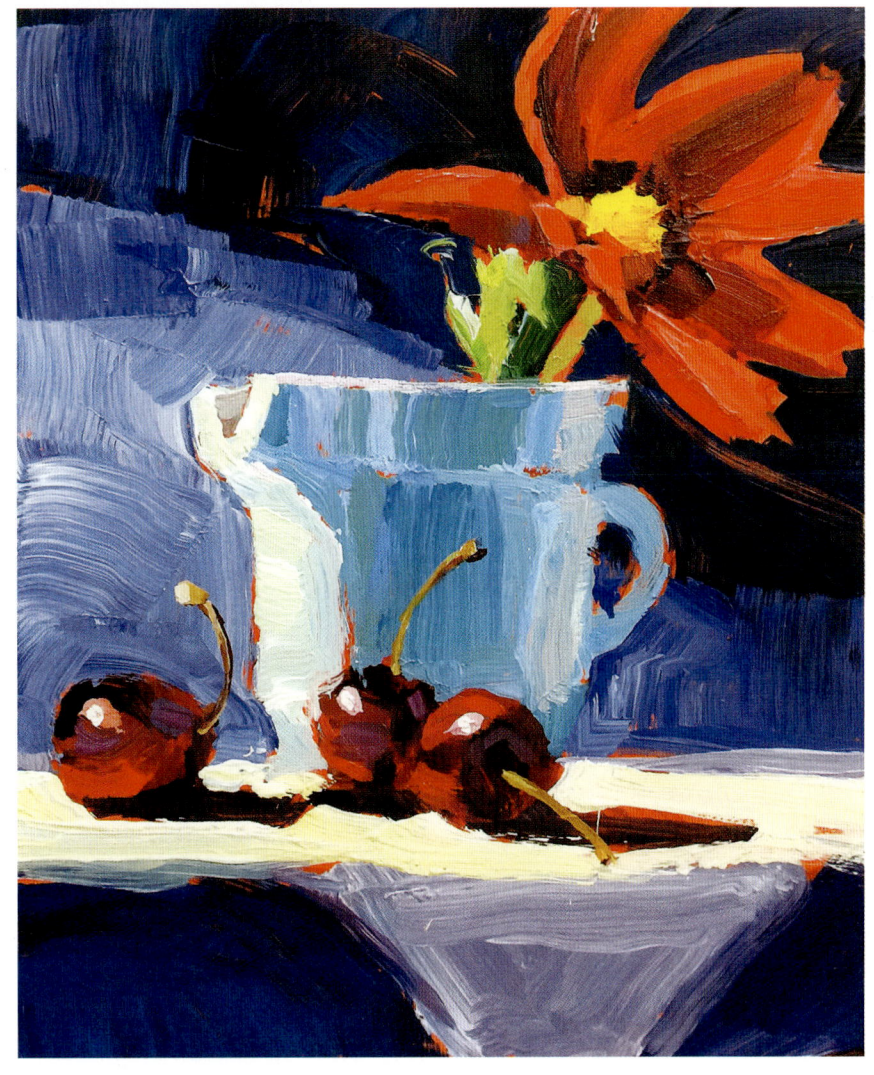

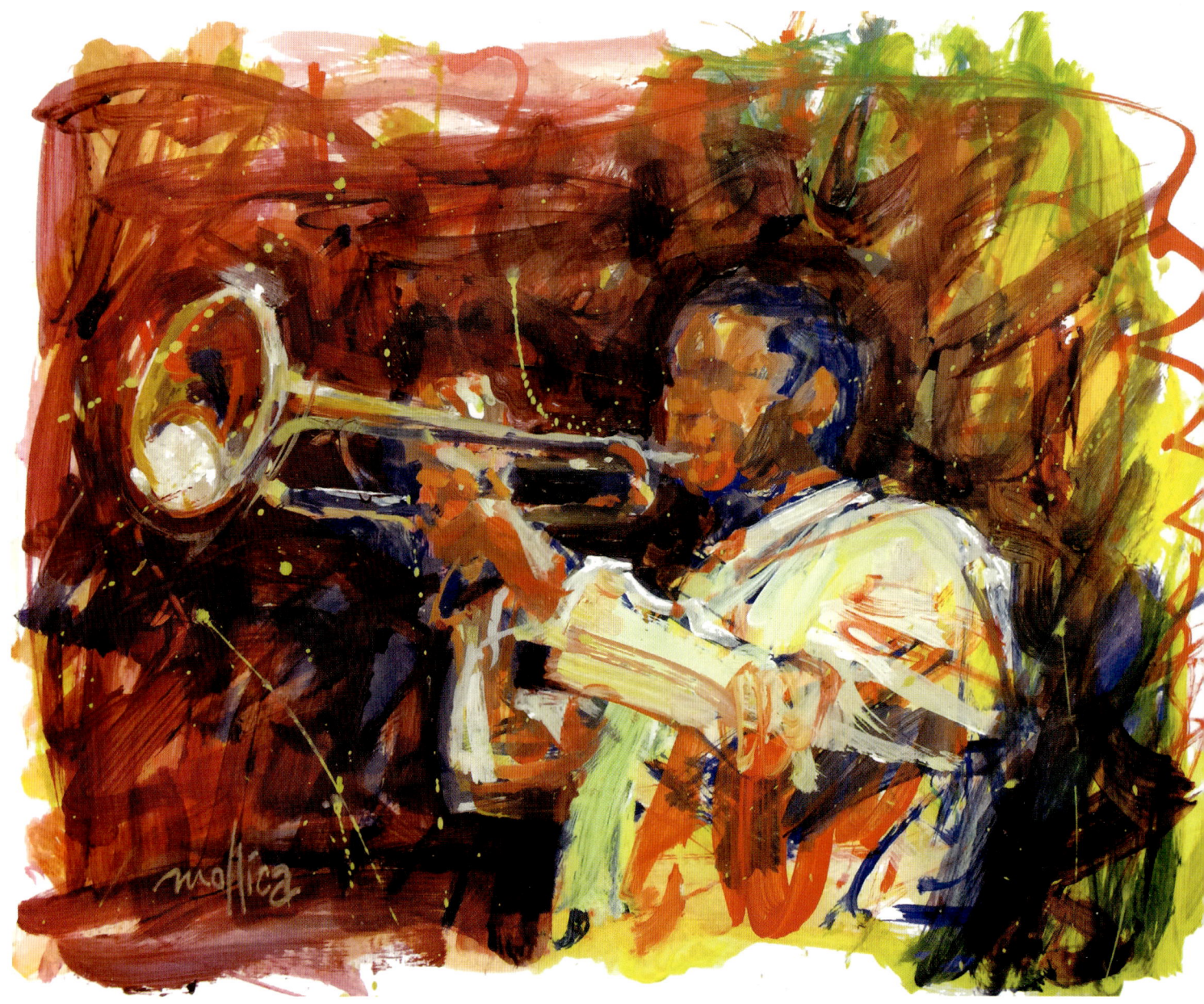

KEEP CONTROL

Even if you intend for your brushwork to look gestural and expressive, you still need to exercise a certain amount of control so that the paint ends up in the approximate place, and shape, you intended.

JAZZ CAT
Acrylic on panel
9" × 12" (23cm × 30cm)
Private collection

Brushes & Brush Effects

Using the correct brushes is a big factor in achieving painterly brushstrokes. There are a variety of brushes available depending on the style you are aiming for. I have found that I can get many types of strokes with wide flat brushes, which give me the control I need.

However every artist must experiment and decide for themselves what brush types feel most comfortable and yield the results they are after. In the following pages, we'll explore various types of brushes and the resulting strokes possible with each.

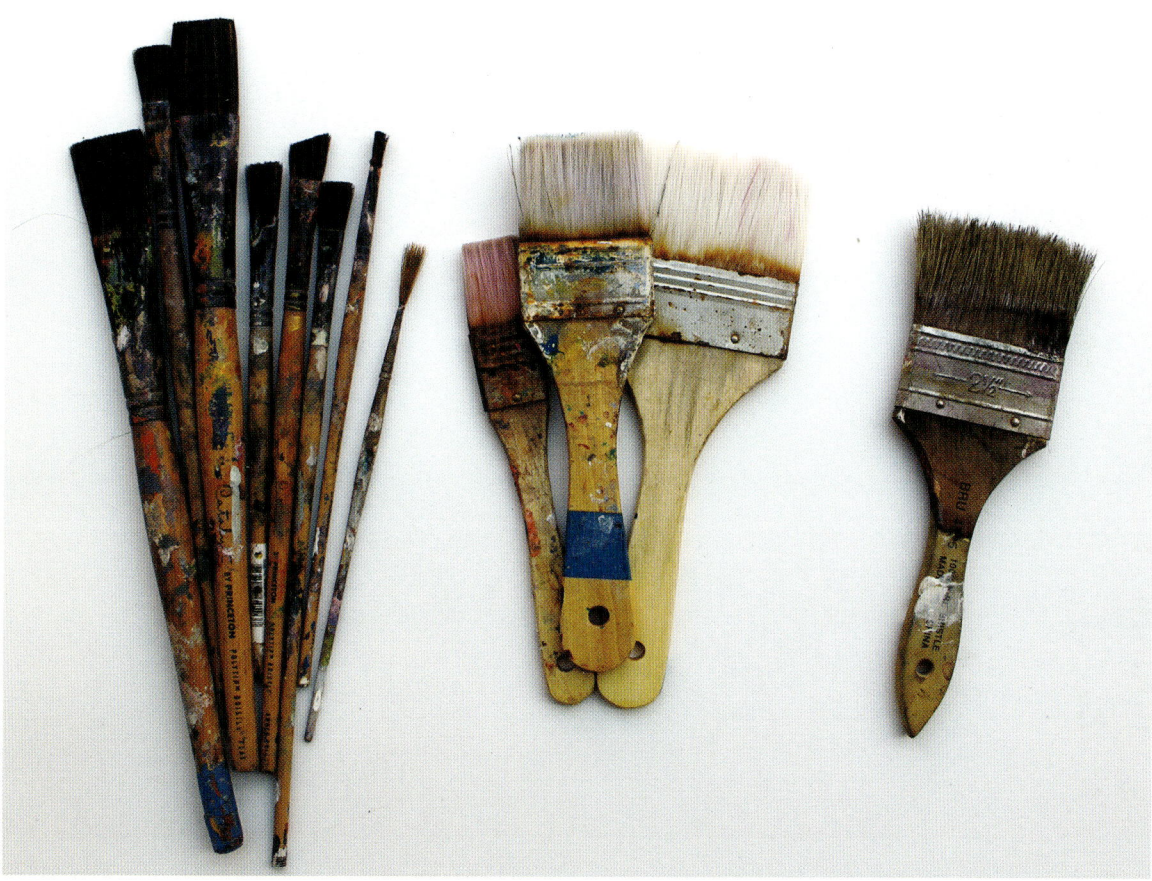

VARIETIES OF BRUSHES

The group of brushes on the left are Catalyst Polytip made by Princeton. By giving each individual hair two to three distinct tips, Polytip bristles are able to hold a higher volume of paint while providing smoother application. When wet, they come to a nice taper for excellent control, but also spring back to their original shape. They are suitable for both oil and acrylic paints. Included at the far right of this group is a synthetic script brush, which comes to a fine point when wet and can be used for small stems, branches and highlights.

The three brushes in the middle are inexpensive craft brushes. They are sold three to a package, in widths of 1-, 2-, and 3-inches (25mm, 51mm and 76mm). They are made of synthetic nylon and are suitable for acrylics, but not for oils. If your budget is a major concern, these can substitute in a pinch. However, the bristles shed and will lose their integrity over time. Just as with paints, you get what you pay for.

The brush on the right is a simple bristle brush from a hardware store that I use only to gesso or tone canvases. These types of brushes are not suitable for painting with any type of precision because the bristles do not taper when wet. Although they may yield a painterly quality, you will not be able to exercise any amount of control in your edges or shapes.

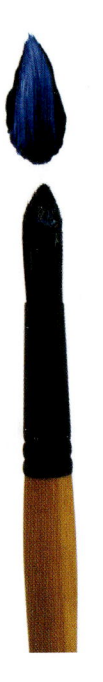

◄ ROUND STIFF BRISTLE

Round brushes have a pointed tip with long, tightly-arranged bristles. The pointed tip is meant for detail work, and the long bristles hold a large volume of paint. This brush style creates thin to thick lines (thin at the tip, becoming wider the more it's pressed down).

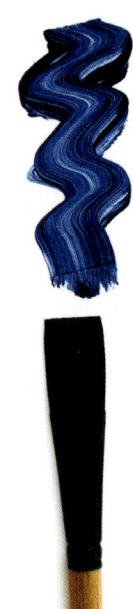

◄ FLAT

Long haired with flat bristles, these brushes are excellent for direct, bold strokes. The long bristles hold a lot of paint. You can use them for fine lines and crisp, straight edges.

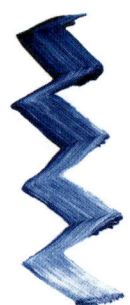

◄ BRIGHT

Brights are like flat brushes but with short, stiff bristles. They are good for short geometric strokes with a thin and thick line ability.

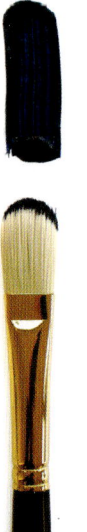

◄ FILBERT

Filbert brushes are dome-shaped on the end and offer a slightly curved stroke.

◄ ROUND SOFT BRISTLE

Many artists use a soft round bristle brush for more exacting shapes. The soft bristles are more flexible and offer great control for small shapes and details.

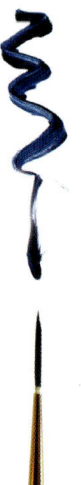

◄ LINER/ SCRIPT

Liners (also known as script brushes) have long, fine soft hairs. They are perfect for painting stems, branches, telephone poles and other linear strokes.

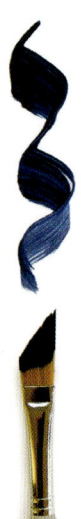

◄ ANGLED

Angled brushes give a thick/ thin calligraphic stroke, depending on the direction and pressure applied.

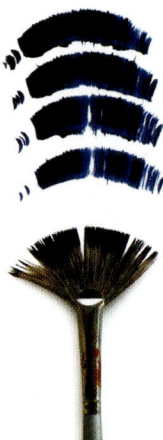

◄ FAN

The curved shape of a fan brush's bristles offers the ability to soften edges as well as create a rounded stroke.

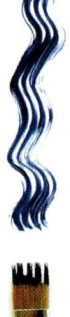
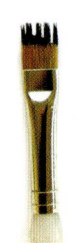

◄ SPECIALTY

There are many types of specialty brushes that offer a variety of unusual effects. Sometimes I cut up old brushes to create the shape I need.

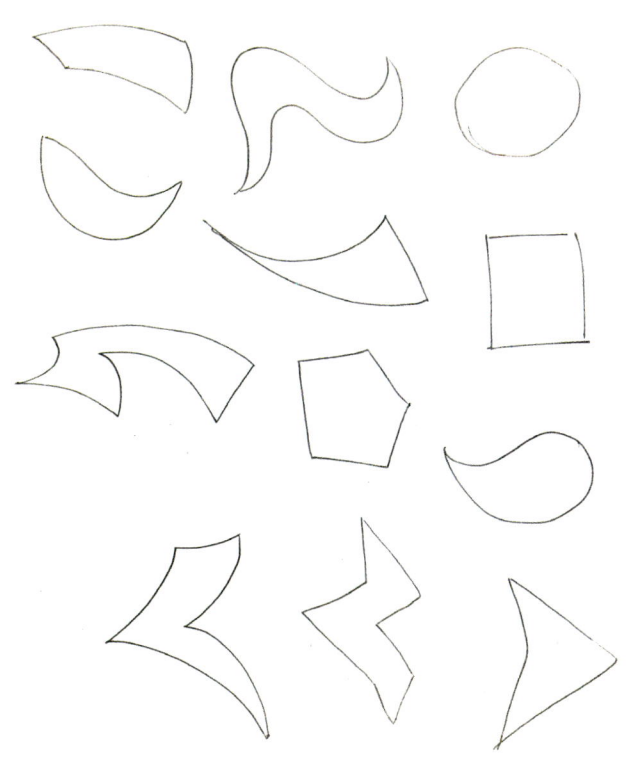

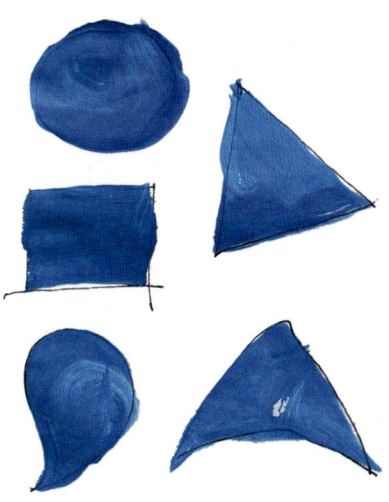

BRUSHSTROKE SHAPES

The blue shapes were made with a flat brush, using only one or two strokes. The brush was loaded with paint, and each time it was lifted up off the surface, a stroke was counted. This is one of the preliminary exercises I give to my students in workshops. It forces them to learn how to use the edges of their brush to create the shapes. By learning to be aware of each side of the brush, and the amount of pressure required to squeeze out the paint that is lodged in the bristles, one learns how to control the brush motion more efficiently, using fewer strokes overall.

It is interesting how many students (and even advanced painters) have never thought to practice brush control using twisting and turning movements. An excellent way to try this is to draw out irregular shapes with a fine tipped marker and fill them in with as few strokes as you can. It will feel a bit like creating calligraphic shapes with your brush—and that's the point—to get control of your brush handling!

A Tip on Brush Tips

One of the most important qualities to look for in a brush is that it tapers to a fine tip when wet. If the bristles are splayed, you will not be able to control your edges with any amount of accuracy.

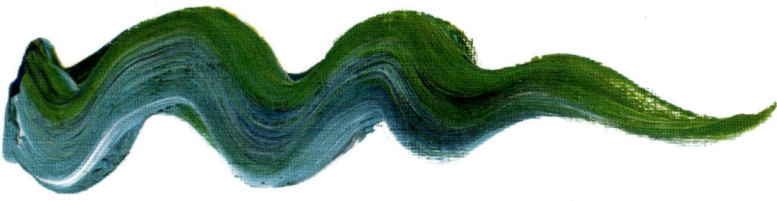

TWIST AND TURN

If you find your brush skipping out of paint before you are done with your stroke, it means you are not using enough. Try to get enough paint on your brush so that you can create one long painterly stroke. Experiment and see what it feels like to really load up with ample paint, especially if you are normally conservative with your paint applications.

Blending & Transitions

In order to create convincing realistic depictions of subjects that convey space and rounded forms, it is necessary to have a variety of edges in a painting—hard, firm, soft and lost edges. Note that it is much easier to create variations in edges when working with oil paints than acrylics, because acrylics dry almost immediately, creating hard edges.

The four most common types of edges found in paintings are

- Hard: When two colors meet and form an abrupt transition between color areas.
- Soft: A blurred and gradual delineation between two colors.
- Lost: A blurred edge that is so gradual it is nearly impossible to see where one color begins and the other ends.
- Optical blending: Series of firm edges adjacent to one another, created by mixing colors/values that are halfway between each color, then painting in a new color adjacent to the previous colors. It creates a choppy look with no lost edges.

Consideration of edges is important when determining where you want to lead your viewer to focus their attention on a specific part of the painting. The eye tends to zero in on the areas where the hardest edges are located, in addition to the parts of the painting that have the most value contrast, such as a very light shape next to a dark shape.

In order to make the focal point of the painting obvious, many artists place their hardest edges and highest value contrast in this area, softening most or all of the others. Depending on the style of painting you are creating, it is your choice whether you need a variety of edges, which are more common in traditional paintings and less prevalent in contemporary styles.

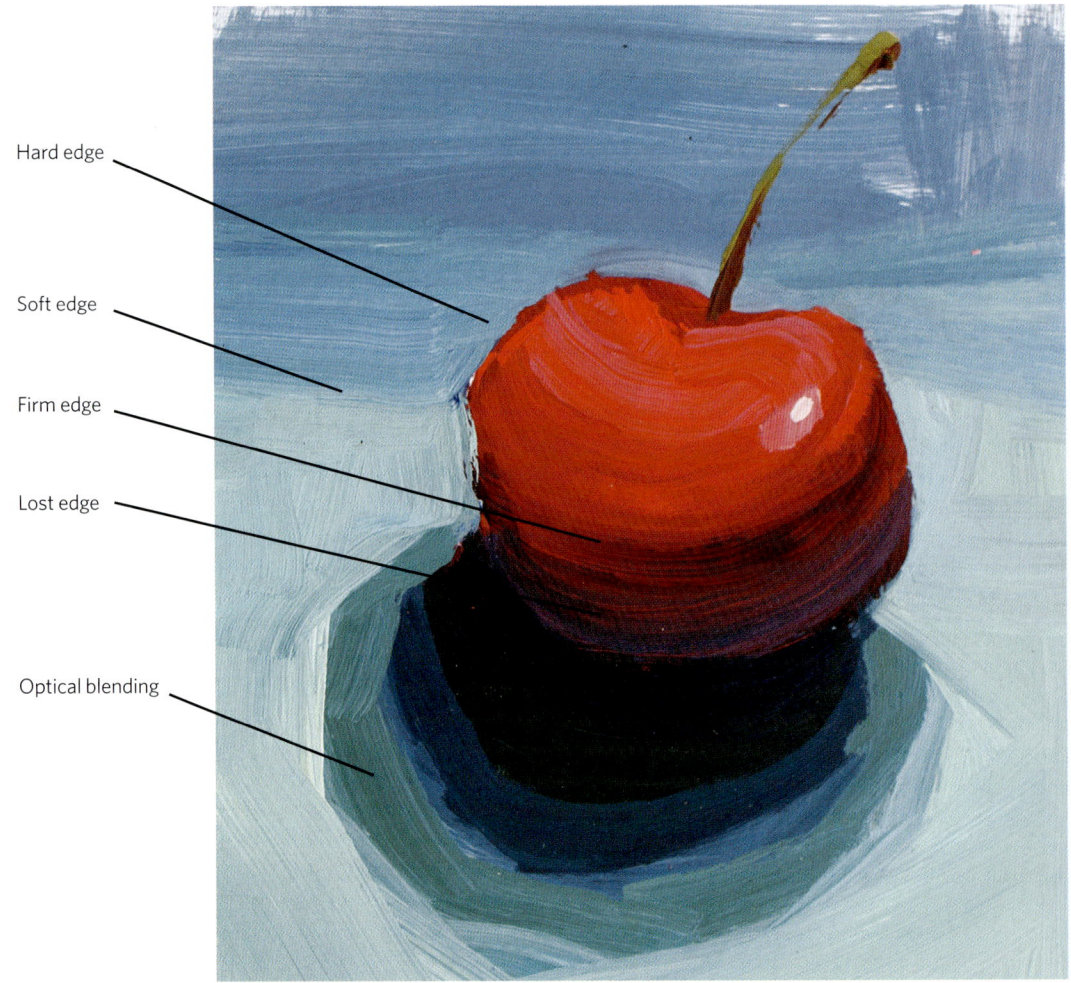

Hard edge

Soft edge

Firm edge

Lost edge

Optical blending

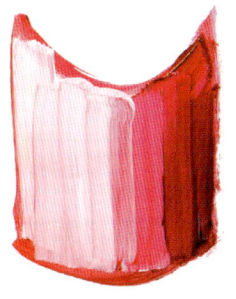
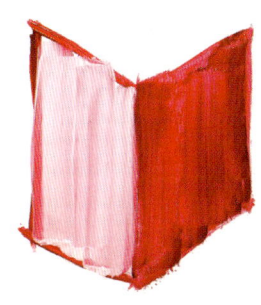

TRANSITIONS

Transitions are important in giving a subject the feeling of a three-dimensional quality and structural believability. The way you depict edges suggests whether you are looking at a surface that is sharp and metallic, soft and fuzzy, or any number of textures in between. A rounded form that is lit on one side will have a soft edge where it starts to turn away from the light. A plane that turns a corner away from the light source in a sharp manner will have a sharp edge.

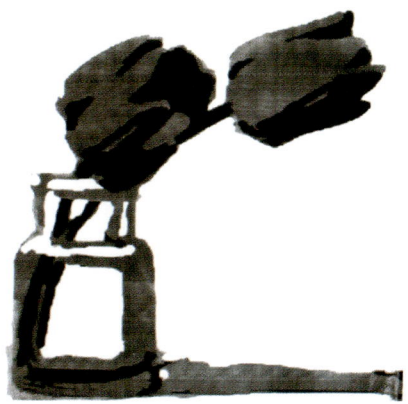
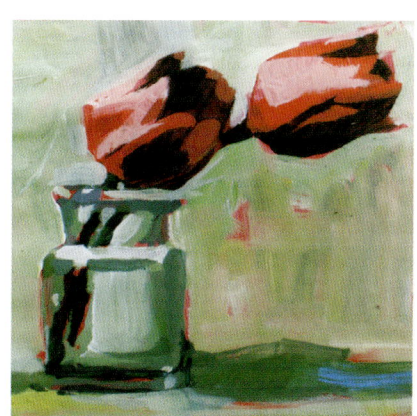
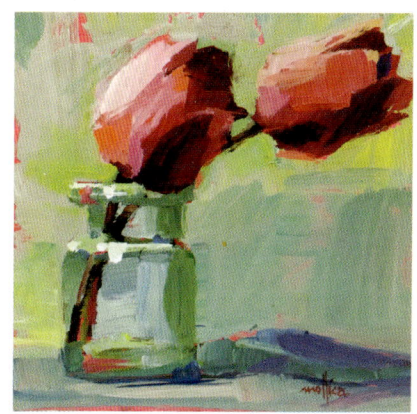

TRANSITIONAL EDGES AND VALUES

The image on the left is a three-value sketch. The middle image is a value sketch translated without soft edges. The image on the right uses a variety of transitional edges and values for a more realistic effect. Although I worked in only three values for the sketch subject, I used additional values in the color stage of the painting, while adhering closely to the values I chose in the sketch.

Beginners often translate three-value sketches verbatim, with sharp, hard edges where one value meets another. This results in flat, graphic interpretations of subjects that lack nuance of structure. For the subject to be believable, transitions between the values need to be present. The best way of making natural transitions in acrylics is to work fast in a wet-into-wet manner so soft, natural edges and transitions can be achieved. (If you're working with oil paint, which dries very slowly, it is not necessary to work quickly since there is plenty of time to create a variety of edges.)

Softening Edges

In this blending exercise, follow the steps to soften the edges between two passages of color.

MATERIALS

Surface
white mat board

Pigments
two colors of your choice

Brushes
small flat

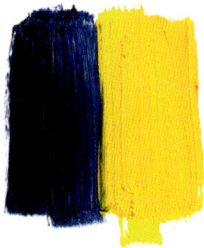

1 LAY DOWN COLORS

Paint two colors side by side.

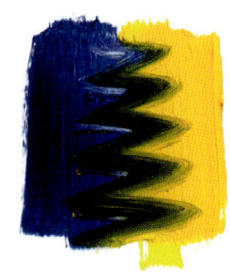

2 ZIG ZAG STROKE

While the paint is still wet and with firm pressure on your brush, apply a zigzag stroke with a downward motion along the line where the two colors meet.

3 DRAG STRAIGHT DOWN

Immediately drag your brush straight down from top to bottom. This will create a firm edge. Then in a continuous motion, brush down several more times, moving slightly to the right, then slightly to the left.

4 REPEAT DRAGGING MOTION

The more times you sweep your strokes from right to left and back, the more you will soften your edge.

It is much easier to create softened edges when the paint is still wet. Once it has dried, you will have to re-create the same colors in order to blend the edges where two colors meet.

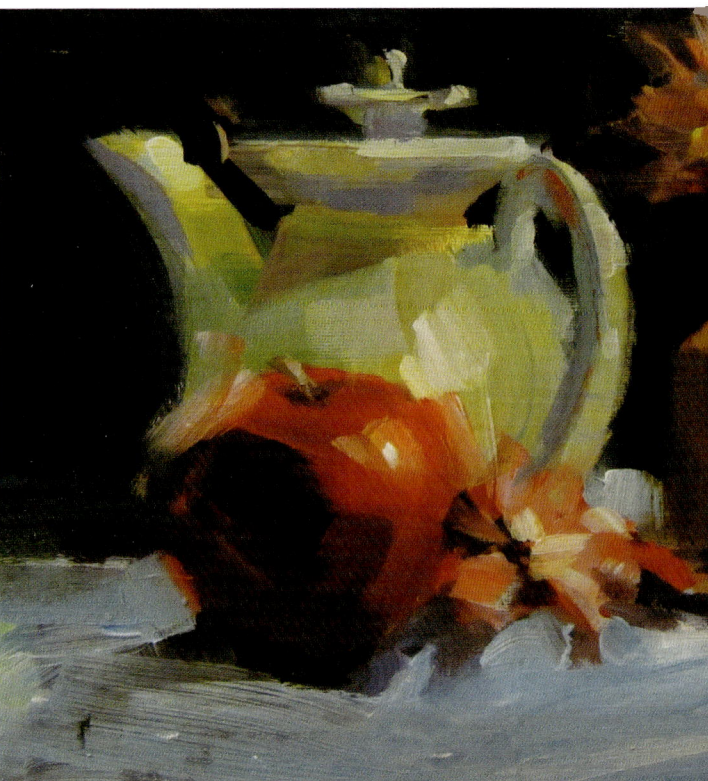

BLURRED EDGES HELP SOFTEN FORMS
Notice the blurred edges around the apple, teapot and flowers. They help soften the forms by implying they are rounded and turn away in space. With oils it is easy to create soft, blended edges by simply smudging with a brush or rag. Due to the fast drying time of acrylics, it takes a little more effort and know-how.

Limited Strokes Exercise

Here is a great exercise in learning how to use more paint. The goal is to depict a scene or still life subject in as few strokes as necessary and keep track of how many strokes it requires to fill in the entire canvas.

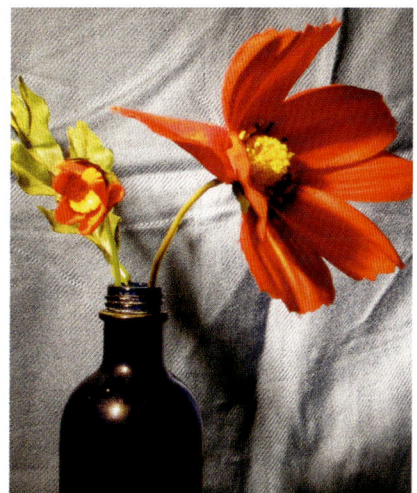

REFERENCE PHOTO

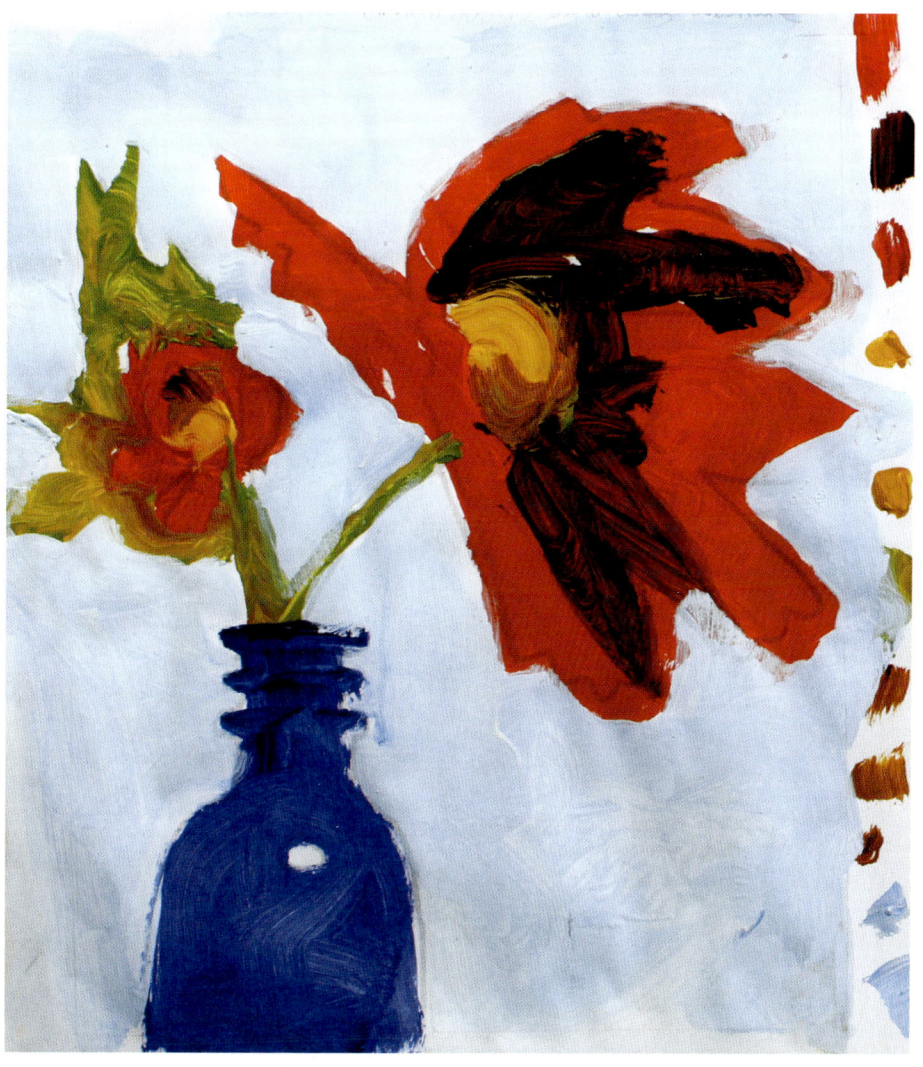

THE PROCESS

Begin by lightly sketching the outlines of your subject. Then paint in the most important elements of the painting. Load your brush with enough paint to cover the area that you are working on. Try to cover as much area as you can in one stroke—as soon as you lift your brush off the canvas, it is considered one stroke. Record your strokes by indicating a dab of the color you used to the right of your canvas. Try to do an entire painting in fifteen strokes or less.

The beauty of this exercise is that you not only learn to use more paint, you also learn how to eliminate the details that are not important. If you normally paint everything you see, this will automatically force you to consider what contributes the most important visual information to your painting. Don't forget to include the background—that counts too!

Practice Painting Faster

Early in my painting career, I used to paint large canvases and work on one painting for weeks or months on end. It was relaxing, meditative—and slow. I'd work on the same painting every day, frequently modifying certain passages or colors or changing whatever struck me as needed.

There is nothing wrong with this approach. However, I felt like I was feeling my way along, somewhat indecisively, rather than approaching my painting with a more definitive vision and goal. This approach also allowed me to avoid the intimidation of a new blank white canvas indefinitely. However, I came to the realization that I would progress faster as a painter by facing "the white challenge" as often as possible, rather than avoiding it. So I decided to start painting more often in smaller sizes. And I found that daily timed painting sessions were the key to progress. Books, videos and workshops are all wonderful ways to learn, but they can't teach you the subtle techniques that can only be realized through the experience of painting.

Painting fast in timed sessions is rather uncomfortable compared to slowly tickling a painting to death, but it will force you to respond to the main compositional challenges quickly and intuitively. You must adopt a priority-driven "triage" approach by tackling the biggest issues first, then gradually honing in on lesser, superfluous details. The beauty in this approach is that it forces simplification.

This is not to say that details are not important—some are. But given endless time, many painters will paint every single detail they see just because they are there. This will result in a painting that looks like a photograph (provided the artist has learned the appropriate skills to render so meticulously). I'm not putting down photo realism, which takes considerable skill. It's just not my personal cup of tea and not the style of painting we have been exploring in this book.

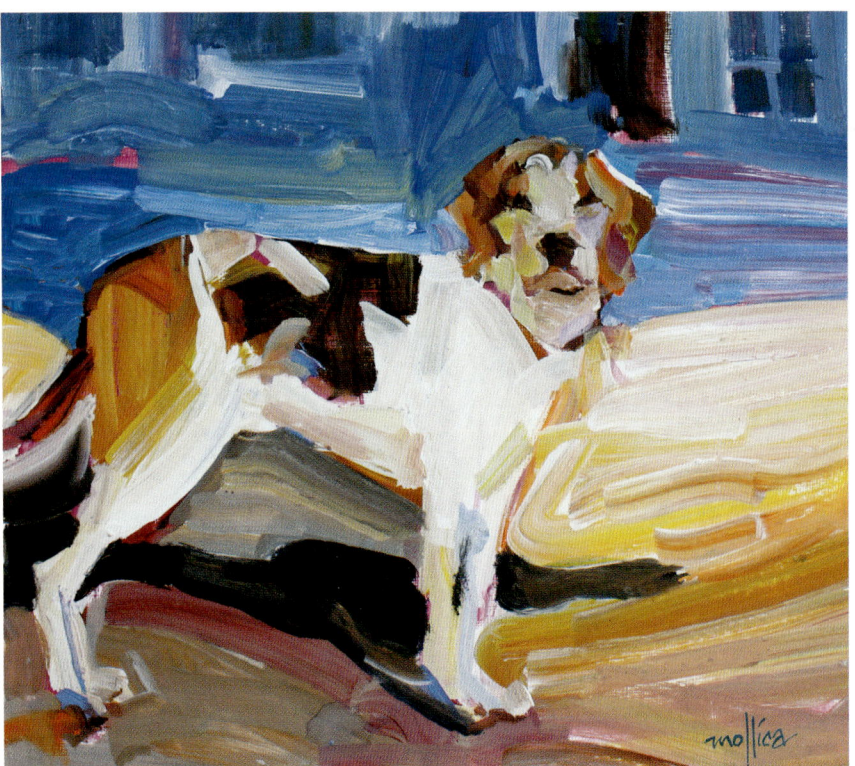

SOMETIMES LESS IS MORE
A representational artist's job is not to account for every detail, but rather include only what strengthens a composition's structure, character and essence. This painting was started and completed in 15 minutes. By simplifying the background shapes, I've kept the focus where I want it—my pooch!

CASEY
Acrylic on panel
12" × 12" (30cm × 30cm)
Private collection

Timed Painting Exercises

One of the best ways to edit out unecessary detail is to work within a short time limit. As simplistic as that may sound, it forces a type of efficiency that results in a simpler, bolder effect.

Follow the steps to get the feel for working faster and more efficiently.

MATERIALS

Surface
6" × 6" (15cm × 15cm) panel

Pigments
colors of your choice

Brushes
½" (13mm), 1" (25mm) and
2" (51mm) flats or filberts

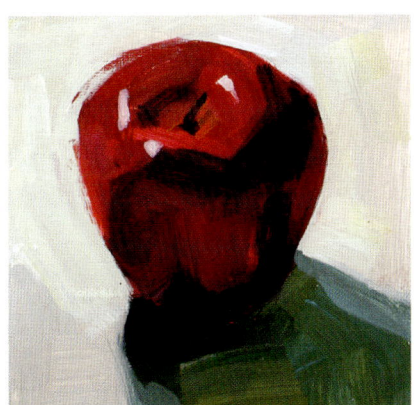

1 45-MINUTE PAINTING

Set up a still life using an object with a simple shape, such as an apple. Shine a light on it so that part is directly lit, and the other side falls into shadow (cast shadow).

Set a kitchen timer for 45 minutes to start and complete the painting. Work on a small canvas board or other support no larger than 8" × 8" (20cm × 20cm). The smaller the size, the faster you can cover the surface.

Do the best you can to get the structural feel of the object. Notice where the light is striking it directly and at what point the plane of the object falls into shadow. Do not worry about perfection; aim for simplicity in depicting a three-dimensional structure. Simply paint what you see in the 45-minute time period.

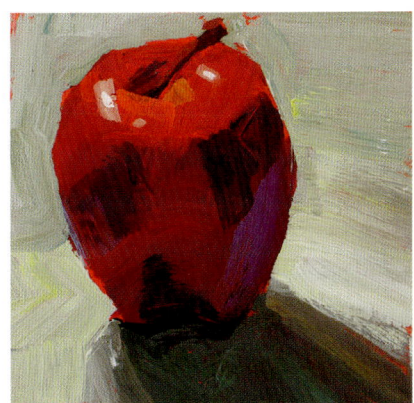

2 30-MINUTE PAINTING

Using the same reference, set the timer for 30 minutes. Since you are now familiar with the subject and the basic colors mixes used, work this to your advantage and try to paint more decisively with fewer strokes.

Use this as an opportunity to push the colors and the gestural manner of your brushwork. Make any amends to the shape or proportions that will give the subject a more appealing or dramatic presence. Aim for a bolder, more confident statement than the 45-minute painting.

In this case, I felt the apple's shape needed to be more streamlined, and the colors needed a boost. I switched the background color to a dull gray-green to enhance the red and magenta colors of the apple.

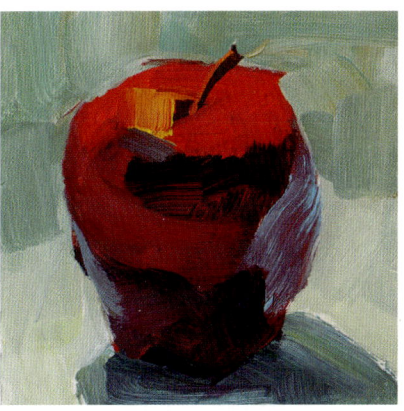

3 15-MINUTE PAINTING

Set a timer for a 15-minutes. Force yourself to be fast and loose with your brushwork. Push the colors further, experimenting with different colors on the reflected light passages. Use this session to really let loose and be playful.

More Timed Painting

Let's practice another 45-minute painting session (not including the value sketch). As I have mentioned earlier, the entire painting process moves along quickly and efficiently once the values have been worked out. However, do not expect to create a masterpiece in any of these fast painting sessions. The goal here is to learn what it feels like to paint swiftly and more consciously. Try not to judge yourself harshly if you don't like the outcome—that type of thinking will sabotage your progress. This is simply an exercise, and the resulting paintings are not meant for framing. Have fun with it!

MATERIALS

Surface
8" × 8" (20cm × 20cm) panel

Pigments
Alizarin Crimson, Burnt Sienna, Burnt Umber, Cadmium Orange, Cadmium Primrose Yellow, Cadmium Red Light, Cadmium Yellow Medium, Carbon Black, Green Gold, Manganese Blue, Medium Magenta, Neutral Gray N6, Quinacridone Magenta, Permanent Green, Sap Green, Teal, Titan Buff, Titanium White, Ultramarine Blue, Yellow Ochre

Brushes
½" (13mm), 1" (25mm) and 2" (51mm) flats or filberts

Other
black vine charcoal, eraser

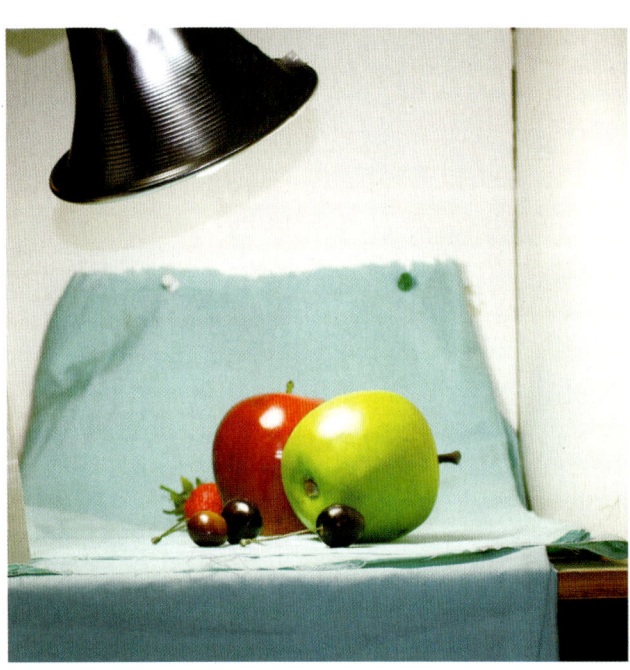

REFERENCE PHOTO

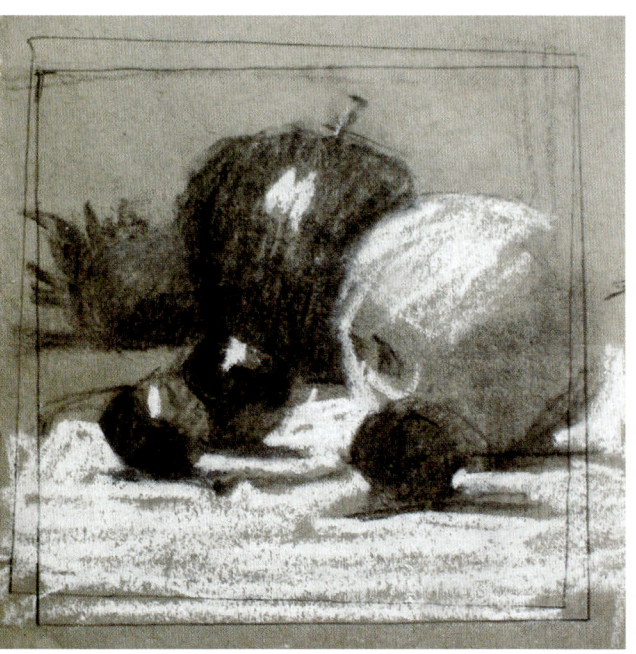

VALUE SKETCH

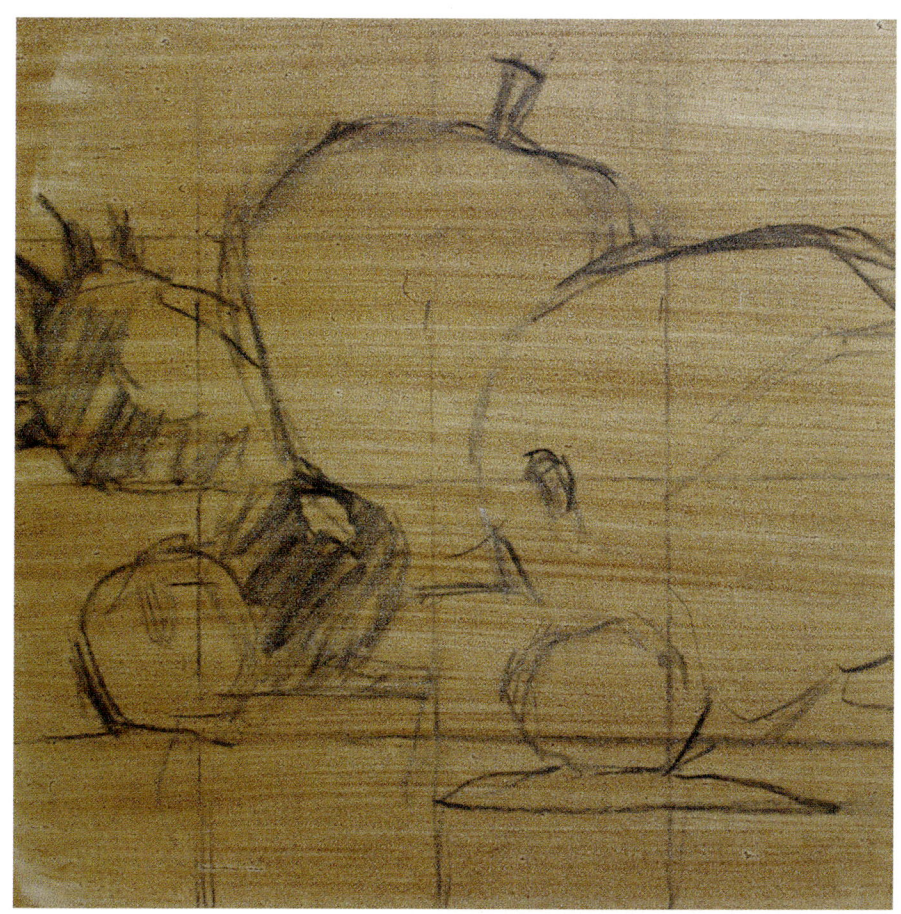

1 TONE THE PANEL AND BLOCK IN THE SHAPES

Tone the panel with a light wash of Burnt Umber. Then lightly draw in the basic shapes with black vine charcoal. This is for positioning only, to get a basic idea of where the objects are placed on the panel.

2 PAINT THE MIDDLE GROUND FRUIT

Paint the apple in the middle ground using a mixture of Sap Green, Cerulean Blue, Teal, Cadmium Yellow Light, Cadmium Yellow Medium and Titanium White.

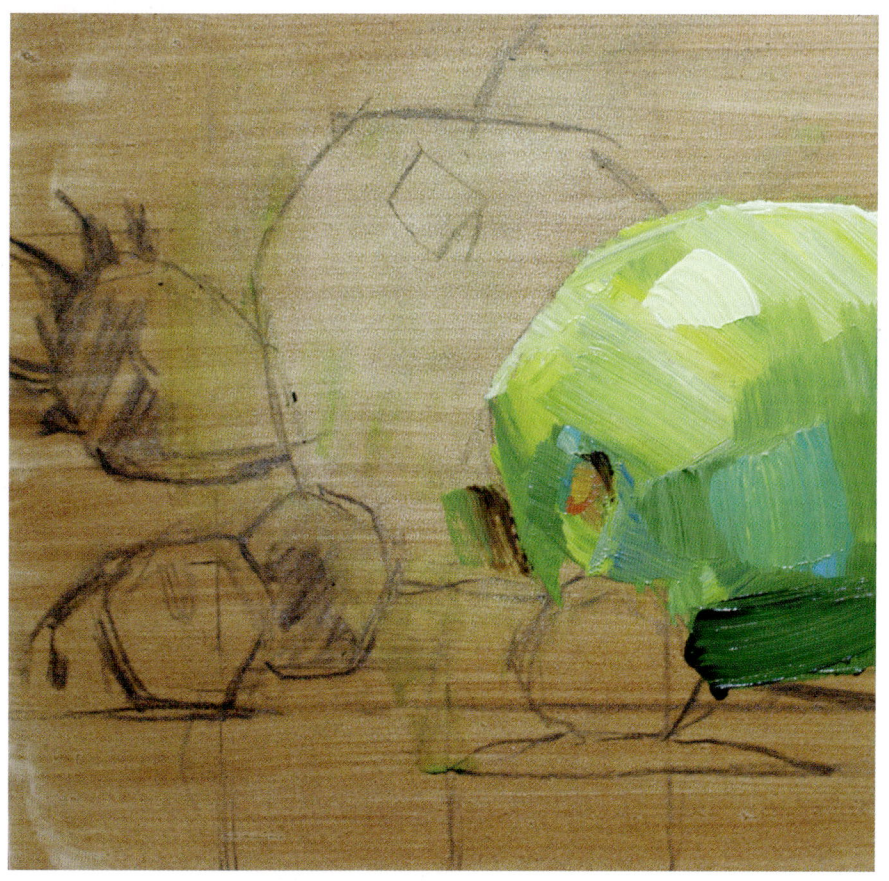

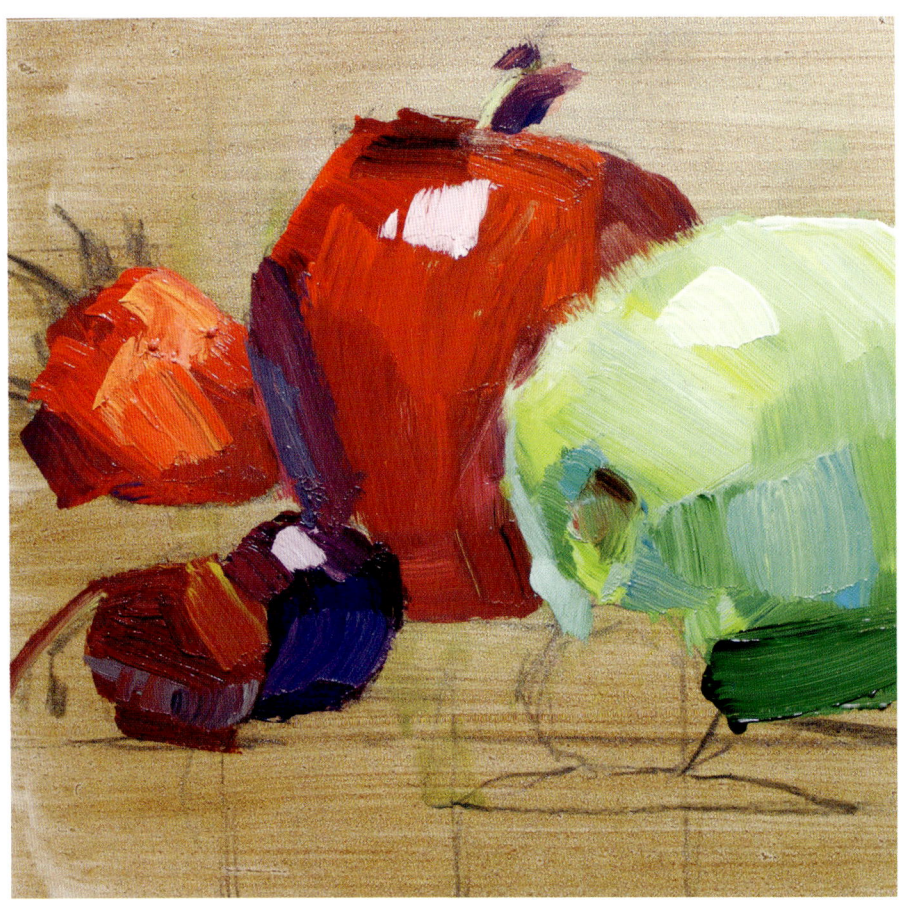

3 CONTINUE PAINTING THE MIDDLE GROUND FRUIT

Paint the red apple, cherries and strawberry with Cadmium Red Light, Alizarin Crimson, Quinacridone Magenta, Ultramarine Blue and a little bit of Titanium White.

At this stage you are just trying to get the values and colors accurate to get a sense of how they will sit together.

4 PAINT THE FOREGROUND FRUIT

Paint the cooler cherries in the foreground with mixtures of Ultramarine Blue, Alizarin Crimson, Quinacridone Magenta and a bit of Titanium White. Paint a lovely reflection on the left cherry with a stroke of Yellow Ochre mixed with Alizarin Crimson and Titanium White. Paint the green petals of the strawberry with Ultramarine Blue, Cadmium Yellow Medium and Titanium White. Add a touch of Cadmium Orange on the right side of the strawberry.

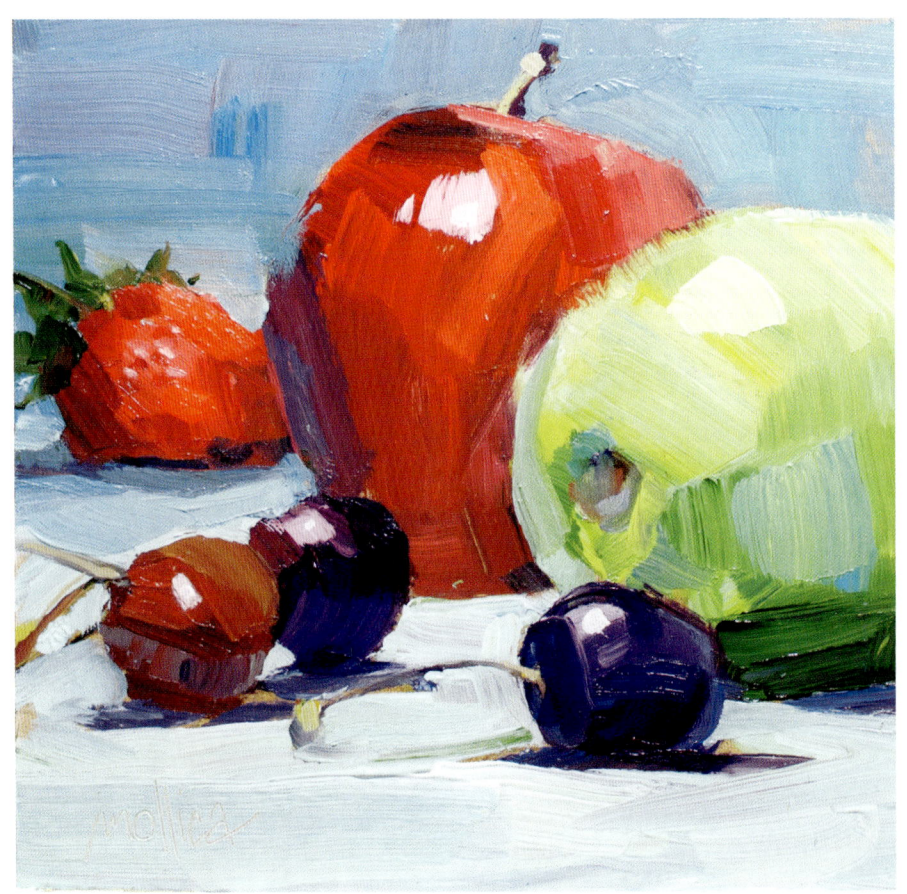

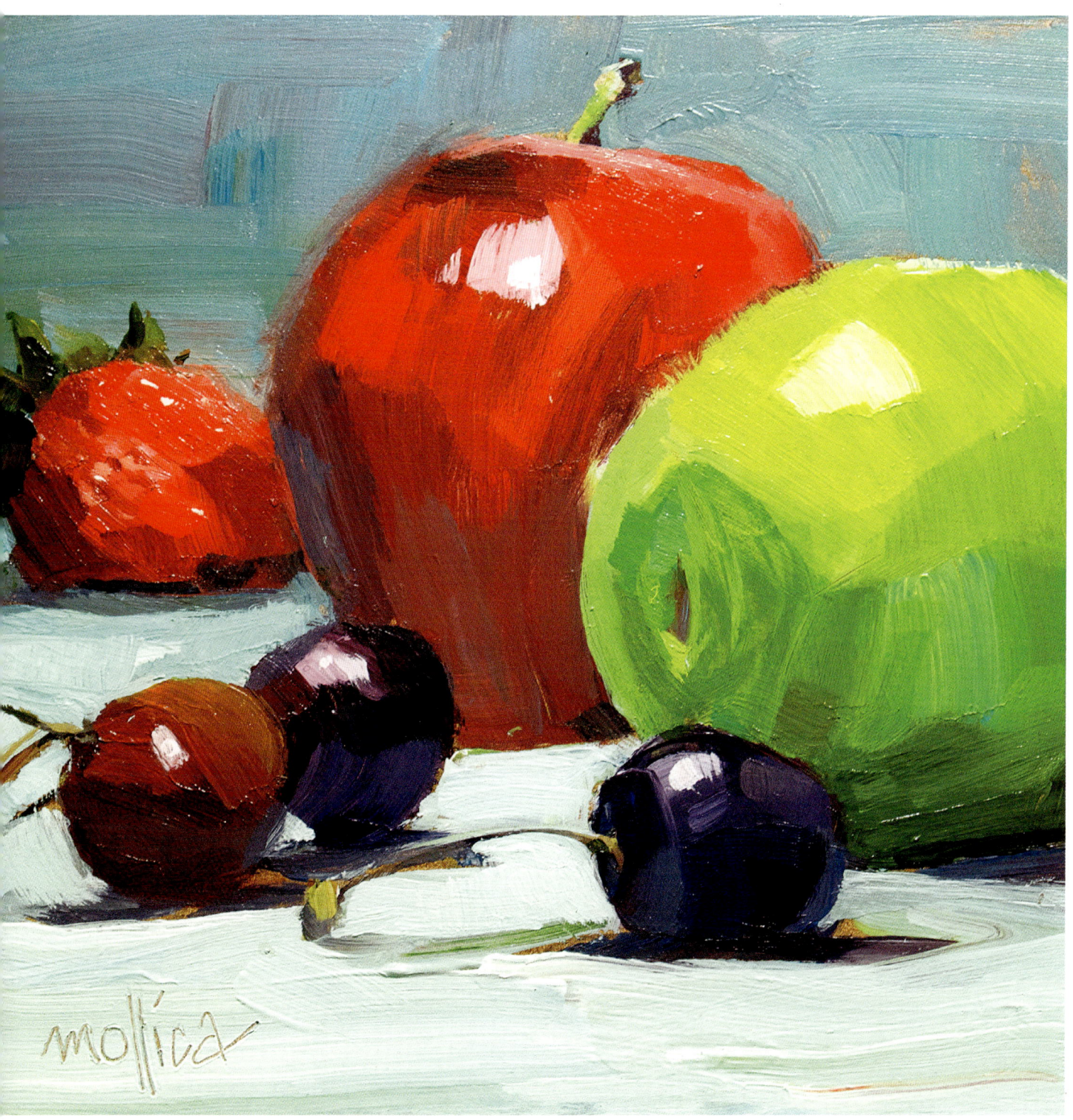

5 MAKE ADJUSTMENTS AND ADD FINAL DETAILS

Paint the cherry stems with Green Gold, Burnt Sienna and Yellow Ochre. Create the background color by mixing Titanium White, Cerulean Blue and a hint of Alizarin Crimson. Add Teal and a hint of Yellow Ochre in the foreground. Once all the main components are in, add small highlights to the strawberry. Finally, add any small touches that will help define the shapes, as well as modify any brushwork and colors that need slight adjusting.

OPPOSITES ATTRACT
Acrylic on panel
8" × 8" (20cm × 20cm)
Collection of Nancy Schuster

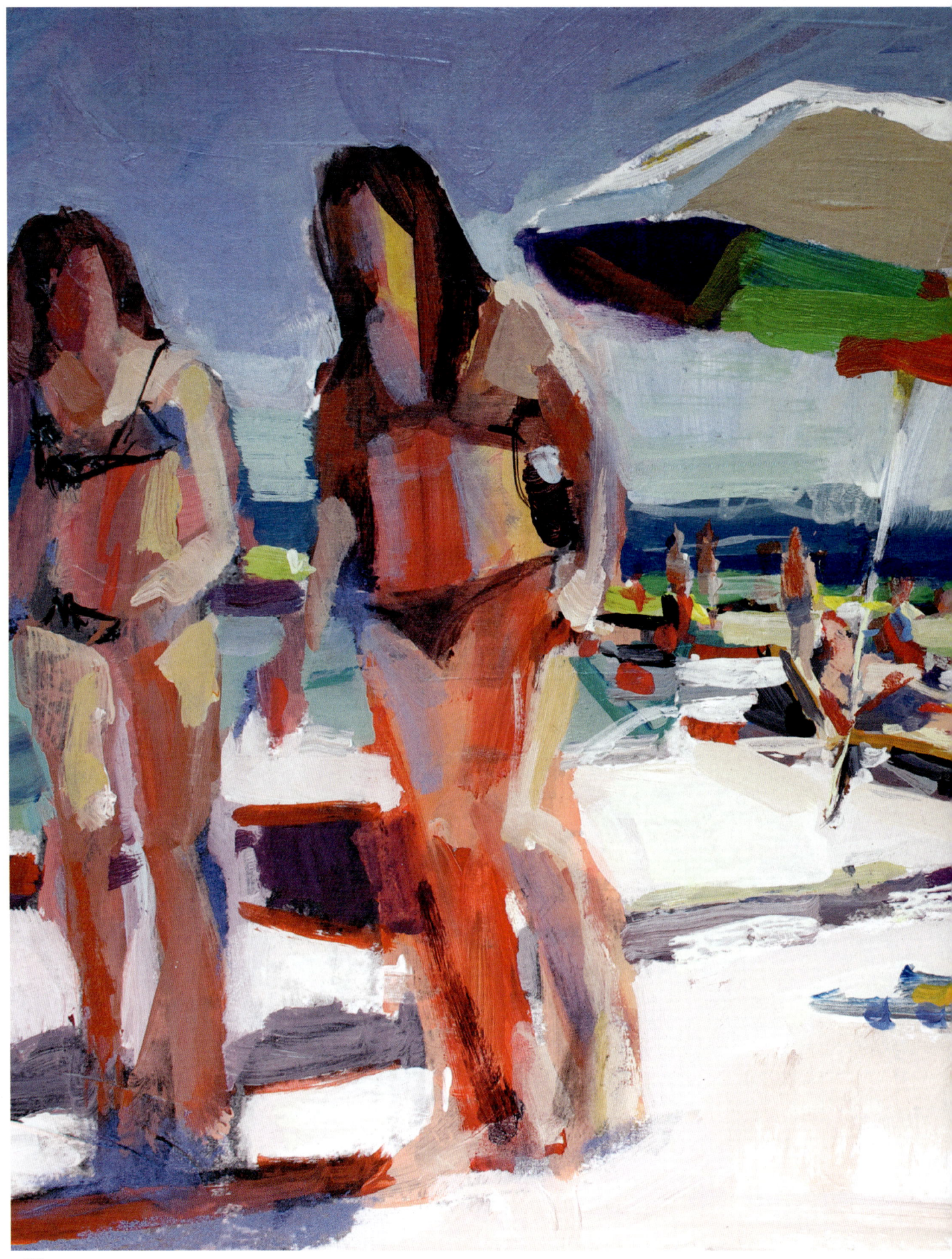

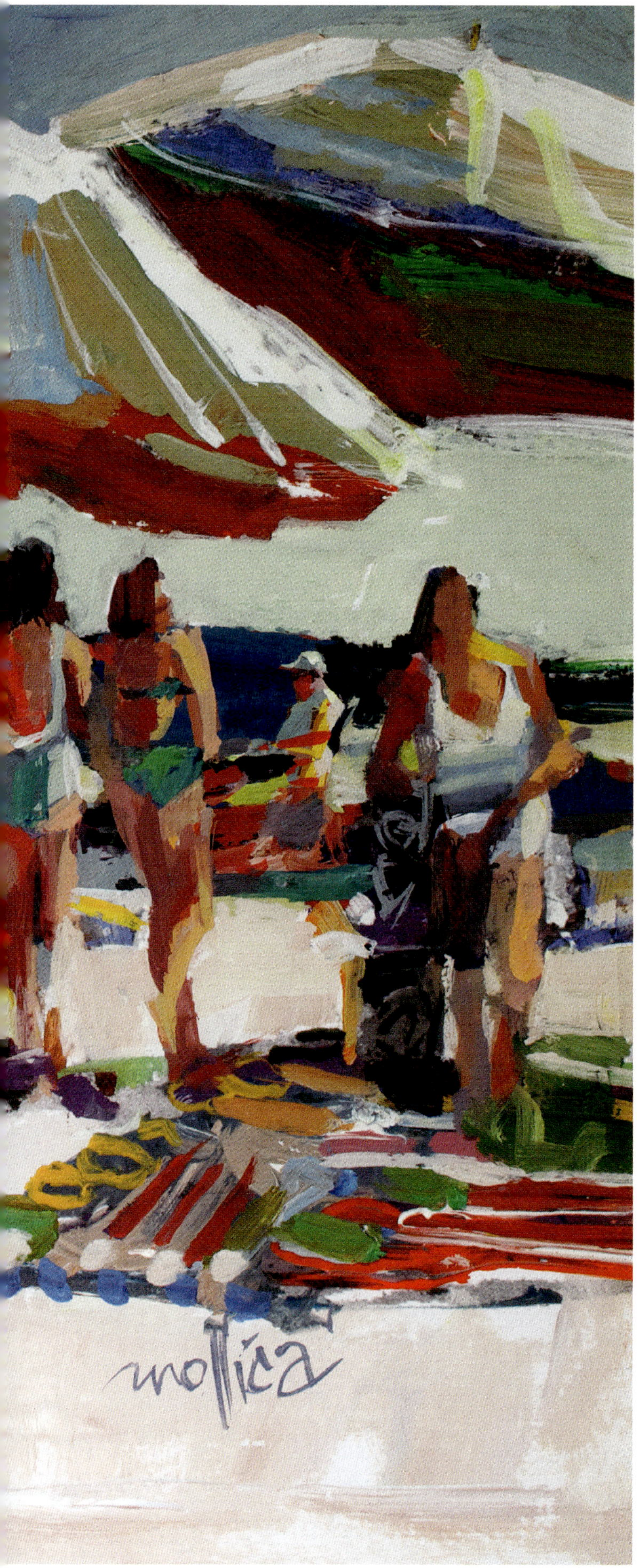

Painting Fast, Loose & Bold

The beauty of working with the methods in this book is that once you have done your homework, you can approach the blank white canvas with more confidence and less apprehension. The value map shows you where you're going. The color mixing principles keep you on track. The brush handling practices keep your strokes fresh. This approach results in paintings that are created quite fast, display a loose, painterly quality, and have bold underlying compositions. It's an approach that has always worked well for me, and with a little practice I'm sure will work for you, too.

In this chapter I will take you through several step-by-step demonstrations to illustrate the process in action.

BEACH WALK
Acrylic on panel
10" × 12" (25cm × 30cm)
Private collection

Good Gourd!

As I mentioned when discussing paints at the beginning of this book, the pigments listed with the materials in these demonstrations include the colors I keep on my palette at all times. However, you will not necessarily be using every color listed in each painting.

Follow the steps to paint a still life of warm-hued fruit contrasted against a cool blue background.

MATERIALS

Surface
10" × 8" (25cm × 20cm) panel

Pigments
Alizarin Crimson, Burnt Sienna, Burnt Umber, Cadmium Orange, Cadmium Lemon Yellow, Cadmium Red Light, Cadmium Yellow Light, Cadmium Yellow Medium, Carbon Black, Green Gold, Manganese Blue, Medium Magenta, Neutral Gray N6, Quinacridone Magenta, Permanent Green, Sap Green, Teal, Titan Buff, Ultramarine Blue, Yellow Ochre

Brushes
¼"–2" (6mm-51mm) flats or filberts

Other
eraser, black vine charcoal

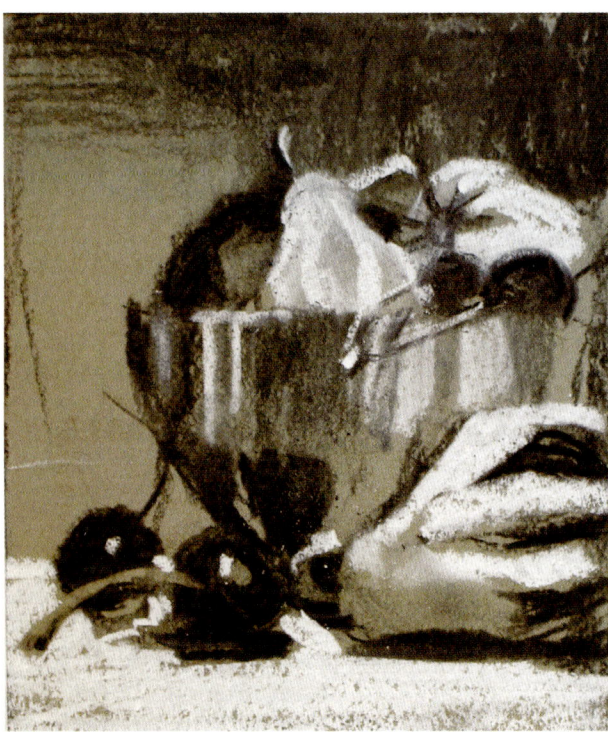

VALUE SKETCH

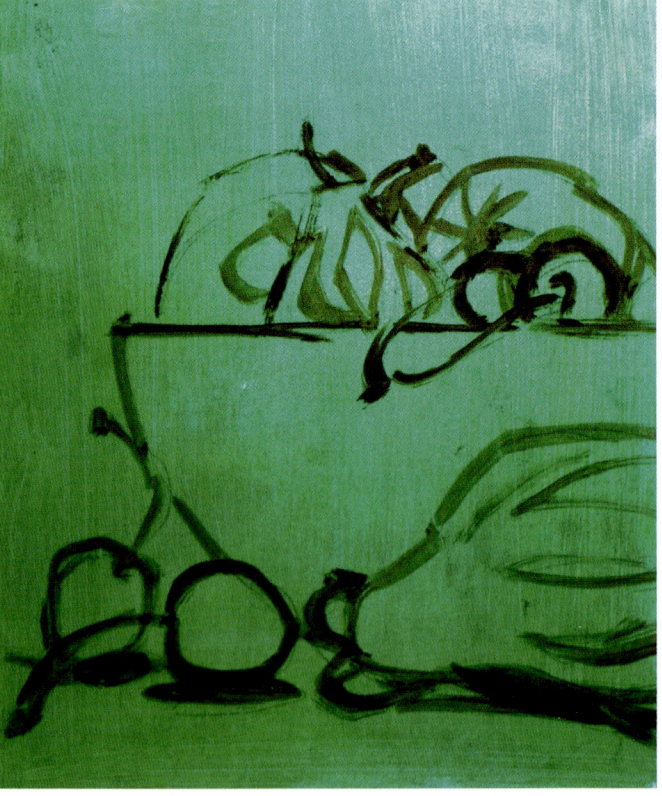

1 PAINT THE BACKGROUND BASE AND SKETCH THE COMPOSITION

Use a 2-inch (51mm) flat to paint the panel with Teal as a background base color. Sketch in the basic outlines of the composition with a ¼-inch (6mm) flat and a dark value color such as Burnt Umber to serve as guidelines.

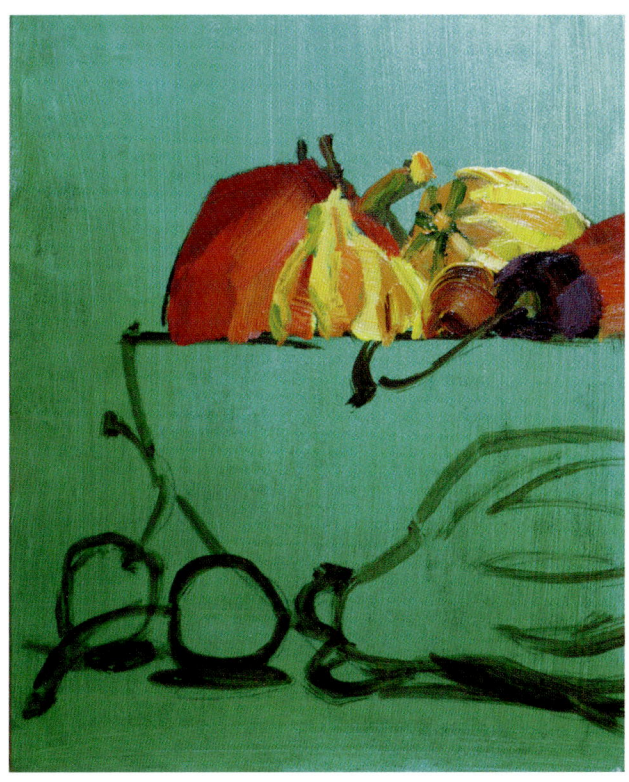

2 BEGIN PAINTING THE FRUIT

Begin painting the composition from the top down. Start with the fruit in the bowl using a 1-inch (25mm) flat. Use color mixtures of Alizarin Crimson, Cadmium Red Light and a little Titanium White with Cadmium Orange mixed in. For the gourd mixtures, add Cadmium Yellow Medium and Yellow Ochre. The dark cherries will require Quinacridone Magenta mixed with Ultramarine Blue and Titanium White. The fruits are mainly warm tones, so work from the same mixed colors for each piece of fruit. This will give the fruit a color unity.

Acrylics dry very quickly, so you will need to work fast when using colors that share the same color family.

3 PAINT THE BOWL

There was a lavender overtone in the reflective surface of the metal bowl that did not show up in the photo. This is the main reason I recommend working from direct observation, especially with still life subjects. Some subtle nuances of color are often only apparent when working from life.

Paint the bowl using ½-inch (13mm) and 1-inch (25mm) flats. Although the bowl has violet undertones, they need to be subdued with a touch of Yellow Ochre. Color wise, it's OK to tend toward overemphasizing what you see. You can always tone it back later if the color becomes too saturated and competes with the subject.

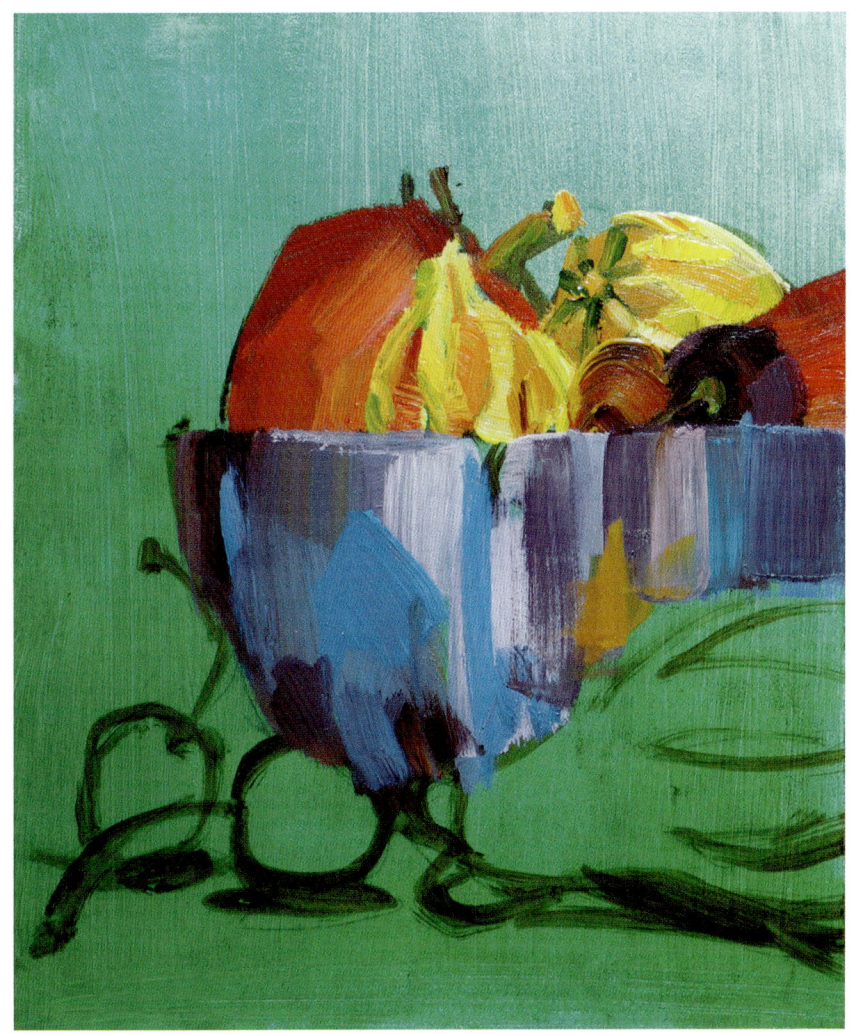

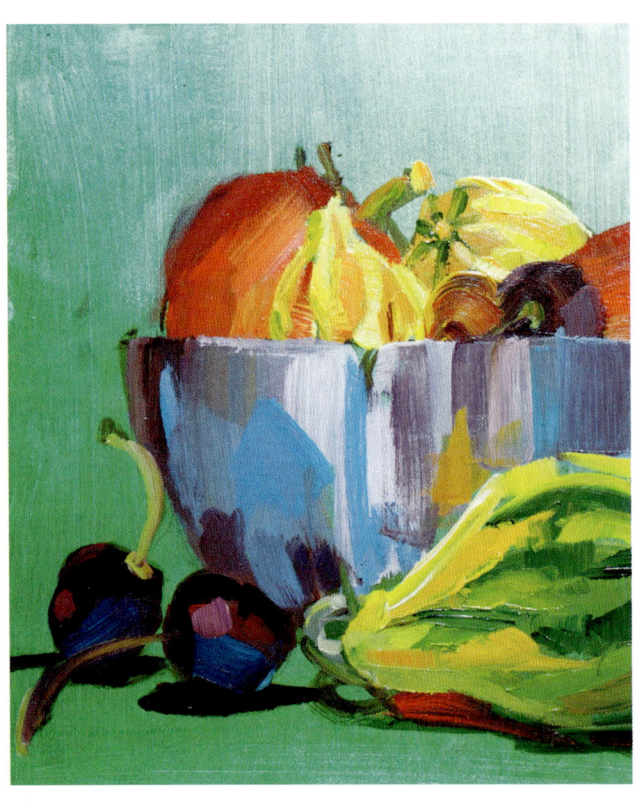

4 CONTINUE PAINTING THE FRUIT

Use ¼-inch (6mm) and ½-inch (13mm) flats to paint the cherries and the gourds. Try to keep your brushstrokes minimal and fresh. Make sure you add the blue color of the bowl reflecting on the underside of the cherries.

5 FINISH THE BACKGROUND AND THE FRUIT

Use 1-inch (25mm) and 2-inch (51mm) flats to paint the background. Mix your colors from mixtures of Manganese Blue, Teal and a bit of Yellow Ochre, plus Titanium White. Applying the background colors allows you to cut around the objects in the painting if the shapes need to be adjusted.

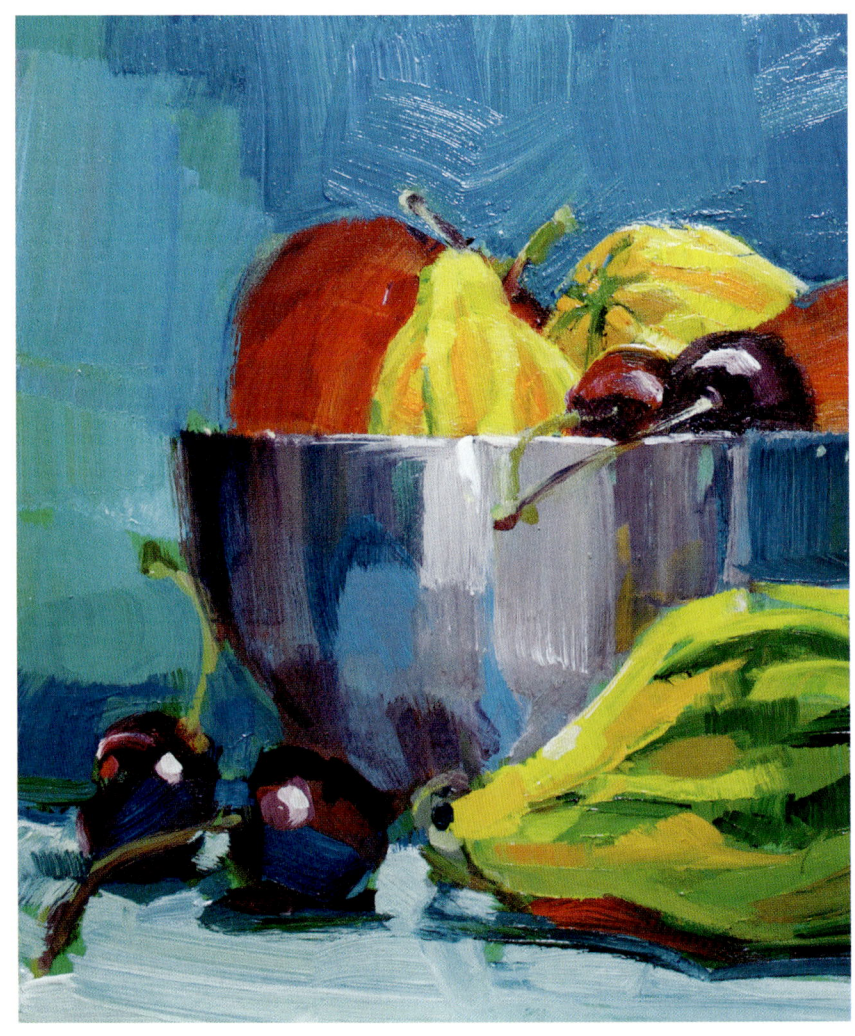

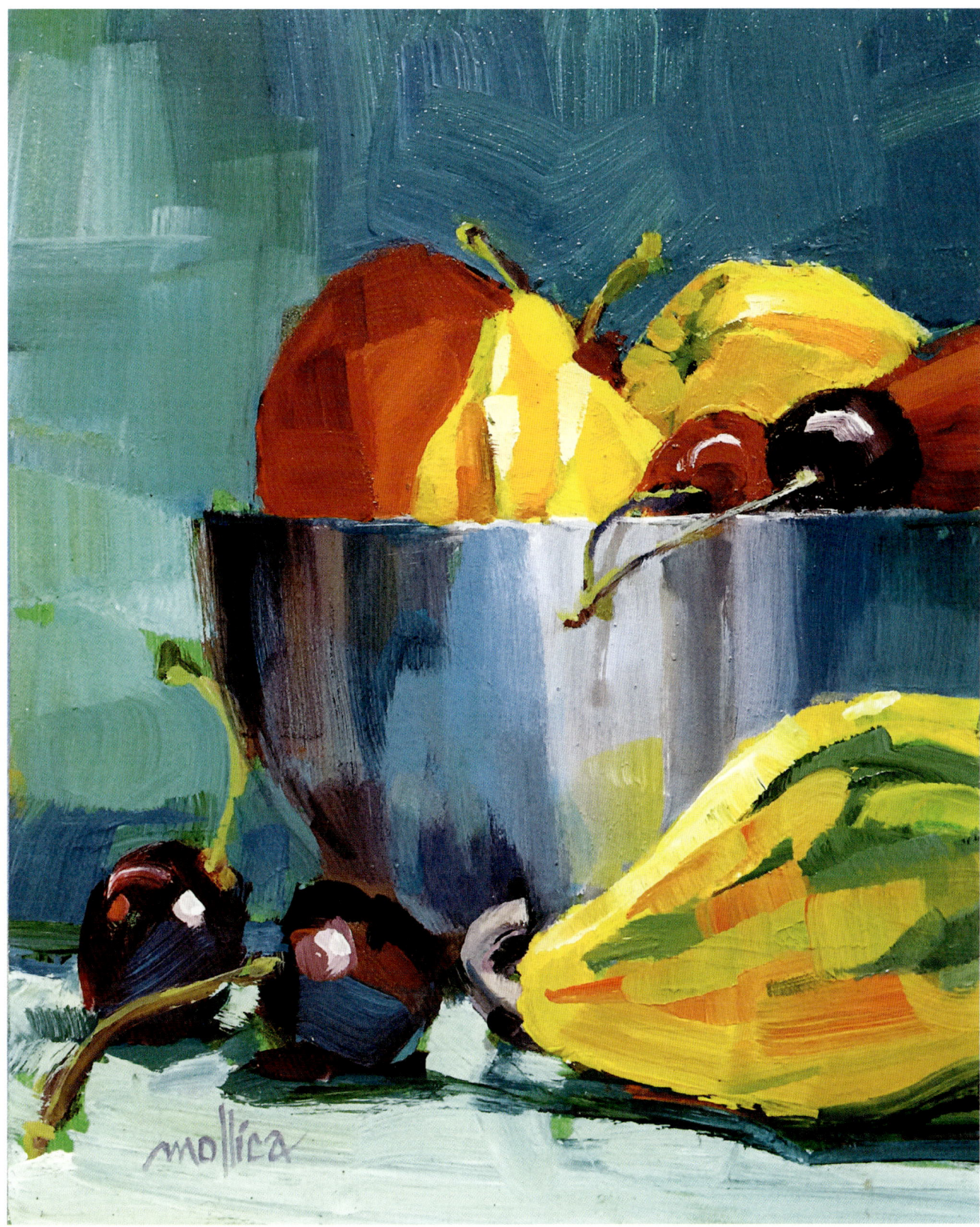

6 **MAKE ADJUSTMENTS AND ADD FINAL DETAILS**
Step back and analyze what needs to be adjusted. If the colors in the background and the metal bowl compete too much with the colors of the fruits, tone down the background, foreground and bowl. Simplify any busy patterns, such as in the foreground gourd. Emphasize the highlights on the pieces of fruit to give them a bit more drama.

GOOD GOURD!
Acrylic on panel
10" × 8" (25cm × 20cm)
Collection of Nancy Smith

Party of Three

Follow the steps to paint this still life in a festive holiday color palette of reds and blue-greens.

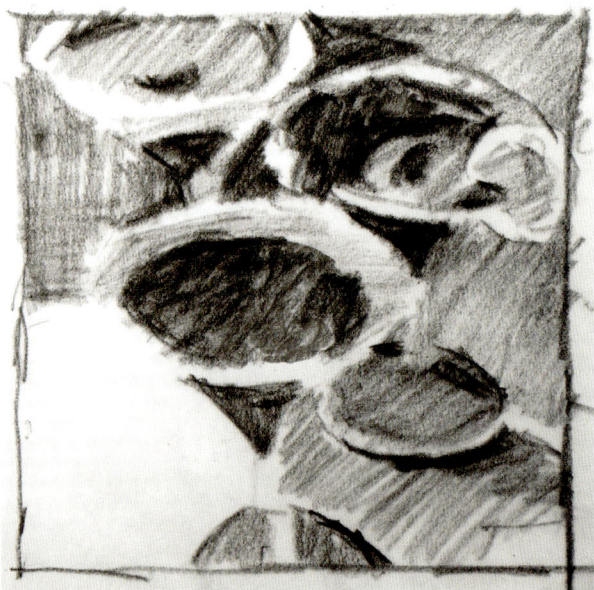

VALUE SKETCH

MATERIALS

Surface
14" × 14" (36cm × 36cm) canvas board

Pigments
Alizarin Crimson, Burnt Sienna, Burnt Umber, Cadmium Orange, Cadmium Lemon Yellow, Cadmium Red Light, Cadmium Yellow Light, Cadmium Yellow Medium, Carbon Black, Green Gold, Manganese Blue, Medium Magenta, Neutral Gray N6, Quinacridone Magenta, Permanent Green, Sap Green, Teal, Titan Buff, Ultramarine Blue, Yellow Ochre

Brushes
¼"–2" (6mm-51mm) flats or filberts

Other
eraser, black vine charcoal

1 TONE THE CANVAS AND SKETCH THE COMPOSITION

Use a 2-inch (51mm) flat to tone the canvas with a bright red color, such as Cadmium Red Light. This will be the dominant color in the painting.

Sketch a faint charcoal grid on the canvas in order to judge your proportions accurately and to ensure that all of the elements will be positioned approximately where you want them. Then sketch in the main shapes of the composition.

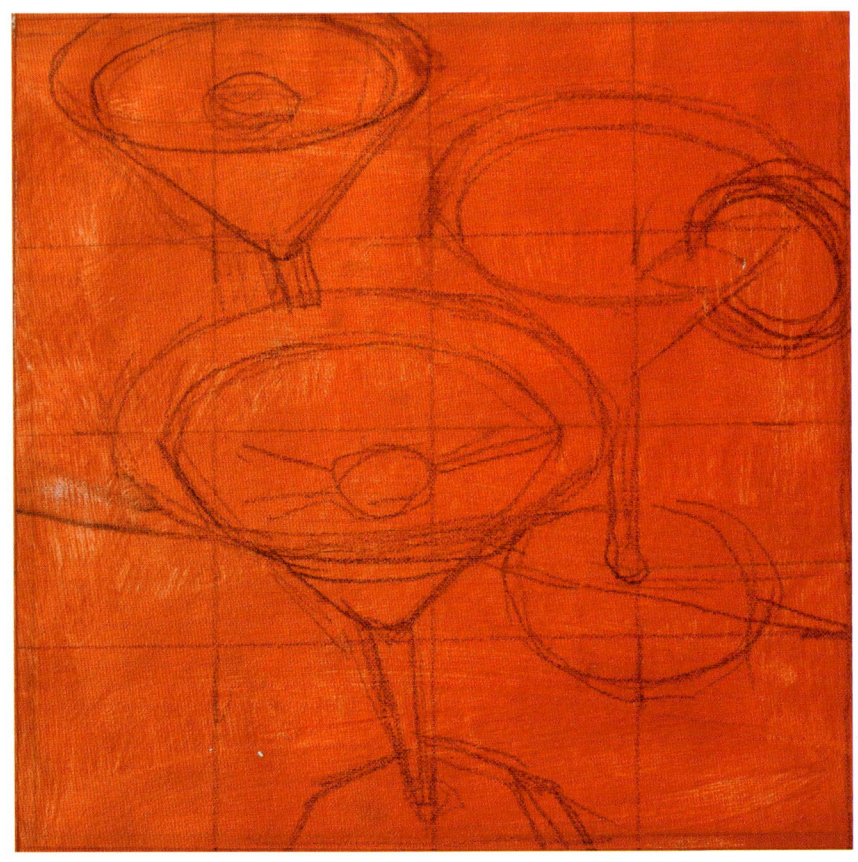

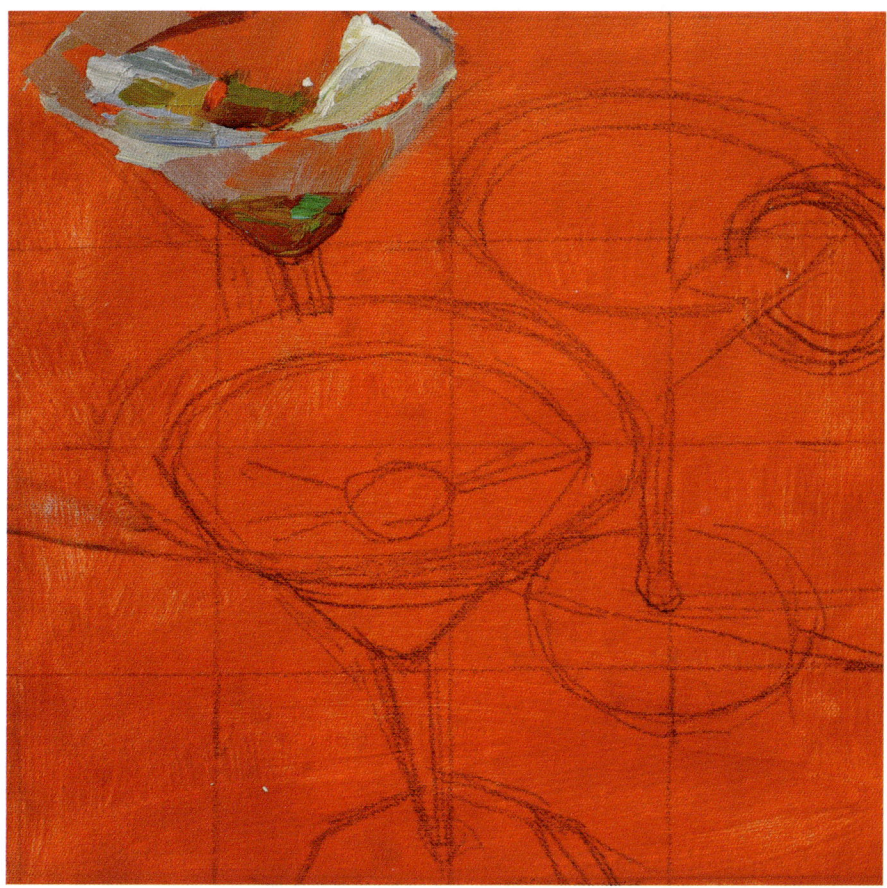

2 PAINT THE DISTANT GLASS

Mix some grayed-down colors with with combinations of Ultramarine Blue, Alizarin Crimson, Yellow Ochre and Titanium White to depict the reflective surface of the most distant glass. If you are not used to mixing grays from primaries, you can start with Neutral Gray N6, which can also be mixed using Carbon Black and Titanium White, and add warm or cool hues to get a variety of neutral colors.

Paint the olive and the other contents of the glass with a ½-inch flat. Use Green Gold and Alizarin Crimson for the olive. Use Cadmium Red Light for the pimento, and a variety of warm and cool grays for the surrounding colors.

3 PAINT THE MIDDLE GLASS

Paint the middle glass with some grayed-down neutrals and a ¼-inch (6mm) flat. Use these same colors to create the flesh of the lemon, and Cadmium Yellow Medium to create the rind. Fill the inside of the glass with Quinacridone Magenta, Cadmium Red Light and Titanium White. Create the stem with Manganese Blue, Teal and Neutral Gray N6.

If you realize at this stage that your shapes are not perfectly drawn, that's OK. The ovals on my glasses were not perfect, but I decided to keep them that way to contribute to the whimsical quality of the subject matter.

Sometimes it is hard to see the forest for the trees, so to speak, when painting a red subject on a red background because it's hard to judge the color values and contrasts. As some of the non-red shapes get filled in later, it will become easier for you to get a sense of the composition and color relationships.

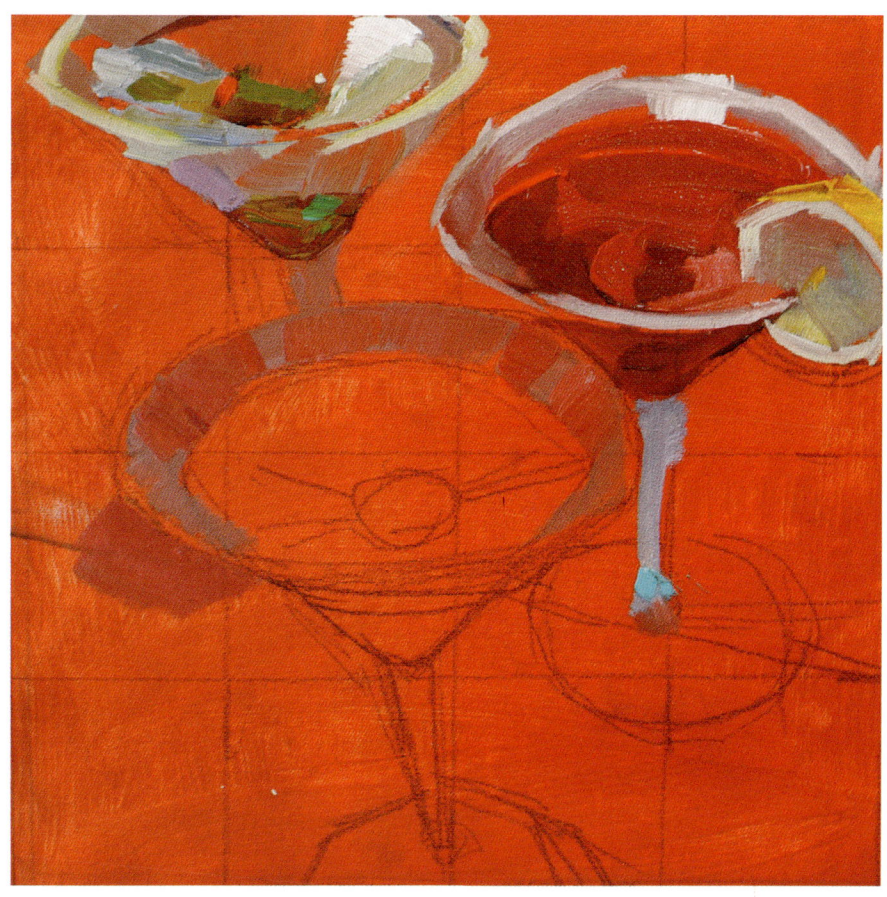

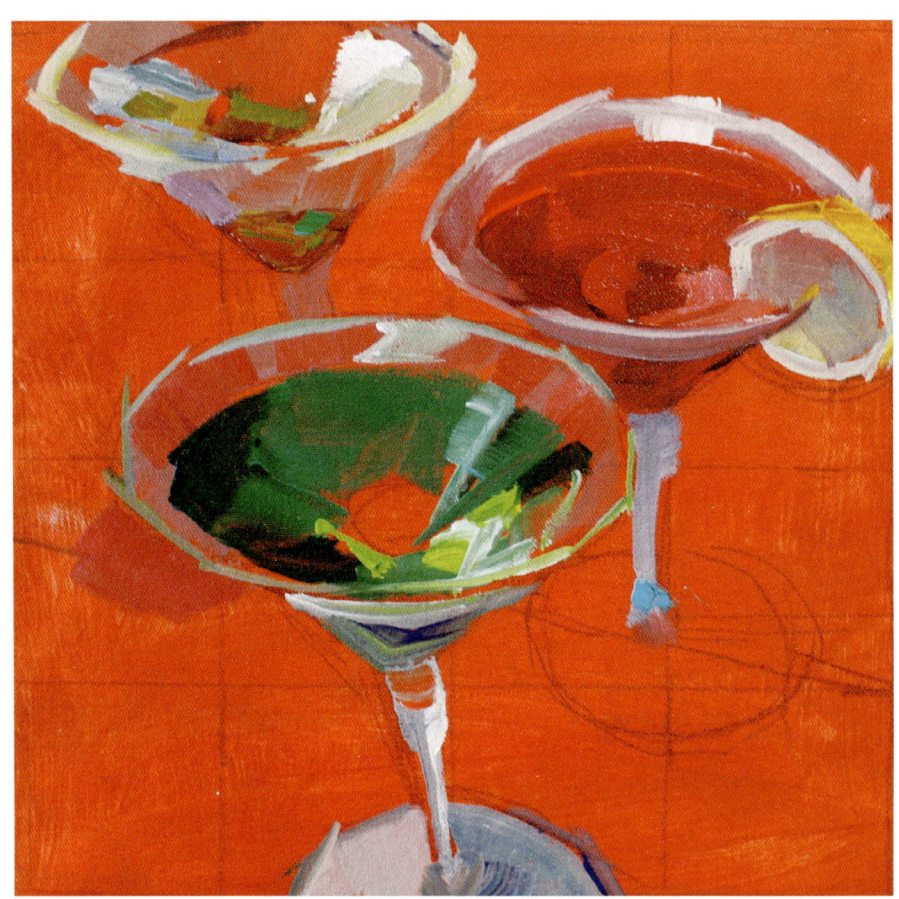

4 PAINT THE CLOSEST GLASS

Use a 1-inch (25mm) flat to paint the closest drink with green hues created by mixing Ultramarine Blue, Cadmium Lemon Yellow, Manganese Blue and Titanium White. The painting will start to come together more, and the composition will make more sense as you finish this step.

5 ADD THE LIGHT VALUES

Create a gray-white mixture with Ultramarine Blue, Quinacridone Magenta, Cadmium Lemon Yellow and Titanium White. Keep the mixture on the violet side. Add Manganese Blue and Titanium White to this mixture to create the blue-gray under the middle glass. Use this mixture to add light values into the foreground with 1-inch (25mm) and 2-inch (51mm) flats. Adding these light values will help to ground the subject and cover up some of the distracting bright red. With the light values in the foreground, it becomes easier to judge how the colors relate to each other.

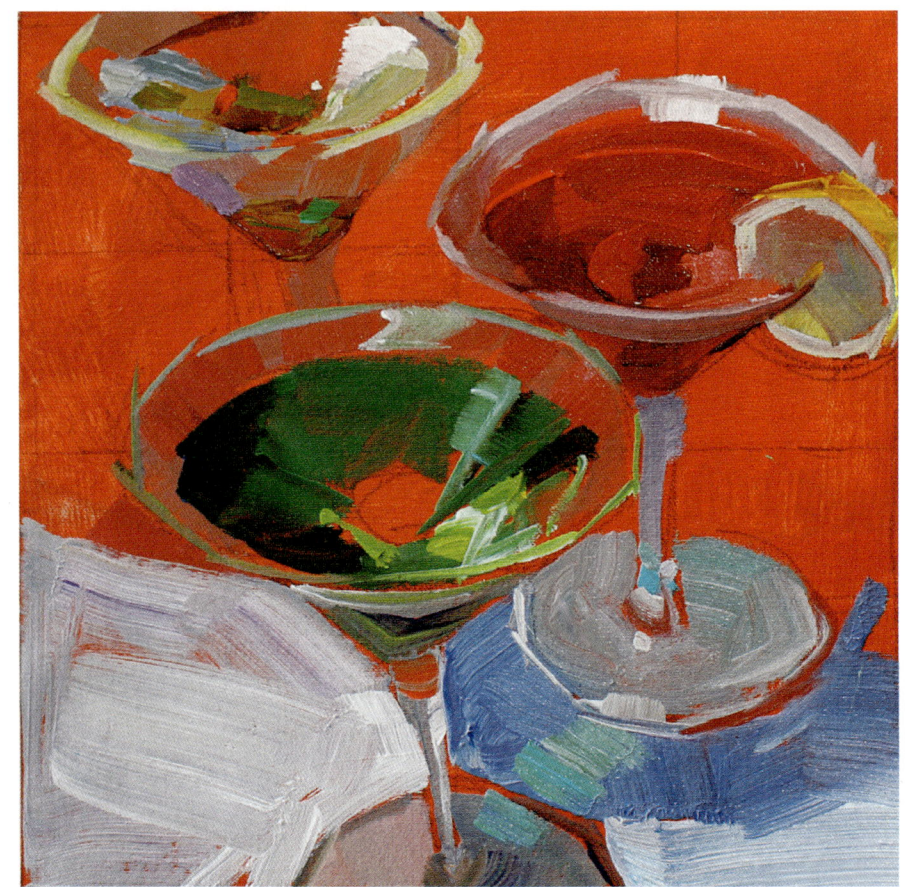

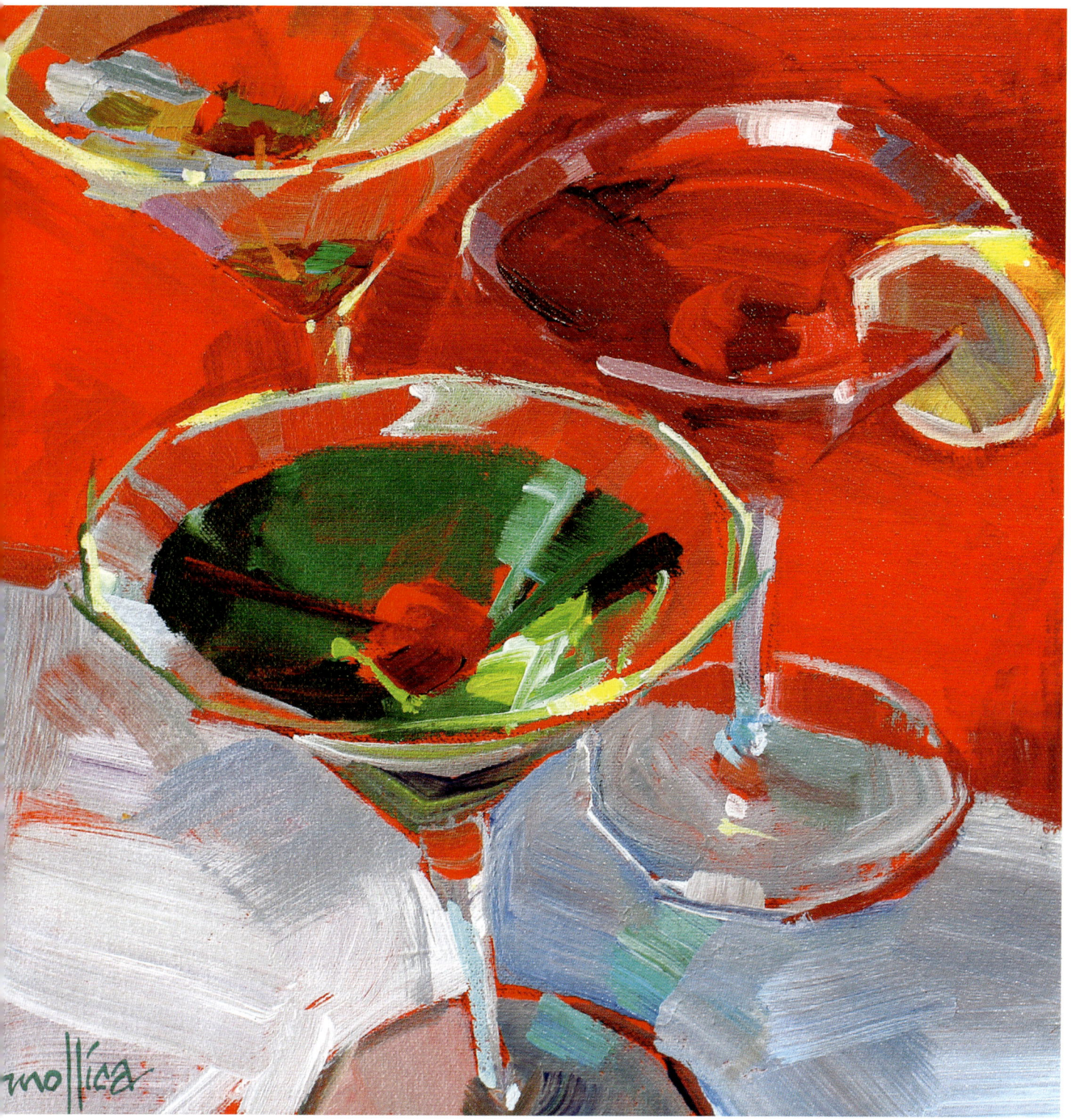

mollica

6 MAKE ADJUSTMENTS AND ADD FINAL DETAILS

Use a 2-inch (51mm) flat with Cadmium Red Light mixed with a bit of Alizarin Crimson to darken the toned background in a few places. Add some zing by painting small, colorful highlights on the crisp reflective planes of glasses with a ¼-inch (6mm) flat. Create warm light colors by mixing Titanium White and Cadmium Yellow Medium. Keep the strokes that go around the rim delicate and minimal.

PARTY OF THREE
Acrylic on canvas
14" × 14" (36cm × 36cm)
Private collection

Stacked

Follow the steps to paint colorful cups against a neutral background.

MATERIALS

Surface
8" × 8" (20cm × 20cm) panel

Pigments
Alizarin Crimson, Burnt Sienna, Burnt Umber, Cadmium Orange, Cadmium Lemon Yellow, Cadmium Red Light, Cadmium Yellow Light, Cadmium Yellow Medium, Carbon Black, Green Gold, Manganese Blue, Medium Magenta, Neutral Gray N6, Quinacridone Magenta, Permanent Green, Sap Green, Teal, Titan Buff, Ultramarine Blue, Yellow Ochre

Brushes
¼"-2" (6mm-51mm) flats or filberts, 1/16" (2mm) script brush

Other
eraser, black vine charcoal

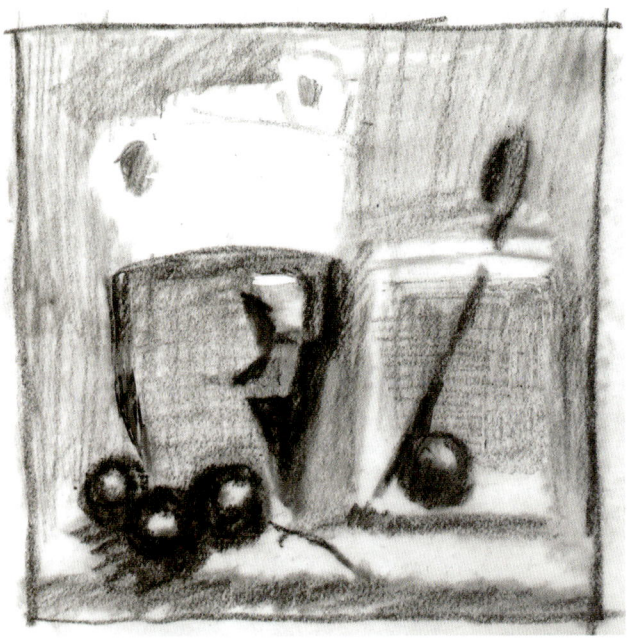

VALUE SKETCH

1 TONE THE PANEL AND SKETCH THE COMPOSITION

Start by toning the panel with Burnt Umber using a 2-inch (51mm) flat. The earth tone will provide a nice neutral underlying foundation color for the multihued cups and transparent glass that will come later.

Sketch your composition on the panel with vine charcoal. It can be easily erased if your proportions need to be adjusted.

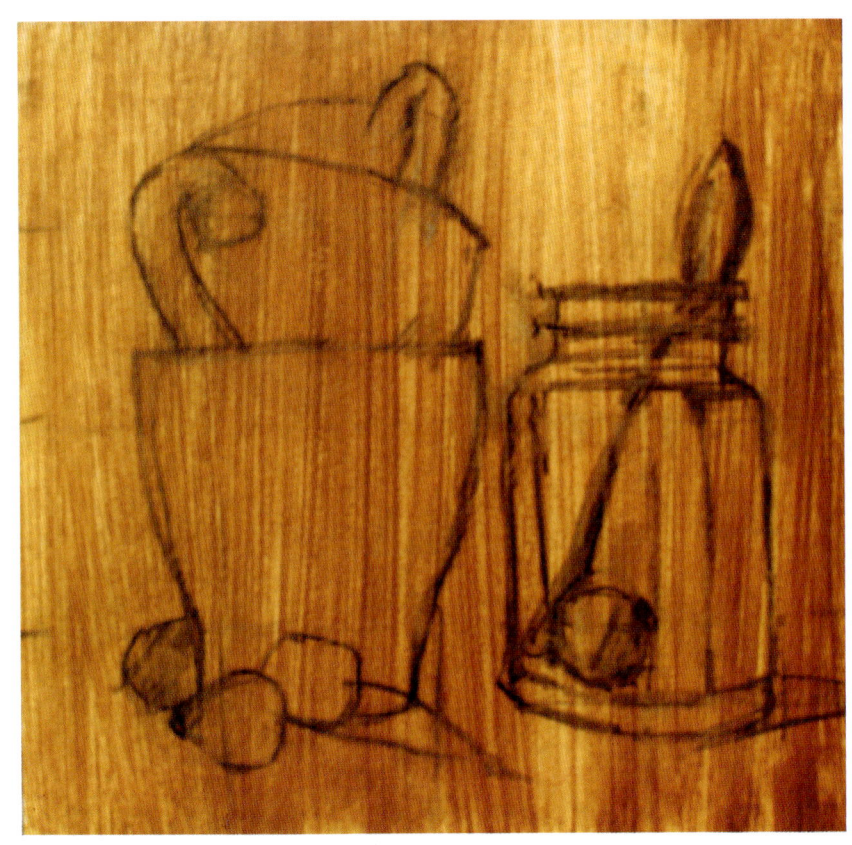

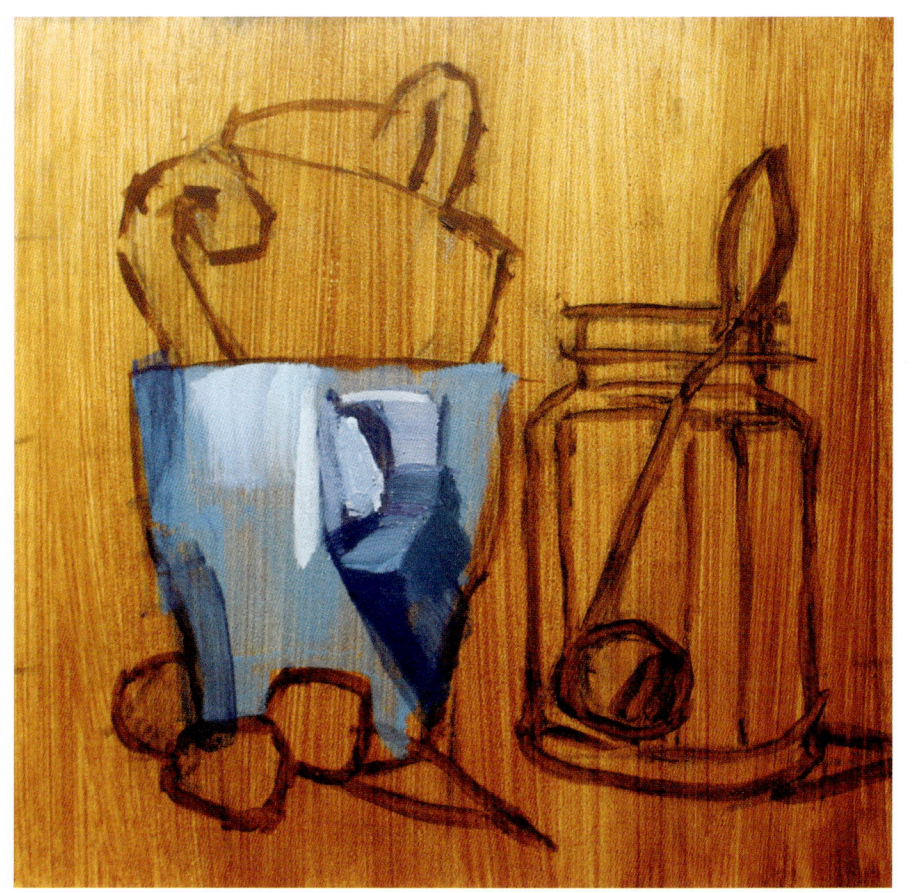

2 PAINT THE BOTTOM CUP
Once you are satisfied with your composition, use a 1-inch (25mm) flat to paint the bottom cup a light blue with Manganese Blue, Ultramarine Blue and Titanium White. Make sure to get a sense of the light-struck areas and planes versus the areas in shadow.

3 BLOCK IN COLORS FOR THE OTHER CUPS
Block in the colors on the other two cups using a 1-inch (25mm) flat. Paint the middle cup an ivory color with a mixture of Cadmium Orange, Manganese Blue and Titanium White. Paint the top cup a mixture of Cadmium Yellow Light, Burnt Umber, and Titanium White. Use Teal for the shadow area. Blocking in the remaining cups will help you judge the accuracy of your color relationships.

At this early stage of the painting, the goal is to simply get the main colors laid in. Don't worry about whether they are exactly right at this point.

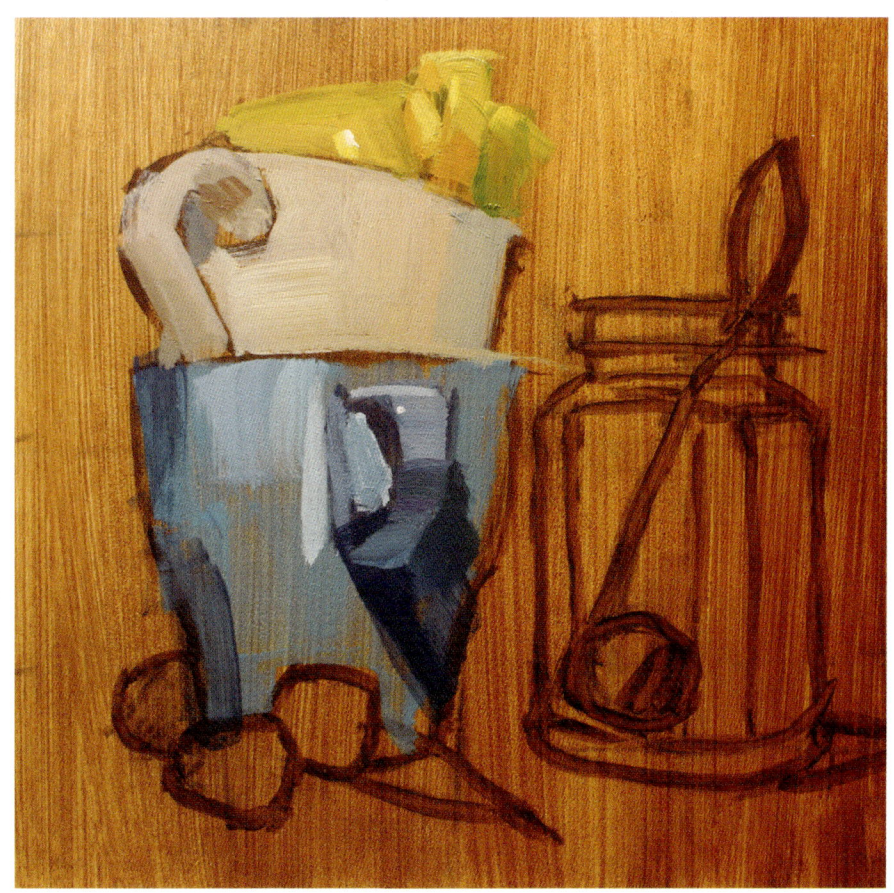

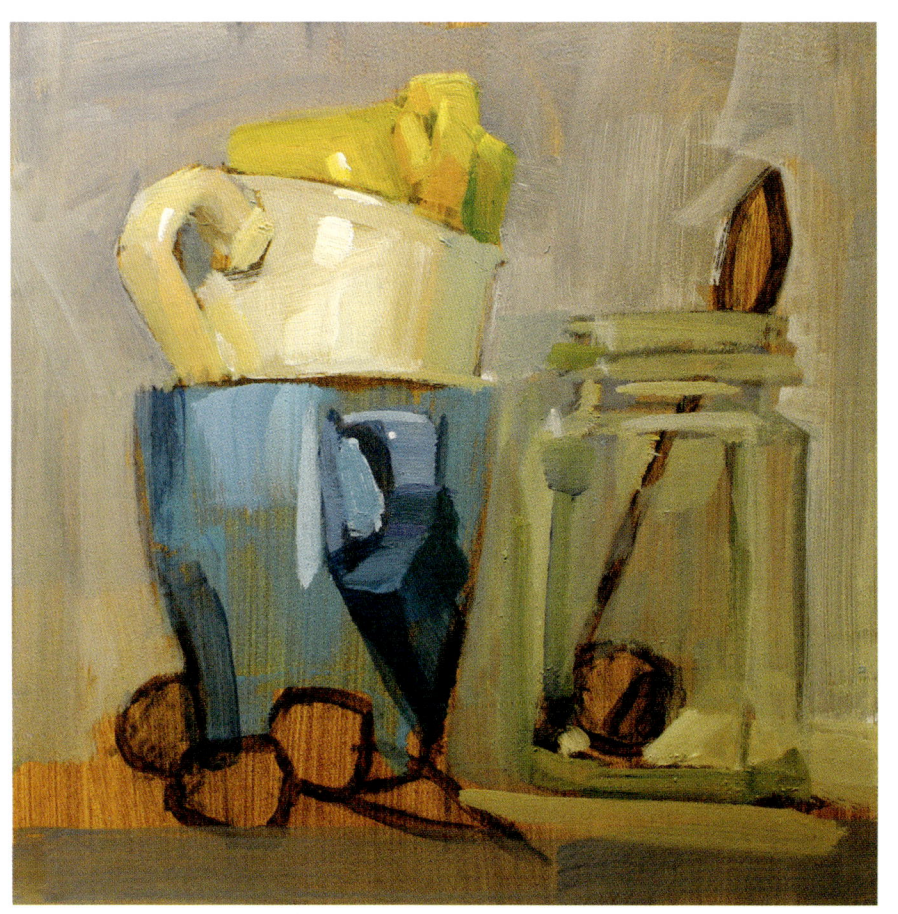

4 FILL IN THE BACKGROUND AND FOREGROUND, START THE GLASS JAR

Fill in the background and foreground with a neutralized gray using a mixture of Ultramarine Blue, Burnt Umber and Titanium White. This is necessary in order to start depicting the glass jar, which is transparent.

Once you have the foreground and background in place, start painting the subtle planes and angles of the glass jar with slightly darker and lighter mixtures of the same colors, but more or less white. Add a touch of Manganese Blue and Yellow Ochre to slightly emphasize the planes.

5 PAINT THE CHERRIES, SPOON AND REFLECTIONS

Start building up the spoon with a dark mixture of Burnt Umber, Manganese Blue and Titanium White using a ½-inch (13mm) brush. Begin painting the cherries using Alizarin Crimson, Yellow Ochre, Cadmium Red Light and Titanium White. This will add a much needed dark value as well as some rounder shapes to help balance the angular shapes of the cups and jar.

With a ¼-inch (6mm) flat and Teal plus a touch of Burnt Umber, paint some small dashes of blue into the bottom plane of the jar to suggest reflections from the blue cup.

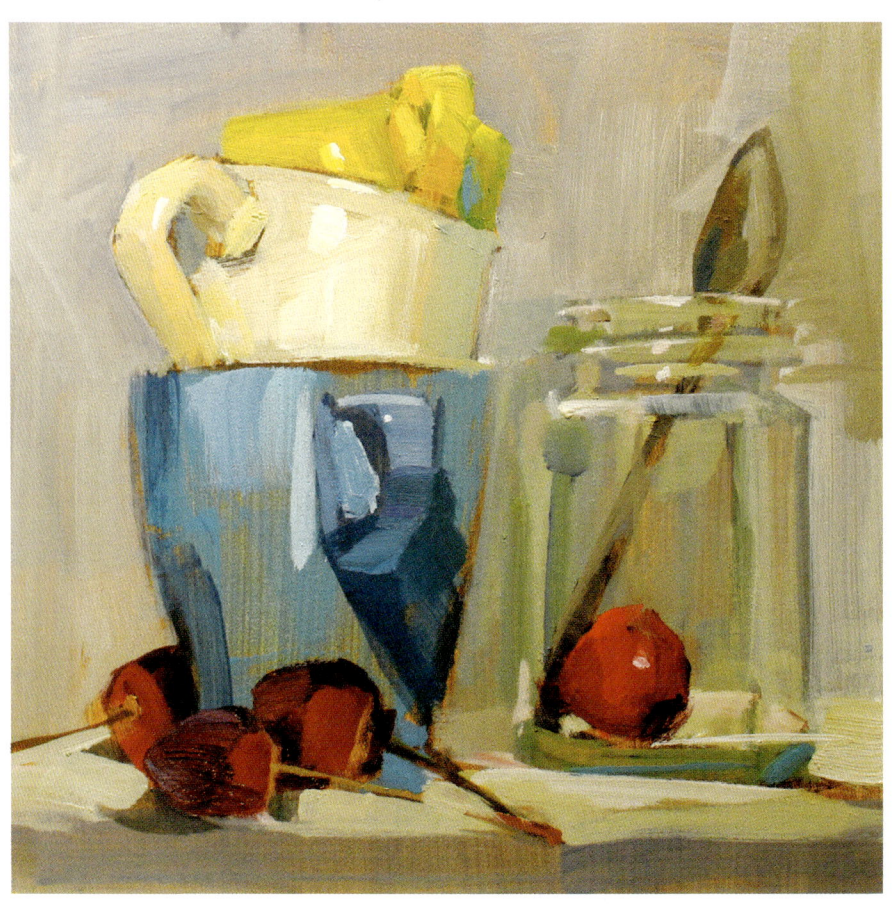

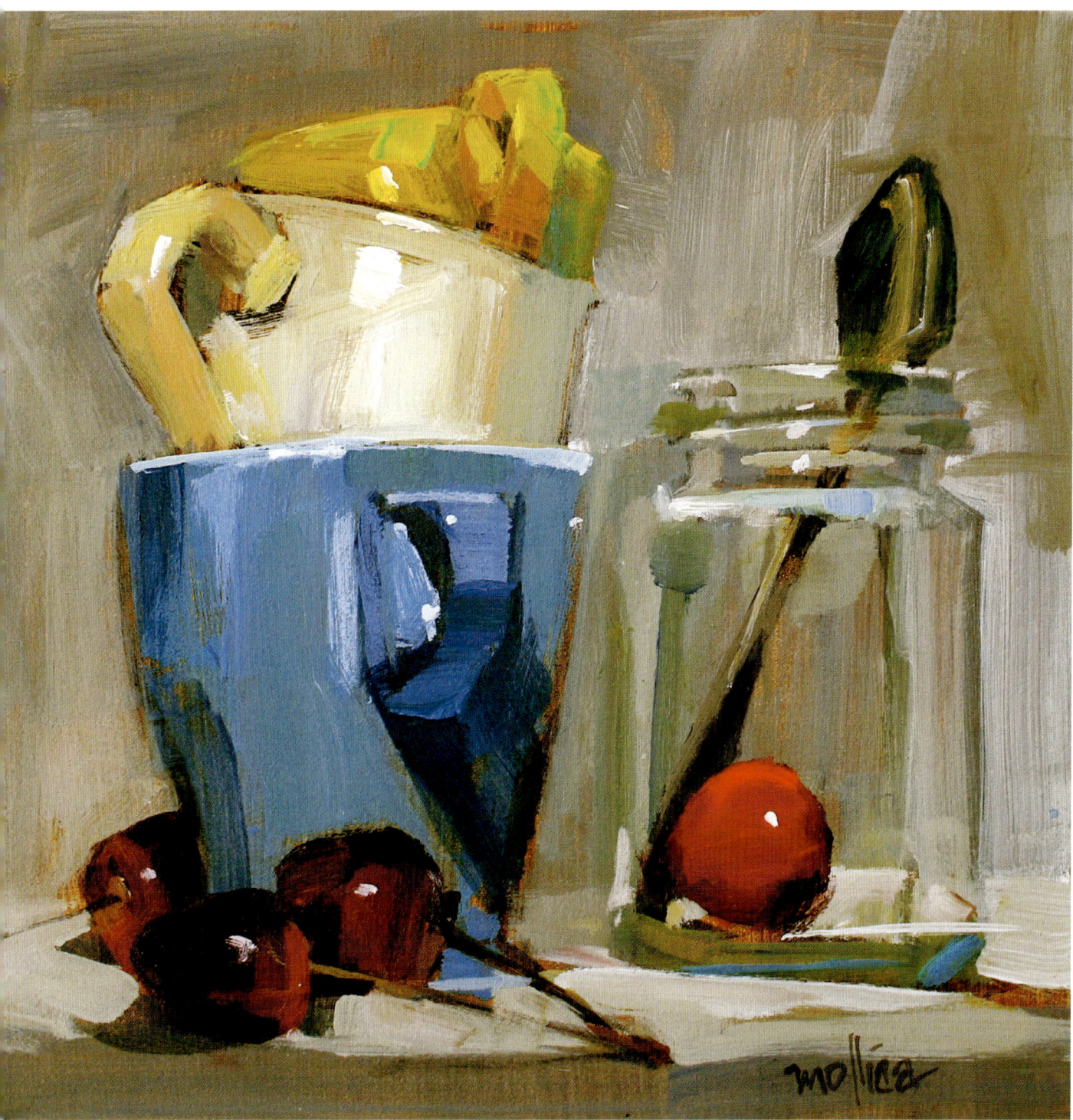

6 CONTINUE BUILDING REFLECTIONS, ADD HIGHLIGHTS AND FINAL DETAILS

Continue building up the reflections. With a script brush and Titanium White, add small highlights to the jar, the blue cup and the cherries to give their reflective areas a shimmer and snap. It's good practice to save the highlights for last and to only paint the most important ones. Too many highlights will make a painting look busy and detract rather than add to a bold outcome.

STACKED
Acrylic on panel
8" × 8" (20cm × 20cm)
Private collection

Grand Canal

I often work from black-and-white images and translate them into the colors of my choice. Follow the steps to paint this scene of the Grand Canal in Venice.

MATERIALS

Surface
16" × 12" (41cm × 30cm) panel

Pigments
Alizarin Crimson, Burnt Sienna, Burnt Umber, Cadmium Orange, Cadmium Lemon Yellow, Cadmium Red Light, Cadmium Yellow Light, Cadmium Yellow Medium, Carbon Black, Green Gold, Manganese Blue, Medium Magenta, Neutral Gray N6, Quinacridone Magenta, Permanent Green, Sap Green, Teal, Titan Buff, Ultramarine Blue, Yellow Ochre

Brushes
¼"–2" (6mm-51mm) flats or filberts

Other
eraser, black vine charcoal

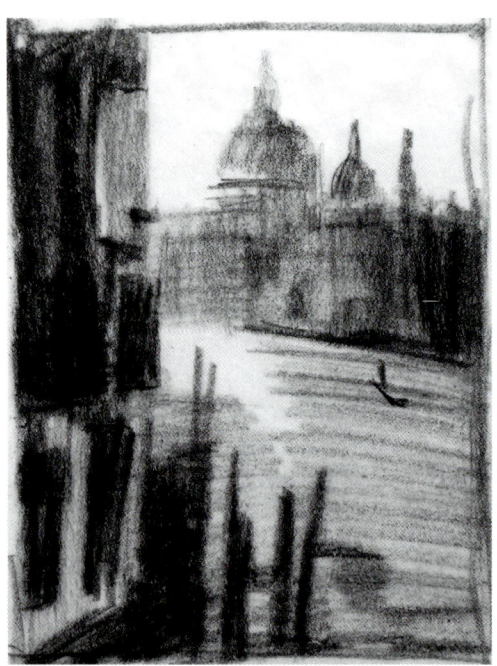

VALUE SKETCH

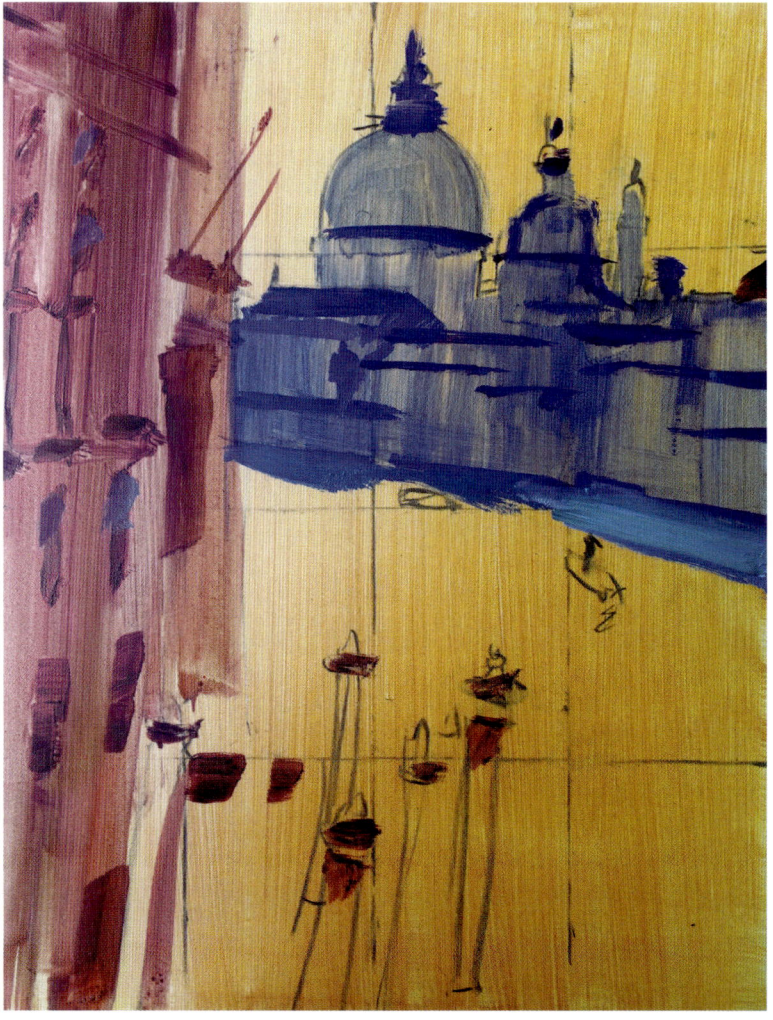

1 TONE THE PANEL AND BLOCK IN THE COMPOSITION

Tone the panel with a light wash of Burnt Sienna using a 2-inch (51mm) flat. Since the water will be completed in cool tones, a warm tone in the background will make a nice base color.

Draw a light grid on the panel with vine charcoal to ensure that your composition proportions will be fairly accurate. Then sketch in the large shapes with vine charcoal.

Begin painting in some rough detail of the architecture with a ½-inch (13mm) flat. Use Alizarin Crimson for the closer building on the left, and Ultramarine Blue, Manganese Blue and Titanium White for the more distant building on the right.

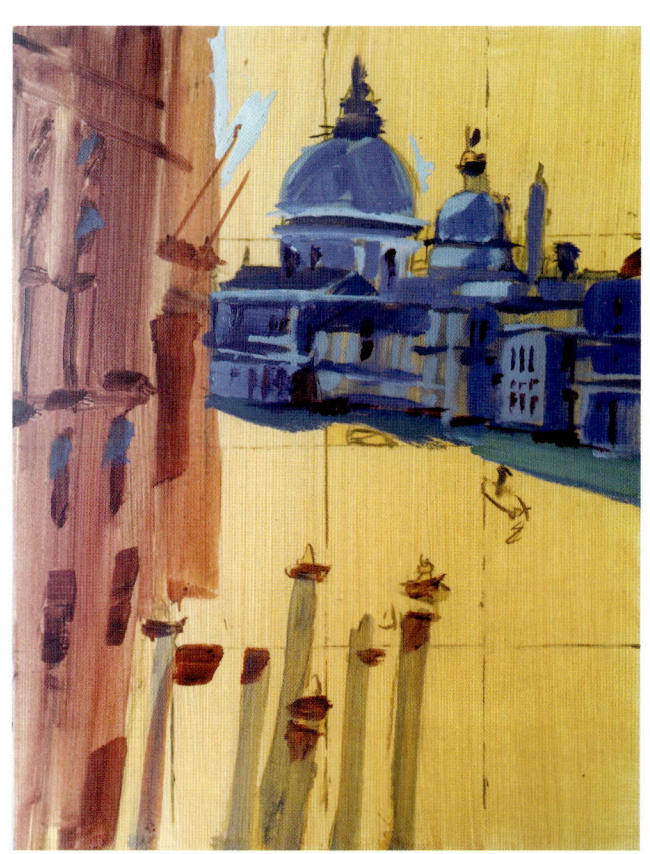

2 DEVELOP THE COLORS AND ARCHITECTURAL DETAILS

Continue developing the colors of the buildings. Paint in more details such as windows and doors using Carbon Black or Alizarin Crimson and a ½-inch (13mm) flat.

It's OK to overstate the colors at this stage because they can always be toned down later. It's also acceptable to put in more details than needed, just so you have some points of reference in the elaborate building.

3 INDICATE THE WATER AND DEVELOP THE RED BUILDING

Indicate the water by laying in a light wash of light blue with Manganese Blue and white. Add Yellow Ochre and Titanium White to the mixture for highlights. Use a 1-inch (25mm) flat and keep the shapes light and loose. This should start to give you a sense of the color relationships in the painting. The warm tones that peek through the light wash will help to neutralize the cool colors a bit.

Further develop the building on the left with warm reds using Alizarin Crimson, Cadmium Red Light a ½-inch (13mm) flat. These colors were chosen so that the foreground structure will appear to advance toward the viewer.

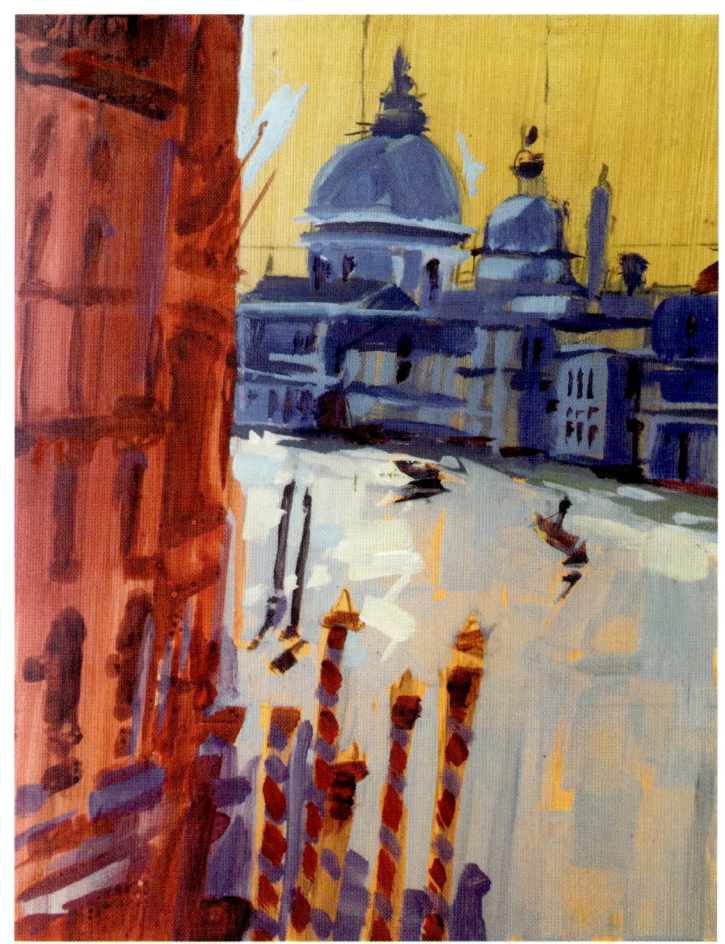

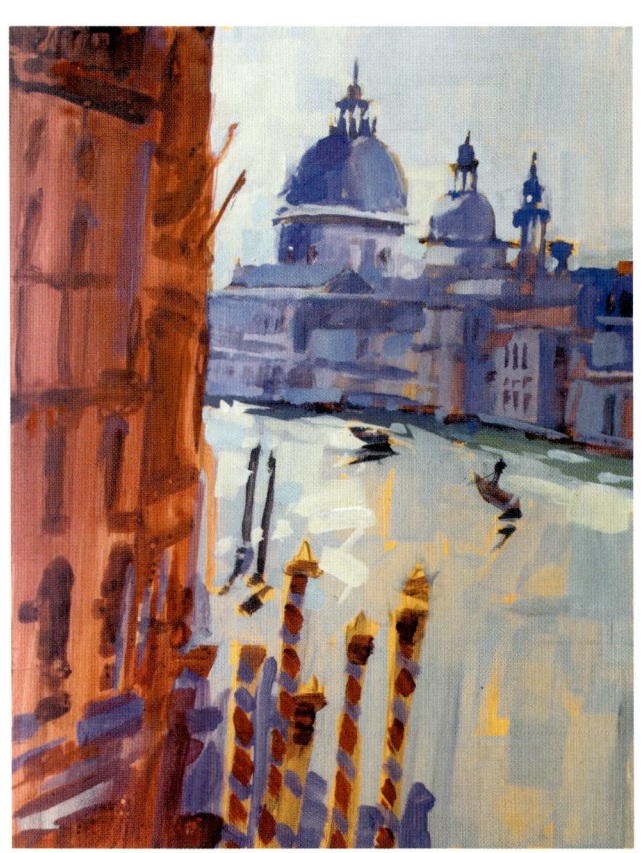

4 PAINT THE SKY AND UNIFY THE BACKGROUND AND FOREGROUND BUILDINGS

Paint in the sky with light value blue-gray hues using a 1-inch (25mm) flat and Manganese Blue plus Burnt Umber, Yellow Ochre and Titanium White. This is the last element needed to be able to accurately judge the color relationships in the painting.

Add in some light purple tones with a ½-inch (13mm) flat to help unify the colors of the foreground and background buildings.

Evaluate your progress. You may find that the background building needs to be pushed back a bit more, and that some of the detail can be eliminated.

5 DEVELOP THE WATER AND GONDOLIER

Develop the water by covering some of the thinner layers using Manganese Blue, Burnt Umber and Titanium White. A few more dashes and dots of white with a ¼-inch (6mm) flat will lead the viewer's eye to the larger reflection and up to the large dome of the cathedral.

Develop the gondolier with a dark value mixture of Burnt Umber, Manganese Blue and Titanium White.

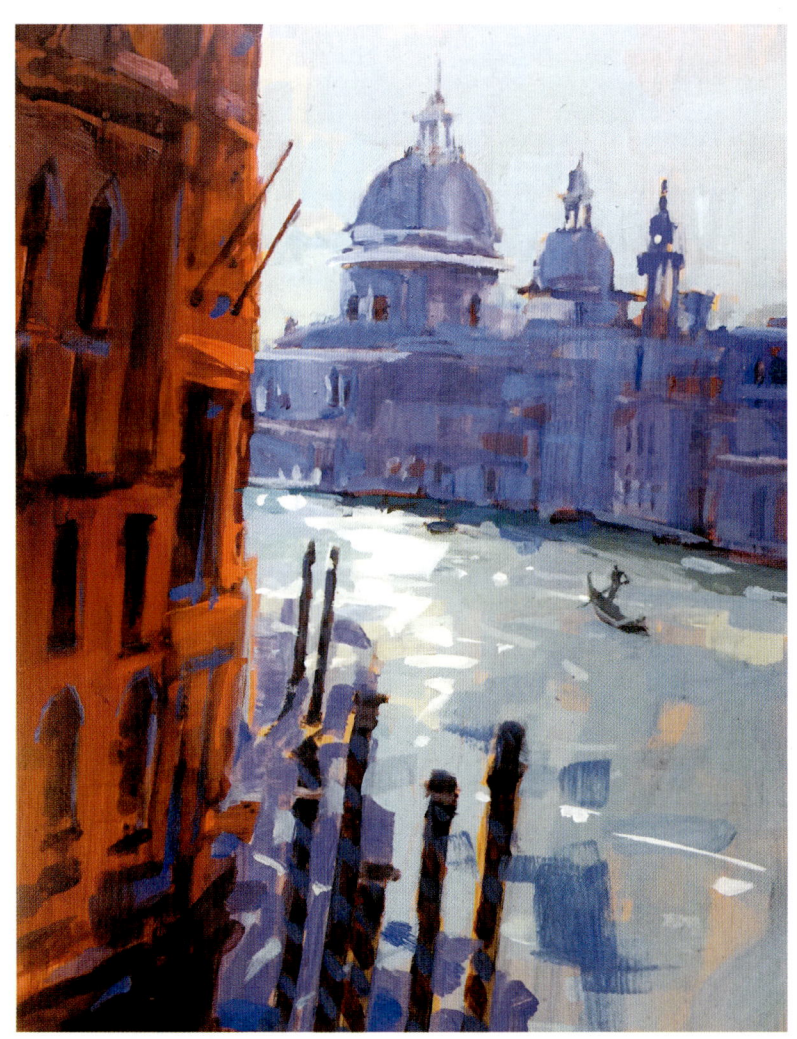

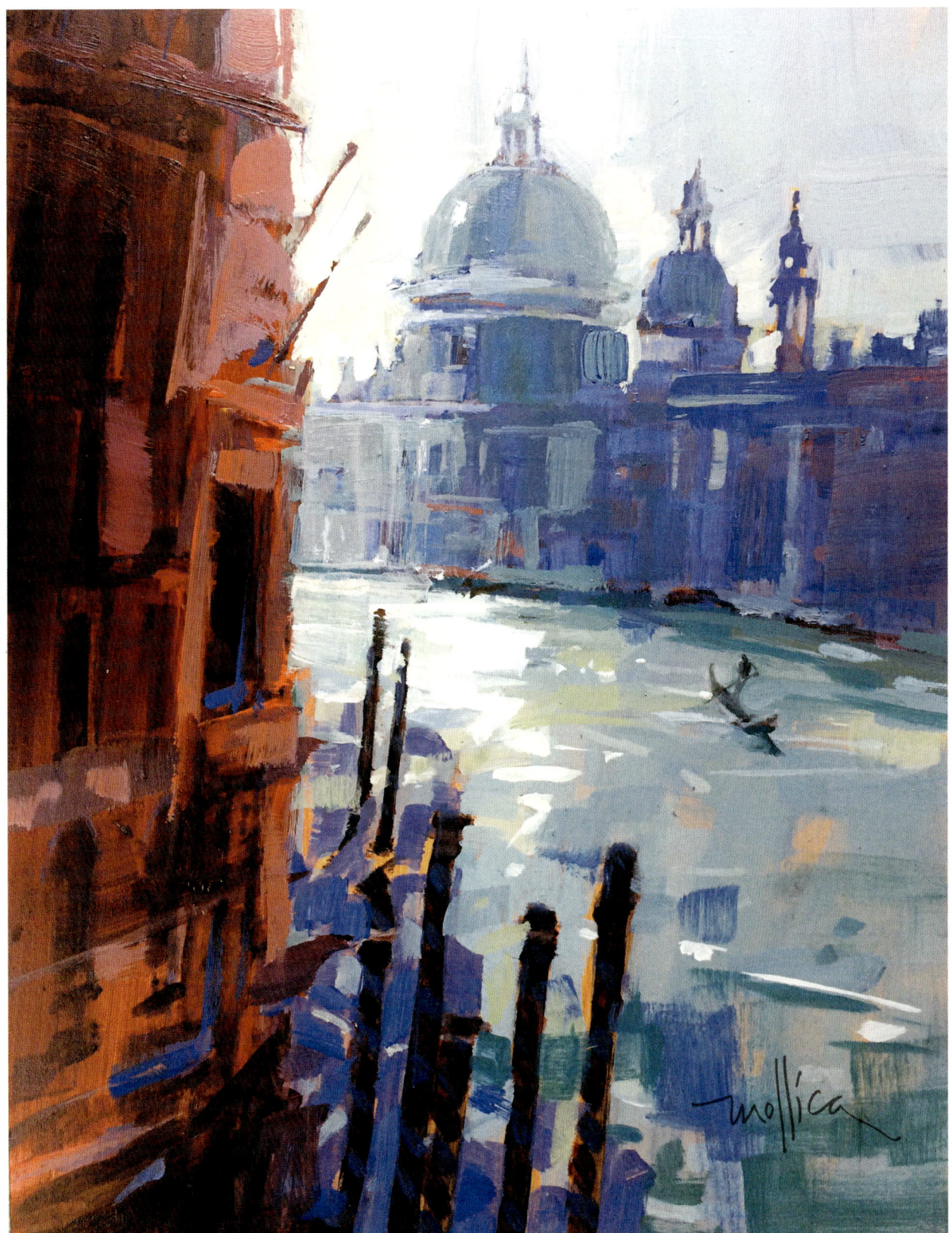

6 FINISH THE SKY AND ADD FINAL DETAILS

Paint a light value warm mixture into the sky using Yellow Ochre and Titanium White plus a touch of Neutral Gray N6. This will give it a late-afternoon feel. Add some warm hues to the building on the right to create the perception that it is closer to the viewer. Add lighter, cooler colors to the building on the left, pushing it back in the distance. Then paint some Teal and purple patches in the water and the blue building to unify both parts of the painting. Small touches of purple in the red building will also help unify it with the background architecture.

GRAND CANAL
Acrylic on panel
16" × 12" (41cm × 30cm)
Private collection

Shopping Buds

The busy street scenes of New York City are some of my favorite subjects to paint. Follow the steps to paint this urban street scene.

MATERIALS

Surface
8" × 8" (20cm × 20cm) panel

Pigments
Alizarin Crimson, Burnt Sienna, Burnt Umber, Cadmium Orange, Cadmium Lemon Yellow, Cadmium Red Light, Cadmium Yellow Light, Cadmium Yellow Medium, Carbon Black, Green Gold, Manganese Blue, Medium Magenta, Neutral Gray N6, Quinacridone Magenta, Permanent Green, Sap Green, Teal, Titan Buff, Ultramarine Blue, Yellow Ochre

Brushes
½"- 2" (6mm-51mm) flats or filberts, 1/16"(2mm) script brush

Other
eraser, white vine charcoal

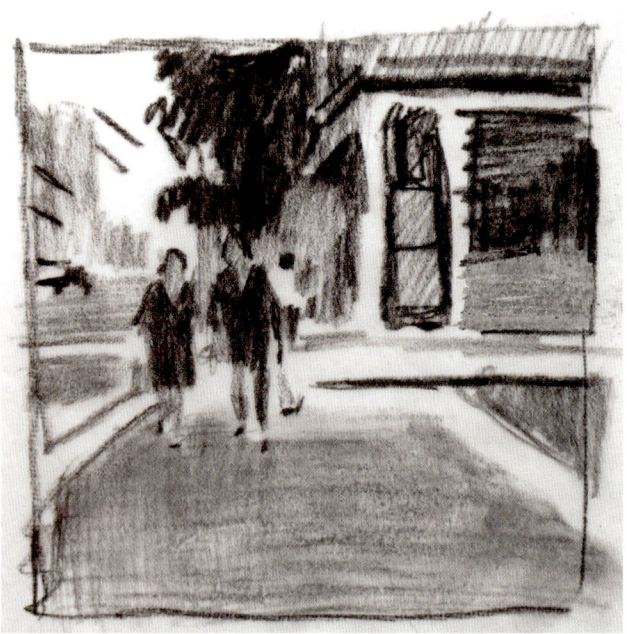

VALUE SKETCH

1 TONE THE PANEL AND SKETCH THE COMPOSITION

When painting urban scenes, working on a dark-toned surface seems to lend itself well to the dark shadows, storefronts and windows of the urban landscape.

Tone the panel with Carbon Black using a 2-inch (51mm) flat. Then sketch a light grid in white vine charcoal and rough in a sketch of your composition. Make sure that you get the positioning of the elements correct before moving on to the next step.

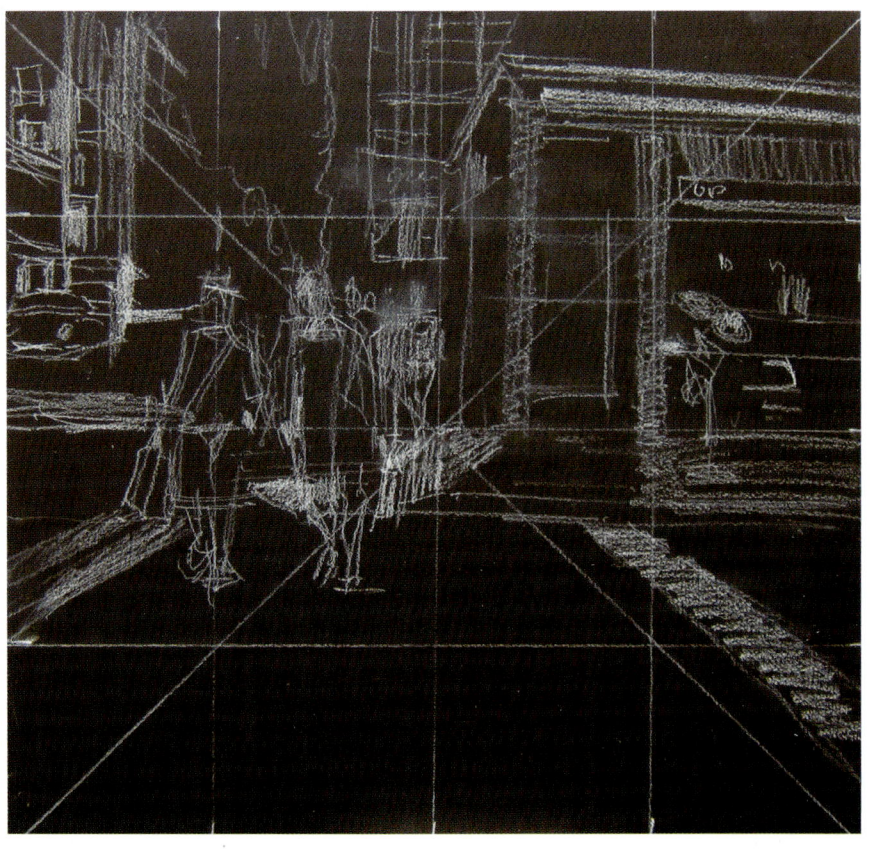

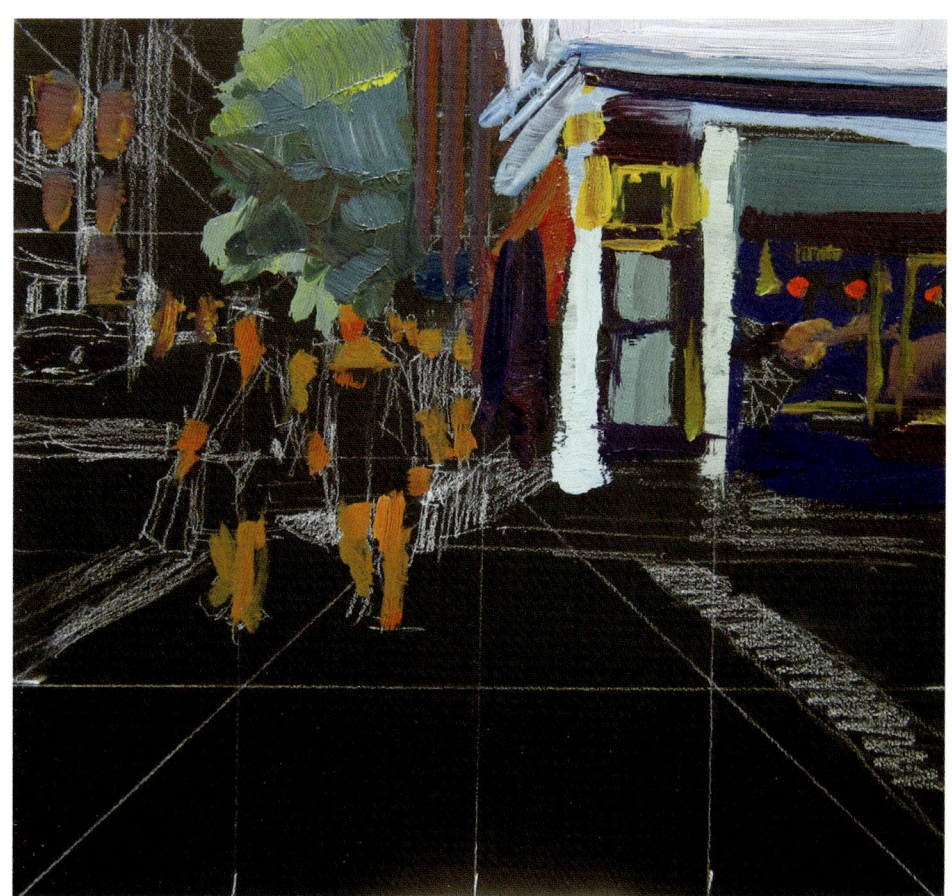

2 BLOCK IN THE MAIN ELEMENTS

Using a 1-inch (25mm) flat, roughly block in the main elements of the painting. Keep your brushwork loose and gestural. Create the greens using a mixture of Ultramarine Blue, Cadmium Lemon Yellow and Titanium White. Apply Yellow Ochre to the traffic signal with a ¼-inch (6mm) flat. Use the same brush to apply Cadmium Red Light in small dabs on the right.

3 BLOCK IN THE LIGHT VALUE BUILDINGS AND TRAFFIC STRIPES

Fill in the light value buildings of the background with a 1-inch (25mm) flat. This will immediately set off the foreground. Create the colors for the background buildings by mixing Burnt Umber, Cadmium Yellow Medium and lots of Titanium White.

Create the traffic stripes and portions of the lavender-gray buidings with Ultramarine Blue, Quinacridone Magenta, Yellow Ochre and Titanium White. Mix it in proportions that skew it cool and light in value. Use a ¼-inch (6mm) flat for this. The traffic stripes and light sidewalk will help draw the viewer's eye and emphasize the focal-point figures.

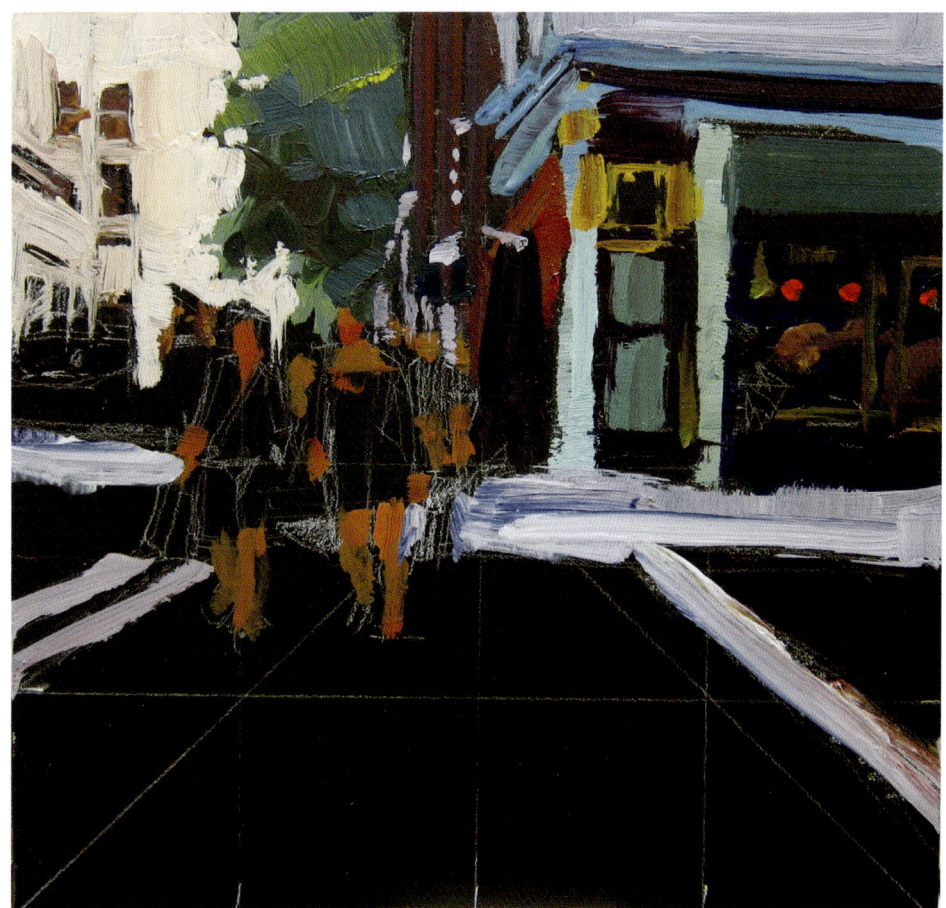

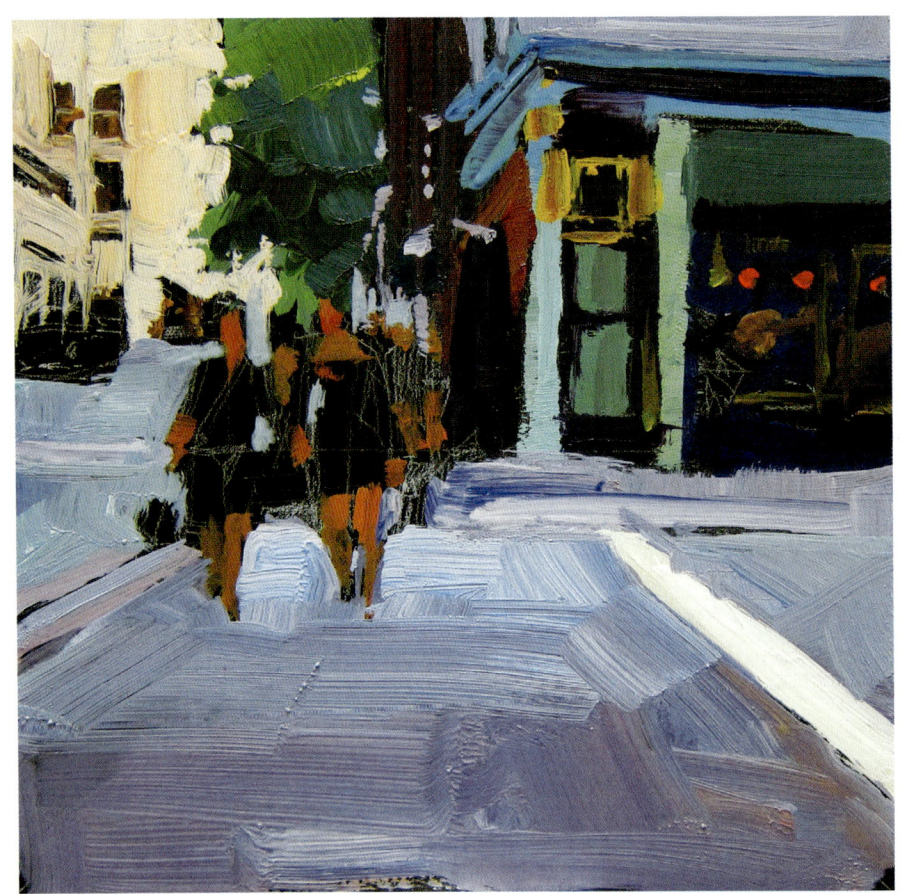

4 PAINT THE MIDDLE VALUES
Paint the middle-value road in a loose manner with a 2-inch (51mm) flat. Use a middle-value mixture of grayed violet for this. Add a bit of Manganese Blue and Titanium White near the figures with a 1-inch (25mm) flat. At this point, you can start to see how your colors are relating overall. Paint the foreground color of the road with warmer tones than the background road, which helps bring it forward.

5 DEVELOP THE FIGURES AND OTHER DETAILS
Develop the figures. Apply Manganese Blue, Ultramarine Blue and Titanium White to the figure on the left with a ¼-inch (6mm) flat. Add some structure and architectural interest to the buildings in the distance using a middle value green-gray color made from Ultramarine Blue, Yellow Ochre and Titanium White.

Indicate the curb with a ¼-inch (6mm) flat and Burnt Umber. This will help to break up and define the foreground. Add some minor details in the foreground store window and the background street activity with a mixture of Ultramarine Blue, Burnt Umber, Alizarin Crimson and Titanium White.

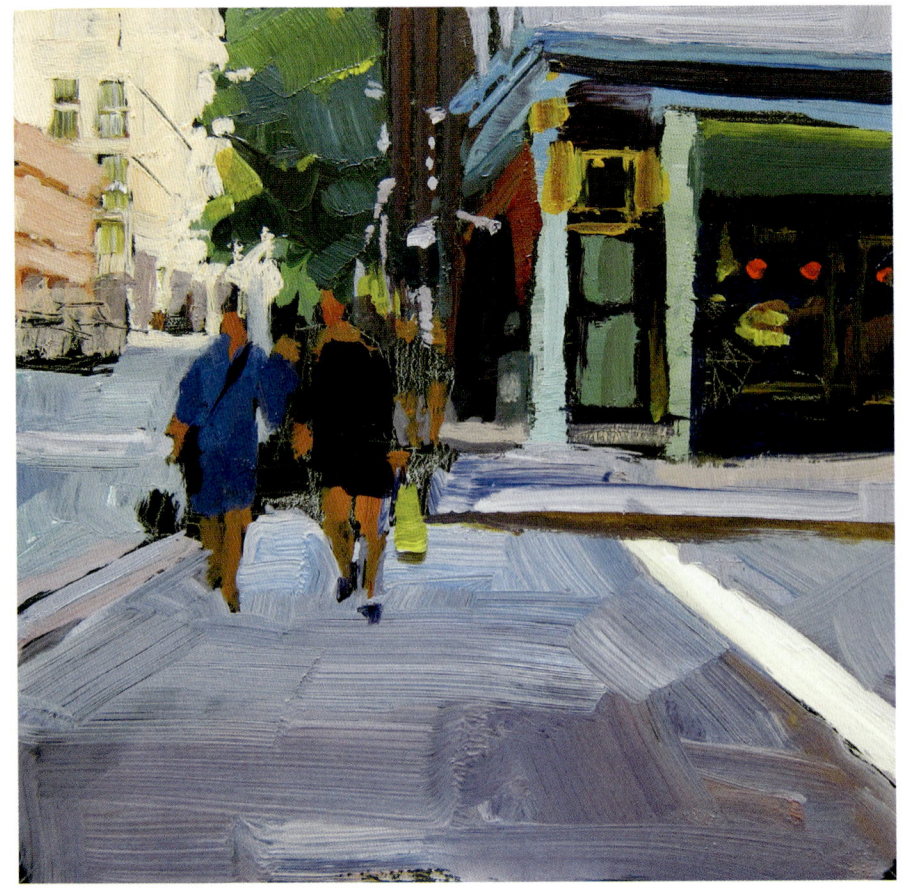

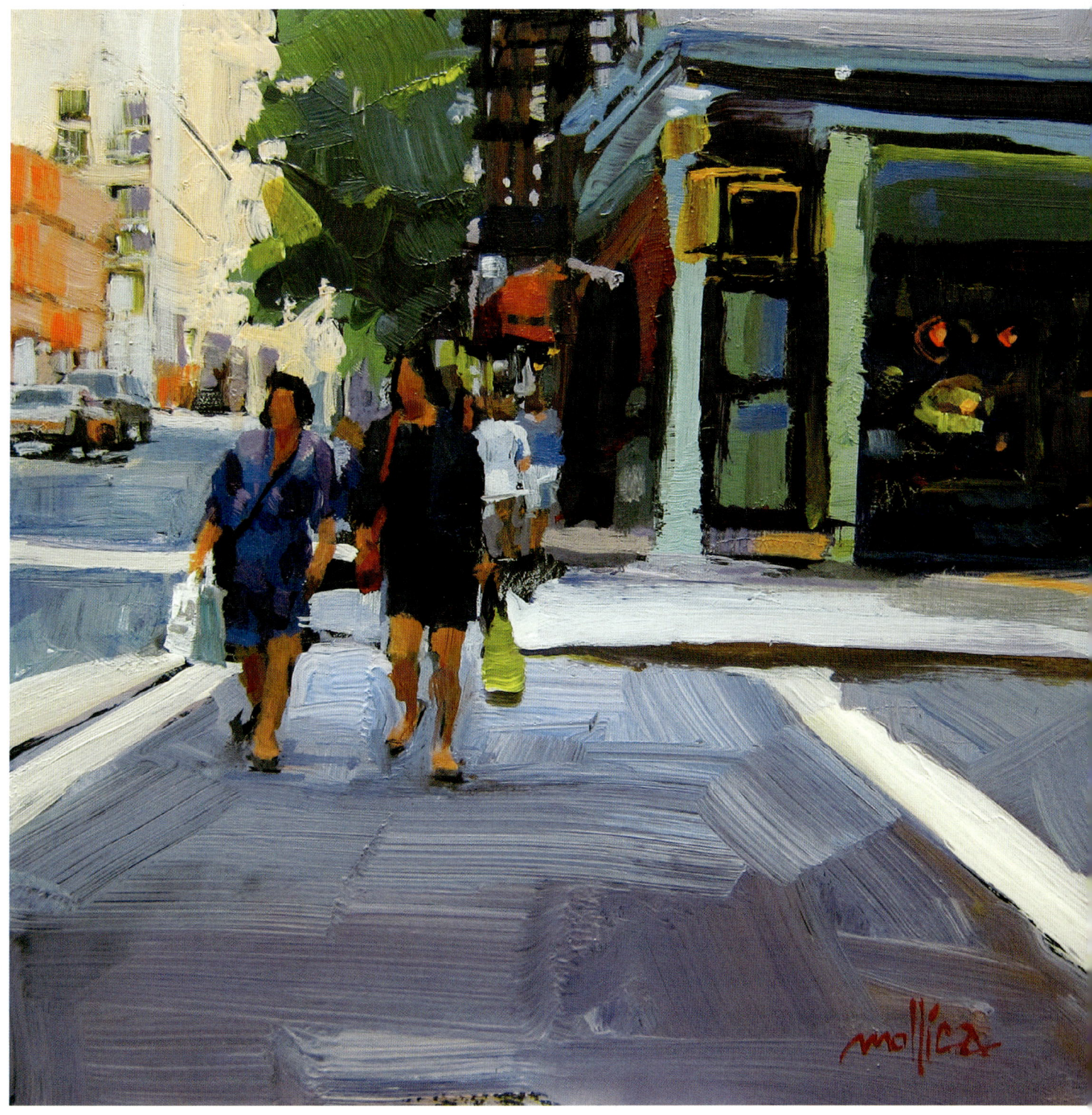

6 ADD FINAL TOUCHES

Add cars using a script brush and any blue-grays and warm grays that are already on your palette from previous mixtures. Then use the same brush and colors to develop small background figures behind the larger focal-point figures. Develop the clothing and accessories of the main subjects. Define the fire escape. Add some pops of color with a red awning mixed from Cadmium Red Light plus Titanium White. Use the same mixture to add a few dabs of bright red on the left to bring that building closer and create some unity with the warm colors on the right. This will also serve to lead the viewer's eye back into the painting.

SHOPPING BUDS
Acrylic on panel
8" × 8" (20cm × 20cm)
Private collection

Index

North Light Books
An imprint of Penguin Random House LLC
penguinrandomhouse.com

Copyright © 2018 by Patti Mollica

Printed in China
10

ISBN 978-1-4403-4210-3

Editor: Christina Richards
Designer: Clare Finney
Production editor: Amy Jones

About the Author

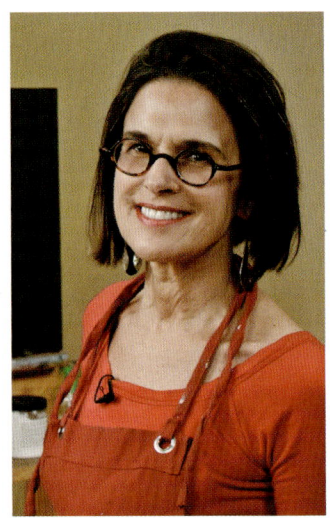

Patti Mollica delights in painting the world around her in a bold, confident style with hues that are vibrant, energetic and contemporary. Her work is known for its fearless use of color and expressive brushwork while still blending a delicate balance between impressionism, abstraction and realism.

Patti's work is included in several galleries as well as the private collections of American Express, Sheraton Hotels, CBS and RCA Records, Penguin Press and many others. Additionally, she is a Certified Teacher for Golden Paints and conducts workshops throughout the U.S. covering topics such as *Innovative Acrylic Techniques Using Golden Paints* as well as *How to Paint Fast, Loose and Bold.*

Patti is the author of three books: *Modern Acrylics, Color Theory* and *Acrylics—Getting Started,* as well as three instructional painting DVDs.

Patti lives in Nyack, New York with her husband and their dog, three cats and four polish chickens.

Visit her website at pattimollica.com.

(*opposite page*)
SUMMER TULIPS
Acrylic on canvas
12" × 12" (30cm × 30cm)
Collection of Angel Cacciola

Metric Conversion Chart

To convert	to	multiply by
Inches	Centimeters	2.54
Centimeters	Inches	0.4
Feet	Centimeters	30.5
Centimeters	Feet	0.03
Yards	Meters	0.9
Meters	Yards	1.1

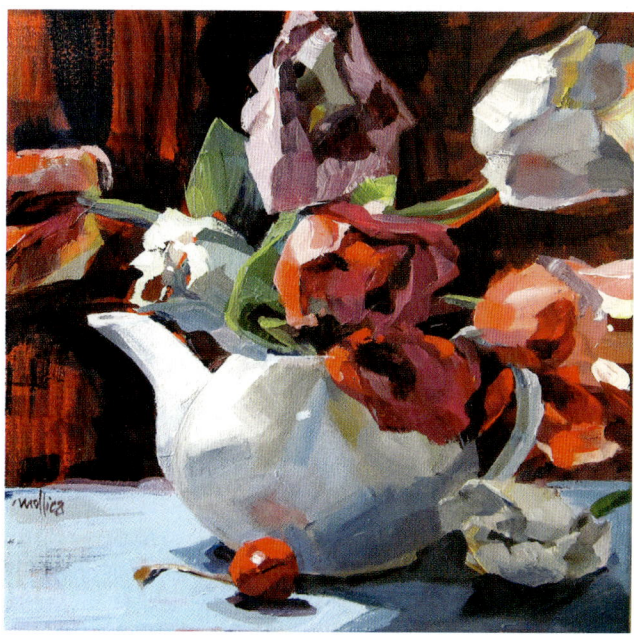

Dedication

To my childhood babysitter, the enchanting Sheila, who always showed up for the gig with sketchbook and pastels in tow. She thoroughly dazzled and inspired this impressionable young girl, and forever changed the course of my life. I have many precious memories of afternoons spent wide-eyed, mesmerized and spell-bound, beholding raw talent flow effortlessly from her fingertips.

To my parents, Jack and Shirley Mollica, who have always whole-heartedly encouraged and supported my interest in being an artist.

To my husband, Mark Hagan, my soul mate and partner in living the artistic life.

Acknowledgments

To Patti Brady of Golden Paints, whose belief in me opened the door to life changes, at the exact time changes were in order.

To my editor, Christina Richards, whose talent, tireless dedication and cheerful spirit helped keep this book—and its author—in order and on track.

To my teacher, John Ruggeri, who taught me I could confront the most chaotic of NYC settings and turn them into art.

To my students, who support, inspire and teach me in more ways than they could know.